"Readable, relatable and above all practical. A fantastic new resource." – Bree Hadley, Queensland University of Technology, Australia

In this accessible introduction to the study of disability arts and culture, Petra Kuppers foregrounds themes, artists and theoretical concepts in this diverse field. Complete with case studies, exercises and questions for further study, the book introduces students to the work of disabled artists and their allies, and explores artful responses to living with physical, cognitive, emotional or sensory difference.

Engaging readers as cultural producers, Kuppers provides useful frameworks for critical analysis and encourages students to explore their own positioning within the frames of gender, race, sexuality, class and disability.

Comprehensive and accessible, this is an essential handbook for undergraduate students or anyone interested in disabled bodies and minds in theatre, performance, creative writing, art and dance.

Petra Kuppers is Professor of English, Theatre and Drama, Art and Design, and Women's Studies at the University of Michigan, USA. She is the author of *The Scar of Visibility: Medical Performances and Contemporary Art*, *Community Performance: An Introduction* and *Disability Culture and Community Performance*, among other titles.

Cover Image Description

If you are reading a hardback version of this book, you can find the cover image online when you go to the Palgrave website for this book. This description tries to model alternative access.

Two figures against a dark background. One face is close up, in white Butoh make-up. Lips are slightly parted, eyes wide, looking beyond. A beard frames the chin. A nose ring catches the light and throws a shadow on the white face. The other figure is further back, frontal, the close-cropped head tilted toward the other dancer. This figure wears a breastplate made out of translucent ventilator tubes: life support systems, ties that bind human to machine, protection, glittering adornment, prosthesis.

In Butoh, a Japanese/transnational art form, the dancer brings surreal images to life by creating energetic fields of embodied concentration. In the dancer's gaze in the photo, the world shifts beyond the frame, something reaches toward an elsewhere.

The two dancers are Yulia Arakelyan, a Russian-speaking Armenian born in Baku, Azerbaijan, and her husband Erik Ferguson, a wheelchair-using anti-virtuoso movement artist living in Portland, Oregon. Arakelyan was first drawn to dance when she saw Light Motion Dance Company in Seattle, and she went on to become the first wheelchair user to graduate with a dance degree from the University of Washington. Ferguson trained in improvisation with Alito Alessi in Trier, Germany. He is a Butoh practitioner who studied with Akira Kasai, Koichi and Hiroko Tamano, Mizu Desierto, and others.

Together, Arakelyan and Ferguson are Wobbly Dance Company, a multimedia company that uses performance, film, improvisation, digital interaction and visual art to create multisensory environments.

Image from *You Too Are Made of Stars*, 2014, costumes by Jenny Ampersand, photographer Ward Shortridge.

G'niimim, zaagijig akiing
You dance, lovers of the world

wewiib, wewini,
quickly, carefully

maashko-waagiziyeg
your curved strength

mino-waawiinjigaazoyeg pane.
is a celebration!

Margaret Noodin

Studying Disability Arts and Culture

An Introduction

Petra Kuppers

First published 2014 by
PALGRAVE MACMILLAN

Palgrave Macmillan in the UK is an imprint of Macmillan Publishers Limited, registered in England, company number 785998, of Houndmills, Basingstoke, Hampshire RG21 6XS.

Palgrave Macmillan in the US is a division of St Martin's Press LLC, 175 Fifth Avenue, New York, NY 10010.

Palgrave Macmillan is the global academic imprint of the above companies and has companies and representatives throughout the world.

Palgrave® and Macmillan® are registered trademarks in the United States, the United Kingdom, Europe and other countries.

ISBN: 978–1–137–41343–7 hardback
ISBN: 978–1–137–41346–8 paperback

This book is printed on paper suitable for recycling and made from fully managed and sustained forest sources. Logging, pulping and manufacturing processes are expected to conform to the environmental regulations of the country of origin.

A catalogue record for this book is available from the British Library.

Library of Congress Cataloging-in-Publication Data
Kuppers, Petra.
  Studying disability arts and culture : an introduction / Petra Kuppers.
     pages cm
  Summary: "In this practical introduction to the study of Disability Arts and Culture, Petra Kuppers draws on a wide range of examples, exercises and activities to introduce the key artists and theoretical concepts in this diverse field. Comprehensive and accessible, this is an essential handbook for anyone interested in the Disabled body in performance"-- Provided by publisher.
  ISBN 978-1-137-41343-7 (hardback)
  1. People with disabilities and the arts. 2. People with disabilities and the performing arts. 3. Arts and society. I. Title.
  NX180.H34K87 2014
  700.87--dc23
                           2014023066

Typeset by Aardvark Editorial Limited, Metfield, Suffolk.

Printed in China

Contents

List of Illustrations

Preface

I dedicate this book to the students in the Disability Culture undergraduate classes at the University of Michigan. We field tested many of the exercises here together, and with the interdisciplinary students of the University of Michigan Initiative on Disability Studies course, a class open to graduates and undergraduates, cross-listed with Architecture, Social Work, Education, Kinesiology, Sociology, English, and Physical Medicine and Rehabilitation. Another willing and friendly test group were artists, community members, graduates, and undergraduates in many disciplines, in disability culture workshops across the world.

Much of what is here has its seeds in some of my early work in disability culture, as a community artist, and a Training the Trainers tutor for Disability Equality Training (DET) workshops in England and Wales, following activists who called for the centrality of the arts and cultural analysis in the fight for disability rights. DET moved away from Disability Awareness Training, with its emphasis on simulation exercises, toward centering disabled expressions, intervening in the perception of disability in mainstream culture.

Special thanks to Beth Currans, Gwen Robertson, and Sara Rofofsky Marcus, who read more or less everything here, and to Neil Marcus, who listened to a lot of it being read out. Thanks to Sadashi Inuzuka for merging ceramics and performance, and for breathing quietly and artfully with me in the middle of semesters. Thanks to the Miskwaasining Nagamojig (Swamp Singers) for communal singing and the drum. Thanks to Stefanie Cohen and the Authentic Movement community for grounding. Thanks to my beloved Olimpias disability culture community for everything. Thanks to Tony McCaffrey, Ian Carter, Ann Fox, Crystal Yin Lie, David Hornibrook, Katy Kidd, Katie Willingham, Jina Kim, Elwyn Murray, Gili Hammer, Tobin Siebers, Gerard Goggin, Julian Levinson, Jane Berliss-Vincent, Liat Ben Moshe, Deanna Adams, Kerrie Divett, Melanie Yergeau, Sharon Siskin, and others who read some of these chapters and trial taught exercises, to my graduate assistant Shannon Walton for all her work, to Maggie Lythgoe, Jenni Burnell, and my editorial team at Palgrave, and to the four anonymous reviewers who offered invaluable suggestions.

We are moving, with curved strength.

Acknowledgments

Some of the chapters in Part II of this book are based on case studies published earlier in much longer form. Our discipline is new, and in process. Revisiting these passages and updating my language and approach provided an excellent learning opportunity for myself. I am grateful to be able to reprint passages of:

"Freak: A Reclamation Project," originally in Kuppers (2003), then in Ine Gevers et al. (eds) (2009) *Difference on Display: Diversity in Arts, Science and Society*. Nai Oio: Rotterdam: 146–56.

"Affect and Blindness: Daredevil's Site/Sight" (2006) *Quarterly Review of Film and Video*, 23(2): 89–96.

"Accessible Education: Aesthetics, Bodies and Disability" (2000) *Research in Dance Education*, 1(2): 119–31.

"Dancing Autism: The Curious Incident of the Dog in the Nighttime and Bedlam" (2007) *Text and Performance Quarterly*, 28(1): 192–205.

"The Rhetoric of the Wheelchair" (2007) *TDR: The Drama Review*, 51(4): 80–8.

Introduction to *Somatic Engagement* (Kuppers, P., ed.) (2011) Oakland, CA: Chainlinks.

"Visiting the Hospital: Disability Culture, Non-Confessional – Jim Ferris's The Hospital Poems." (2007) *Valparaiso Review*, 8(2).

I also acknowledge reprint permission for:

Julie Passanante Elman's exercise, The Accessible Date, from her blog http://disabilitysexuality.blogspot.com/p/accessible-dates.html.

Johnson Cheu's poem "Oats and May", *Red River Review*, 2005, August 26.

Jim Ferris's poems, in *Hospital Poems* (2004). Charlotte, NC: Main Street Rag.

Lynn Manning's poem "The Magic Wand", *International Journal of Inclusive Education*, 2009, 13(7): 785.

Neil Marcus's poem "Disabled Country", written in the mid-1980s, reprinted in *Cripple Poetics: A Love Story* (2008). Petra Kuppers and Neil Marcus, with photographer Lisa Steichmann. Ypsilanti: Homofactus Press.

Excerpt from Cheryl Marie Wade's "Disability Culture Rap." In Shaw, B. (ed.) *The Ragged Edge: The Disability Experience from the Pages of the First Fifteen Years of The Disability Rag* (1994). Louisville, KY: Avocado Press.

Excerpt from Eli Clare's *Exile and Pride: Disability, Queerness, and Liberation* (1999). Boston, MA: South End Press.

Excerpt from A Different Light Company's *Still Lives* play (unpublished manuscript, courtesy of the company).

Finally, I would like to thank my friend and collaborator Margaret Noodin, who sent me the epigraph poem as a gift, on the day I finished this book manuscript.

Part I

1 Setting Up

In this chapter, you will gain some beginning insights into these issues:

- Disability accommodations
- Fuzzy communication and multimodal classrooms
- Classroom conventions and interdependence
- Disclosure and privilege
- Ethics of accommodation and their complexities

It's the first meeting of a disability studies classroom, or the beginning of a course section on the theme. You are likely among a predominantly non-disability-identified group in the room, maybe with some people who are easily externally identified as disabled, plus some who come out as disabled over time. It is pretty likely that you have people among you who choose for a variety of reasons not to out themselves. A lot of you might have experiences of disability in your families, or other personal connections to disability. There is a lot of knowledge among you.

Your teacher will likely have been informed of sensory access issues before classes start, and there might be a sign language interpreter or a CART (Computer Assisted Real-time Translation) reader set up in the room, either for the whole group or assisting a particular student. There might be a student's note taker in the room, other assistants, or service animals.

EXERCISE 1.1   ## Disability Accommodations: What Is Out There?

List all the accommodations you have encountered in classrooms you have been in. As we are now living in a world that reaches more and more toward disability inclusion, most of you will have had contact with disabled peers over your careers in school settings. So, as a classroom community, we should be able to create a long list here.

When done with the list, research the technologies you are not familiar with, which might be ones like communication boards, screen readers, induction loops, or the like. Also look at mechanisms not usually included in accommodation lists, such as stimming devices, compression vests, scent-free environments, or interaction badges.

If your institution has a disability access provision hub, visit it, and see what kind of accommodations and services are provided or organized there. Are there low-stimulation quiet rooms, for instance? Do you think that gender-neutral bathrooms fall under the category of accommodations?

• •

The CART transcriber usually sits somewhere to the side of the class, and she takes down everything I say and types it. The type appears as text on a screen behind me. Studying and teaching with CART shakes things up in interesting ways. Here's my experience, from the teacher's side.

As I am saying hello to my students in the first class, I can see their eyes doing all kinds of interesting things. Some are being riveted by my wheelchair, and by the spectacle I present in it, and I know that they will hardly hear what I say at that point. Some eyes leave my talking face and drift up and sideways, to where the text of my welcome appears as moving type on a screen. And I address this: eyes move to screens, away from faces, disrupting ideas of normative communication protocol, setting up new communicative spaces and new ways of doing things.

A lot of us as students and teachers are used to reliable text. CART, on the other hand, is useful, but hardly reliable; it needs to be read with a grain of salt. Much gets garbled, in particular if speakers speak too fast for the scribe to keep track, or if a lot of unfamiliar words are used. CART can drop whole lines. There's a whole genre of jokes about CART transcription out there in disability culture land.

In a disability-focused classroom, whether equipped with CART or not, we can learn that information is unreliable, and that all communication is complex. This is true for audio access, too. Information is fuzzy, and those of us who rely on hearing do not hear everything, are distracted, shift in our seat, miss a beat, hear something that sounded familiar but might have been something else.

Multimodal approaches can embrace these interesting diversities of learning styles and ubiquitous communication gaps. Is it easier or harder to follow an argument when it gets charted live as a diagram on a blackboard, whiteboard, or Smart Board? What are good ways of using presentation software to structure complex arguments and support audio input?

A multimodal classroom that combines visual, audio, experiential, and other information avenues prepares us for fuzziness, redundancy, and diversity. Our access technologies can help us understand the complicated make-up of all communication, and the meaning-making activities we are engaged in every time we are reaching from our own mental world into another person's world.

EXERCISE 1.2 **Playing with Classroom Conventions**

• •

Rearrange yourself. Get up, and change your position in the classroom: find a body shape and a part of the room in which you can make a comfortable temporary home. What does your body position look like?

Look around. Some of you might be curled up, some stretched out, some leaning comfortably into corners, some hovering on window sills. Some probably continue to sit in a chair, some are away from others, some are in a group. You might choose to put the lights out, and experience non-artificial light, if you are in a room with windows.

Shift again, to take up a new position. Go through this a few times. You are becoming familiar with your classroom in a different way, and you are exploring new spatial relations to one another.

Development Option

Come together – but do so on the ground, in a space created between the tables (if you are in a room with movable furniture). Create a loose star, lying on your bellies, facing inward. Whoever is uncomfortable on the floor, or finds it hard to take up this particular shape, can orient themselves in a different way. The star responds to their position, including them wherever they are. Take note of how it feels to be so close. Nice/uncomfortable/complicated?

Now shift onto your backs, if you are easily able to do so, and look up at the ceiling – everybody is now in their own visual domain, without the demand for eye contact. You can experience the freedom of not having to respond visually/physically to people as they speak, listening without having to do the small movements of nodding or blinking that we use to communicate that we are following a speaker. What happens in this position? Do you drift, or does your attention sharpen?

Feedback

Eventually, move back to the relative safety and comfort of chairs. Have a brief discussion, not a fully developed one, as much of the information gained in these early experiential sessions is emotional and reflective, not something easily shared in quick responses:

- What kind of information style works best for you?
- What impact do various spatial orientations have on you?
- What makes you feel safer and more connected – visual access or auditory access, a mixture, something else?
- Do you like being closer to or further away from people?
- How does freedom from eye contact impact your sense of wellbeing?
- What are the rituals with which we sustain classrooms?

. . . .

As you find your way through this study guide, see if you can reach back to these embodied exercises, and find ways of holding against normative rules for classroom engagements, in agreement with your teacher and fellow students.

Maybe get up to sit by the window, taking in sunshine while participating, or lean against a wall for a while. Turn off florescent light, if that is workable, and does not interfere with clear sightlines for people who lip-read. If you know that you can experience panic attacks, maybe you can share some information about social management with a fellow student. And that might just be to say to the rest of the room, "she is having a panic attack. Just let her be." Even if you choose not to do so, reflect on that choice, and about what it says about the different kinds of pressure you are operating under.

Some openings in classroom can be discussed and analyzed, and some can more easily be intuited. As students, you are co-creators of your classroom, and you can work out rules for engagement with each other.

PRACTICING INTERDEPENDENCY

Kristina Knoll, a women's studies researcher, writes about her feminist disability pedagogy:

> To escape some of the ableistic restrictions on learning, I teach and practice what I call 'interdependency' in the class room (Doe 11). I model interdependency from the onset of a course by acknowledging to the students that I, the instructor, am dependent on them in order to have a positive learning community together.

> I have someone read the syllabus aloud, and I explain to the students that I will need to depend upon them from time to time to read visual material aloud. This can really impact a student, as the university instructor is sometimes considered a pinnacle of able- and mindedness. Instructors can come up with additional ways to demonstrate their relation to interdependency, like having one or two students help with monitoring class time, or writing things on an overhead as the instructor dictates a mathematical equation. (Knoll, 2009: 129)

SAFER SPACE

Experiential and multimodal classrooms are works in progress, and they continue to provide many challenges. We still operate within the constraints of the university as an institution, and within the contours of a largely inaccessible world that has denigrated disabled people and many others for a very long time. Given these histories and realities, it is important to be clear about limits, too:

> The term safer (rather than safe) refers to the idea that no space is ever truly safe for all possible users/participants, and as such it emphasizes flexibility and adaptability for a variety of users and participants. The term safer also encourages an attitude of improvement and the idea that creating accessible spaces is a process of evolving attitudes and practices, rather than an unattainable end goal in which a space is fully welcome and accessible to all people at all times. (Yergeau et al., 2013; see also Price, 2011, for discussions of safety and mental disability in university settings)

Having loosened parts of our ideas of classrooms a bit, can you go further?

- Who is not in the room with you? Why?
- What ideas of education, access, communication practices, and definitions of knowledge have created the particular classroom communities we find ourselves in today?

- How do racism, sexism, ableism, homophobia, classism, and other ways of defining "the norm" shape what we learn, and how we are shaped as learners?
- Who would not have been in this space with you 20 years ago? 50 years ago? 100 years ago?
- How have our cultural ideas of who is human, and who is educable, changed over time, and how do they continue to change?
- What alternatives to a university classroom exist? How else do people educate themselves? How does disability fit in there?

In the chapters that follow, intersectional perspectives on disability will give you more insights into how different kinds of oppression work together and through concepts of disability.

DISABILITY DISCLOSURE AND PRIVILEGE

In a blog post about an academic conference on Disability Disclosure in/and Higher Education, US-based rhetoricians Stephanie Kerschbaum and Margaret Price speak about how privilege and disclosure inform one another.

As you read through this excerpt and reflect on the topic, think about who is economically enabled to claim disability accommodation – testing for learning differences might be expenses carried by parents, and much educational advocacy work can only be engaged in by people with the time and educational means to do so.

Think about other ways in which power, privilege, and histories of oppression might shape who can feel comfortable claiming disability.

We ... confronted the ways that disability literacy deeply engages intersections between disability and other identity categories. Whiteness provides both of us enormous privilege, and affords us, in many cases, the energy and inclination to call out our disabilities and to engage in work that will expand access – for ourselves and for others – across myriad institutional spaces. Both of us make choices every day regarding the degree to which we will call attention to – or keep under wraps – our experiences of disability, and we also make choices about how much to invite others to think about their own experience of disability through interactions with us. (Kerschbaum and Price, 2014)

CASE STUDY   ## An Ethic of Accommodation

One more challenge. What kind of classroom do you want to be in? How open can you be, given where you are, and what you want to do with your life?

Here are the words of three US-based theatre practitioners, Terry Galloway, Donna Marie Nudd, and Carrie Sandahl, and their manifesto for an ethic of accommodation. You can find links to their work online, videos created in the community theatre workshops of the Mickee Faust Club. They write:

this ethic is not abstract to us, but integral to our work and lives. We have all been affected by traditional practices of theatre that still ensure that disabled, queer, female, non-white bodies remain a rarity on stage, except in roles that reinforce the most demeaning stereotypes. We feel the exclusion personally because of our own bodies (Terry is deaf and Carrie has an orthopedic disability), because of our queer and radical politics (Donna and Terry are lesbians), and because of our families (Carrie has a transracial family formed through adoption). We three share a commitment to social justice and in the spheres we can influence, we attempt to make structural changes toward flexibility and openness. (Galloway et al., 2007: 228)

Below is the manifesto the three put forward. As you read through this, think about theatre practices you are familiar with, and about working methods, ways in which a play is created and performed. What opportunities for difference can emerge from this manifesto? Think about the implications for adopting a similar stance for yourself, in a school, a university, or in a creative production setting.

Is this ethic a good thing to work toward, always, or is it complicated? Why? Would this be challenging to you, and how can you think about these challenges?

1   At its core, an Ethic of Accommodation means that the majority does not rule. Instead, accommodation means including everyone wanting to participate, often necessitating that the majority make difficult changes in its practices and environment. These changes are not made begrudgingly, but with goodwill, creativity, and a strong dose of humor, elements that often find expression in the performances themselves.

2   The ethic includes the politics of listening as well as the politics of speaking. Whereas most minority groups maintain that they have been 'silenced' by the majority and thus place speaking at a premium, disability communities often place listening on the same plane. People with disabilities often feel they have not been listened to or even addressed. In this context, listening does not have to happen with the ears. Listening, here, means being taking into consideration, being attended to.

3   The Ethic of Accommodation means making room for difference possible, letting go of preconceived notions of perfectability, and negotiating complex sets of needs. Often these 'needs' compete with one another. Accommodating disability or other forms of difference often does not seem practical or marketable, since doing so often raises costs or necessitates work that seemingly benefits only a few. Marketability is not our concern.

4   The Ethic of Accommodation inspires creative aesthetic choices from casting, choreography and costuming, and also the use of space for the creation of new material. Practicing the ethic enhances theatrical practice. (Galloway et al., 2007: 229)

Can an ethic of accommodation inform a classroom environment? Would you want to modify this manifesto? Why and how? You might wish to come back to this statement as you move through this study guide.

In the pages that follow, we can search for provisional answers to issues of access as an action, an ethic, and a co-created interdependent agenda, rather than a fixed state.

2 *Languages of Disability*

In this chapter, you will gain insights into these issues:

- Studying disability means dealing with ambivalence and uncertainty
- Any definition of disability is already a political statement
- Different groups employ different languages around disability
- Disclosure and "coming out" as disabled are complex processes, as disability has historically been denigrated and has negative associations
- Artists can and do play with words and their associations, and can bring out undertones, new insights, and opportunities for engagement

This is the beginning of our journey. Here is the place where there should be legends, information that will allow you to decode the maps of our travels. "Legend" is the name for the charts that decode what specific symbols on a map mean – this is a lake, this is a river, this is a small town, this is a city. So here, you might expect definitions of disability.

Instead, you will find different kinds of legends: narratives and stories that do not offer truth, but exploration and experience. Legends are stories that are told again and again, and that contain something that needs handling, something that sticks out, that somehow needs smoothing into the flow. Disability is something that sticks out.

This is the first thing to embrace: there is no certainty here, there are no right answers, no strict definitions. This book is a collaborative field of investigation, one that allows you to think differently about yourself and your cultural world – whether you identify as non-disabled or disabled. Together, through readings and exercises, we will reflect on our environment and the attitudes that surround us and help us narrate ourselves.

You already know a lot about disability: it is one of the organizing principles of what we think it means to be human, and how a society organizes itself. This book hopes to make these knowledges more complex.

EXERCISE 2.1 ## Association Map

Take a sheet of paper, or use a blackboard. Write down all the associations you have with the term "disability." Try not to censor yourself: let your mind freely associate. You will likely find insults and "bad language" among the material you garner – let that be OK, for now, as we need to acknowledge all the histories we bring to disability. When you are done, group the terms together in categories that make sense to you. What kind of concept map emerges?

So, as you make your way through this book, you will not find definitions for particular medical labels, impairments, or specific disabilities. Instead, you will find out how disabled people themselves employ their differences, the ways they are seen as different from some definitions of "normality," and how people with disabilities make art out of these differences. We will also see how non-disabled people use disability imagery and metaphors in their art practice, in ways that can be more or less respectful to people who actually live disabled lives. You will see how disabled people incite older art forms, become their subjects, and undermine conventional art practices, opening the range of expressive possibilities.

In all that, though, you will likely not come up with a single firm definition of disability – throughout this book, "disability" will be a machine rather than an entity, something to do stuff with, to move with, to think with – not something one can name and nail down.

UNSTABLE IDENTITIES

US theorist Tobin Siebers offers this perspective on instability, disability, and identity in his influential *Disability Theory*. Think through its implications. What are the differences between disability as an identity and the other identities mentioned? How do all these categories shift and slide, when one starts thinking about it?

> *The presence of disability creates a different picture of identity – one less stable than identities associated with gender, race, sexuality, nation, and class – and therefore presenting the opportunity to rethink how human identity works. (Siebers, 2008: 5)*

Now think through Siebers' quote together with this older piece of writing by Stuart Hall, Jamaican-born and UK-based scholar of cultural studies and race. How does Hall frame instability?

> *Cultural identity … is a matter of 'becoming' as well as of 'being'. It belongs to the future as much as to the past. It is not something which already exists, transcending place, time, history and culture. Cultural identities come from somewhere, have histories. But, like everything which is historical, they undergo constant transformation. Far from being eternally fixed in some essentialised past, they are subject to the continuous 'play' of history, culture and power. Far from being grounded in a mere 'recovery' of the past, which is waiting to be found, and which, when found, will secure our sense of ourselves into eternity, identities are the names we give to the different ways we are positioned by, and position ourselves within, the narratives of the past. (Hall, 1990: 225)*

Languages shift and change in tune with new social arrangements and cultural values, and the journey of the term "disability" shows this malleability of our concepts. The world can change: the value of a refusal of definitional clarity lies in the potential for creative investigation.

Living Languages

The first few pages of this book circle and play with the languages of disability:

- What do you call these people?
- What do you call someone like me, the author of this book, a writer/teacher/dancer who uses a wheelchair?
- Is there a "these people"? And, if there is, what do they share?
- What do you call them if you are one of them? What if you are not?
- What does the "they" say about an "us"?

The pedagogical agenda here is for you to own discomfort, to live with uncertainty, to understand the serious and playful potential of language.

By reading and researching, by watching TV and surfing the net, you will encounter terms like "differently abled," "handicapped," "Down Syndrome child," "wheelchair-bound," "crazy," and "exceptional." Reading through this study guide, you will be able to work out for yourself the problems with these terms:

- Why do some people prefer "person with a disability," and others "disabled person"?
- Are others "non-disabled people", "normal," "normate" or "TAB: temporarily able-bodied"?
- Is a particular term more likely used in a service environment, in a care facility, by parents of disabled children?
- Is it a self-identifying label?

EXERCISE 2.2 ## Group Agreement

Think about a way you can agree on ways of marking discomfort in your shared classroom (if you are reading this book in a class). Is there a way to do this that does not require "offended" people to out themselves, or "offenders" to be embarrassed? Think about a mechanism that can work for your group, and make an agreement to revisit this mechanism when appropriate.

NORMATE

Rosemarie Garland-Thomson coined the term "normate" in an early and influential US disability studies text. The term does a lot of useful labor in disability studies: as a word, it marks a comfortable subject position that is made uncomfortable. Many people might be OK to be called "normal," but would you like to be called "normate"?

As I examine the disabled figure, I will also trouble the mutually constituting figure this study coins: the normate. This neologism names the veiled subject position of cultural self, the figure outlined by the array of deviant others whose marked bodies shore up the normate's boundaries. The term normate usefully designates the social figure through which people can represent themselves as definite human beings. Normate, then, is the constructed identity of those who, by way of the bodily configurations and cultural capital they assume, can step into a position of authority and wield the power it grants them. If one attempts to define the normate position by peeling away all the marked traits within the social order at this historical moment, what emerges is a very narrowly defined profile that describes only a minority of actual people. (Garland-Thomson, 1997: 8)

One of the most important learning goals of this study guide is an understanding that language changes just as our cultures do, and that how we feel ourselves to be human is deeply intertwined with issues of cultural representation. You will begin to understand that words are relational, are wielded differently at different times, and by different people, for different purposes.

EXERCISE 2.3 **Coming Out**

Languages and behaviors are acts that repeat again and again. Ellen Samuels writes about the relational and ongoing nature of "coming out" – linking "coming out" as gay or queer in complex ways to "coming out" as disabled. Research and think about issues of passing, disclosure, and "coming out" in your classroom: Can it happen, what is useful about coming out, how and why? What are the costs and opportunities of it? Think about hidden or ostracizing disabilities, and run through a range of scenarios to allow you to understand the complexity of choices. Samuels posits that:

> *[Coming out is not] an over-the-rainbow shift that divides one's life before and after the event. Certainly, there must be some people who experience such momentous comings out, but I believe that the majority of us find that, even after our own internal shift, and even after a dozen gay pride marches, we must still make decisions about coming out on a daily basis, in personal, professional, and political contexts. (Samuels, 2003: 237)*

Living Change

In your lifetime, as students in a classroom today, the world has shifted. In the US in 1990, the Americans with Disabilities Act came into force, after decades of campaigning. Similar legislation is transforming many other nations. Everybody working in disability studies today has experienced in some form the world-changing impact of these acts: ramps, speaking elevators, curb cuts, parking places, the growth of Sign Language as a recognized language in university settings, a slowly growing popular cultural visibility of disability as a lived experience. As students and teachers, we are part of this change, and we can make change happen. That is the baseline of language discussions around disability: we are growing, with a hopeful agenda, and we are powerful.

So there we are, at the beginning of the 21st century, with "people first" language like "people with disabilities" and with the more politicized group identification that the phrase "disabled people" implies for many. And just in case you are looking for answers, these two descriptors are least likely to offend today – although this might well change. The best thing to do, whenever possible: ask a person what descriptor they like to have used.

And there are other words, before person with disability, person with disabilities, and disabled person: cripple, retard, spaz, mute. They provide the deeper sediment for a discussion around language, they hold pain and, rarely, newly recovered pride. Literature and language artists have begun to mine the representations of disability in ways that do not merely renounce oppressive structures, but find play within them. The swing in our words is part of the energy of the discovery projects in disability arts and culture.

EXERCISE 2.4   ## Neurodiversity

Autistic author and educator Nick Walker shares perspectives on language change from within the neurodiversity movement. Discuss the relationship between the term "neurodiversity" and concepts of "autism," or medical categories such as "low/high functioning" – terms usually seen as undesirable and stigmatizing by many autistic self-advocates.

The Neurodiversity Paradigm

Here's how I'd articulate the fundamental principles of the neurodiversity paradigm:

1   *Neurodiversity – the diversity of brains and minds – is a natural, healthy, and valuable form of human diversity. There is no 'normal' style of human brain or human mind, any more than there is one 'normal' race, ethnicity, gender, or culture.*

2   *All of the diversity dynamics (e.g., dynamics of power, privilege, and marginalization) that manifest in society in relation to other forms of human diversity (e.g., racial, cultural, sexual orientation, and gender diversity) also manifest in relation to neurodiversity. (Walker, 2012: 228)*

EXERCISE 2.5   ## deaf/hearing impaired/Deaf

Many disability studies writings make a distinction between deaf and Deaf. The capital D Deaf refers to people who use American, British or other Sign Language, who have a shared cultural history, who engage in specific Deaf art forms like Sign Language Poetry, and common social forms, like clubs.

The small "d" refers to deafness as a biological marker, as "not hearing."

A term like "hard of hearing" or "hearing impaired" would not necessarily apply to a Deaf person, who might not see her- or himself as being impaired, or in some relation to hearing culture.

If in doubt, ask what the preferred term might be, and be aware of the power relations inherent in naming a particular way of being in the world as normal ("hearing culture").

Shared cultural markers make for cultural cohesion. There are many shared markers in Deaf history. Choose one of these historical moments or cultural groups, and research it. Bring your research material back to the classroom, and discuss your findings in pairs: Where did you find your answers? Who do you think wrote it? Are different perspectives evident in the material you found?

- oralist versus manual teaching
- Deaf President Now and the history of Gallaudet University
- World Federation of the Deaf
- British Deaf History Society
- Deaf villages, like Benkala in Indonesia
- performance companies:
  - Flying Words Project, with Peter Cook and Kenny Lerner
  - Common Ground Sign Dance Theatre (Liverpool, England)
  - National Theatre of the Deaf (West Hartford, Connecticut)
  - Deaf West Theatre (North Hollywood, California)
  - Deaf Youth Theatre (Glasgow, Scotland)

DESIGN AND LANGUAGE CHOICE

In this passage, British designer Graham Pullin makes a particular language and register choice – note how access to a different kind of language can have effects. What is so funny and so radical about this story?

In order to communicate with other people, Somiya Shabban uses a dialogue book, in which she points to words or images. This is versatile, but it can be laborious. When Somiya was still at school, Johanna Van Daalen from the design group Electricwig worked with her to help her express herself more fully. In particular, Somiya wanted the freedom to express frustration more spontaneously, so together they designed a badge that she could activate using a switch next to her head, whenever she wanted to.

When she does this, the badge lights up with the words 'Somiya says SOD OFF.'

This message is wonderfully direct and disarming, and yet the badge expresses so much more besides this information. It also communicates that she is the kind of person who will use this language; that she is the kind of person to whom this is important enough to dedicate a button to; and that she doesn't mind who knows this. Perhaps it seems inefficient to produce such a limited communication device, and one that can only be used for one sentence. But this is to ignore its other role: the short-term utterance is also a long-term badge – a label of Somiya's own devising, to express her individuality and identity rather than any stereotype associated with her impairment. (Pullin, 2009: 177)

Language Change

Let us look at some of this language change and revaluation in action. Here are four instances of disability arts and culture. As you look through these, chart similarities and differences. What hopes are expressed, what desires emerge? How is language used to offer hope and ways forward? How does the concept of disability and the words associated with it go on a historical journey in each piece? How does humor feature in these pieces?

Example 1 Disabled Country

Read this poem out loud (and find the video of the poem online, listen to Marcus speak the poem in his own real time, as someone with a speech difference). What happens when words out of different contexts align? What is the effect of saying "disabled/love" or "disabled/mountains" together? What is the effect of using the word "country" here – and how is that different (or the same) as "group," "minority," "state," "tribe," or "nation?"

Neil Marcus, "Disabled Country" (mid-1980s, reprinted in *Cripple Poetics*, Kuppers and Marcus, 2008: 155)

> If there was a country called disabled,
> I would be from there.
> I'd live disabled culture, eat disabled food,
> make disabled love, cry disabled tears,
> climb disabled mountains and tell disabled stories.
> If there was a country called disabled,
> I would say she has immigrants that come to her
> from as far back as time remembers.
> If there was a country called disabled,
> then I am one of its citizens.
> I came there at age 8. I tried to leave.
> Was encouraged by doctors to leave.
> I tried to surgically remove myself from disabled country
> but found myself, in the end, staying and living there.
> If there was a country called disabled,
> I would always have to remind myself that I came from
> there.
> I often want to forget.
> I would have to remember … to remember.
> In my life's journey
> I am making myself
> at home in my country.

Example 2 Disability Culture Rap

This passage is a rap. What does that mean, in this context? The previous example and this one also exist in video form, with the creator performing the material. How does the form of this rap embody aspects of what "rapping" has come to mean? How does the phrase "pass the word" resonate for you here – can you perform this piece in a group, "passing the word"?

Cheryl Marie Wade, *from "Disability Culture Rap"*

> Disability culture. Say what? Aren't disabled people just isolated victims of nature or circumstance? Yes and no. True, we are far too often isolated. Locked away in the pits, closets and institutions of enlightened societies everywhere. But there is a growing consciousness among us: "that is not acceptable." Because there is always an underground. Notes get passed among survivors. And the notes we're passing these days say, "there's power in difference. Power. Pass the word."
>
> Culture. It's about passing the word. And disability culture is passing the word that there's a new definition of disability, and it includes power.
>
> Culture. New definitions, new inflections. No longer just "poor cripple." Now also "CRIPPLE" and, yes, just "cripple." A body happening. But on a real good day, why not C*R*I*P*P*L*E; a body, hap-pen-ing. (Dig it or not.)
>
> Culture. It's finding a history, naming and claiming ancestors, heroes. As "invisibles," our history is hidden from us, our heroes buried in the pages, unnamed, unrecognized. Disability culture is about naming, about recognizing. (Wade, 1994: 15)

Example 3 Krip-Hop

In this excerpt, Leroy Moore describes his activist agenda, and its roots in searching for people who share his own experiences as a black disabled man. You can find his performance work online, in particular in the group Sins Invalid, which he co-founded with Patricia Berne (see Chapter 3). Pay attention to the cross-cultural reverberations around the term "crip/krip," and follow Moore's origin story for this term.

Leroy F. Moore, Jr., *from "Krip-Hop Nation is Moore than Music"*

> Krip-Hop Nation came from my experiences as a young Black disabled boy growing up in the late 1970's and 80's in a White suburb of Connecticut. Always being the only Black disabled youth in almost everything I did from special education to being mainstreamed, from playing with White non-disabled kids in my neighborhood to my early days in activism with my parents, to my many years of volunteering in disability non-profits to college classes In all of these experiences I always had the same question: Where were the other people who looked like me as a Black disabled young man? With this continuous question of race and disability along with my love of poetry and music, I started to question the arena of music and performance around the representation of musicians with disabilities, especially disabled musicians of color. ...
>
> Krip-Hop Nation must give love to Poor Magazine in San Francisco where Krip-Hop Nation was born on Poor Magazine, Poor News Network, Radio show on KPFA 94.1 FM in Berkeley, where we invited Hip-Hop artists with

disabilities on the show, and where for the first time my writings on race and disability gained an audience under my own online column Illin-N-Chillin. Poor Magazine led me to being involved for almost three years on a disability radio collective called Pushing Limits at the same station. At Pushing Limits on KPFA 94.1 FM in Berkeley, CA, I proposed a three part series with a co/host, Safi wa Nairobi, on Hip-Hop and artists with disabilities in the year of 2000. The show had Hip-Hop artists who were Deaf like Sho Roc and WAWA, Keith Jones who makes beats with his feet because of his cerebral palsy and DJ Quad who became disabled while he was surfing. The show was so successful that I wanted somehow to keep it going. Thus the birth of Krip-Hop Nation.

The last but important concept of Krip-Hop Nation is the title. Why Krip with a K? Like I wrote above, Krip-Hop Nation is more than music and "bling bling", it is about advocacy and education and taking back what has been taken from us to oppress us. Language, like other oppressed groups, was taken from people with disabilities and the language was turned on us to oppress us. Before people with disabilities had civil rights, a movement and arts, many had placed labels on us like "crazy", "lame", "cripple" and "retarded", etc. Of course, now with our civil rights and disability studies and culture, we have named ourselves and have used the negative terms to our own benefit to not only shock people but to respect that these words are our history and we must reclaim them.

After realizing that the term Crip has a long history of negativity to being used for Black gangs in LA (The Crips & The Bloods and knowing that one of the gang members had a disability so they called him Cripple that become Crip) to now being remade in Crip Culture (Disability Culture) and also talking it over in New York with a follow disabled advocate and cultural critic, Lawrence Carter-Long, I wanted to again reclaim the term Crip to advocate and educate with a proud framework of the music and struggles of Hip-Hop artists with disabilities. Just like in Hip-Hop you turn something that the so-called mainstream has discarded with a fresh spotlight thus changing the C to a K in what we know today as Krip-Hop (Moore, 2012).

Example 4 Deaf Gain

In this excerpt of an academic essay by Deaf scholars H-Dirksen Bauman and Joseph Murray, they draw on a deaf performance artist, Aaron Williamson. Performance and enactment are central here: chart how issues of embodied language and reception flow in this passage. Also, how does this passage challenge an easy multiculturalism? What does it mean to think of diversity not only as an add-on game?

As a development, research Aaron Williamson's art practices, his installations, and his work with Katherine Araniello in The Disabled Avant-Garde (some work is collected on the DVDs in Keidan and Mitchell, 2012). For writing about his art practice, see Davidson (2008), Kochhar-Lindgren (2006), and Kuppers (2003).

H-Dirksen Bauman and Joseph Murray, *"Reframing: From Hearing Loss to Deaf Gain" (translated from ASL)*

The first mention of Deaf Gain was by an Englishman named Aaron Williamson. Williamson, a performance artist, gave a presentation to Dirksen Bauman's graduate class, Enforcing Normalcy: Deaf and Disability Studies in the spring of 2005, where he told of his experience of going deaf later in life. At the onset of his deafness, Williamson consulted many doctors, and they all told him the same thing: "You're losing your hearing." He wondered why it was that not a single doctor told him he was gaining *his deafness.*

Deaf Gain is defined as a reframing of "deaf" as a form of sensory and cognitive diversity that has the potential to contribute to the greater good of humanity. There are three different signs that we use to mean Deaf Gain. The first can be glossed as DEAF INCREASE, and it expresses the opposite notion of hearing "loss". It emphasizes that Deaf people have something of importance. The second sign can be glossed as DEAF BENEFIT, and it emphasizes that deafness is not just a loss but a benefit as well. The third sign can be glossed as DEAF CONTRIBUTE. This sign emphasizes the importance of considering all the ways that Deaf people contribute to humankind. We will use all three of these signs in our discussion of Deaf Gain, choosing the sign that best fits the context.

Applying the new frame of Deaf Gain helps provide an answer to the question, "Why should we continue to value the existence of Deaf people?" This is a bioethical question, and it can be answered by using one of two different approaches, as proposed by Theresa Burke (2006). The first is an intrinsic argument that says that Deaf culture ought to be valued and preserved for its own sake. The other, an extrinsic argument, states that Deaf people should be cherished because they have something to contribute to the general society. Traditionally, the intrinsic argument has held sway. The preservation of Deaf culture clearly benefits Deaf people, but there has been little consideration given to how Deaf culture can contribute to the general good of humanity. (2009: 3–4) ...

In addition to the benefit to society, there is a direct benefit – a Deaf-gain – to Deaf people who use a visual-based language. Research has shown that, among other things, they have more well-developed peripheral vision, a greater ability to form quick mental images, and better facial recognition skills. Deaf Studies scholar Ben Bahan (2008) notes that Deaf people are visually-oriented to the world around them. One example that he provides is of a father and a daughter who are out by a busy street packed with pedestrians. The father asks his daughter if she can spot the Deaf pedestrian, and she does so easily. The Deaf pedestrian stands out because he is constantly scanning his surroundings as he walks. He is orienting himself to the world visually, and the Deaf-gain to him, as to all Deaf people, is a different way of perceiving and understanding the world. (Bauman and Murray, 2009: 5–6)

The Serious Play of Language

In this exercise, work in a small group. Write down all the disability labels you found in the texts above. This is your raw material.

Create a theatrical scene with these labels. Find out what it feels like to speak a particular word or put it into your fingers – if you have ASL/BSL/other Sign Language speakers among you. Address each other. How does it feel to find them applied to you?

The object here is to explore language in an embodied way: it is likely that certain meanings and association fields will only become apparent to you as you put them into action.

Your group should figure out theatrical mechanisms to work with these feelings, creating a scene that can be performed in front of the class. Can you create change in the "feeling" of these words? Maybe you can use your voice differently, or your body, setting up groupings, chanting together. You are welcome to add more words, or to focus on just a few.

Take about 20 minutes to create your scene, making sure that there are at least three different energies, feeling states, in the group, and that they are clearly delineated. Show your piece to your wider class. Discuss the process of creating these scenes together.

Access Note

Not everybody is comfortable performing for others. In setting up groups like these, it might be useful for one group to designate itself as a non-performing group, so that people who do not wish to perform can work without peer pressure. Here are some example of non-performance approaches: you can take photos on camera phones, record sounds and create a music/sound piece, or create a sound poem. You can then send your products to a class website, so others can engage with your group's work and comment on it.

Development

Later, away from class, and outside the energy created by the group work, do you still feel something resonating? What about this exercise stuck with you? Why is that? Are there more personal connections coming up for you, experiences of power, of bullies and name-calling, of reclamation and pride? Write about these more private echoes, maybe for sharing, maybe just for yourself.

Media Images

After reading the four examples of artful disability language change above, work in a small group. Grab a handful of magazines, and find images of disabled people. Note whether it takes a while to find them, how you recognize them, and if you find cues to non-visible disabilities, too. Do you need to find other magazines? Which ones?

Now create a grid of categories based on the four readings, and sort the media images into them. This will involve a lot of improvisation:

- What are "disabled mountains"?
- What is the visual style of krip as opposed to "crip," or "disabled person?"
- How can a concept like "Deaf Gain" appear in visual terms?
- What are contemporary images of madness?

Go with improvisations, push yourself to make unusual connections. You might need to go back to the magazines and begin to transform other images, maybe images unmarked by disability. This is supposed to be a playful exercise, so see what assemblages you can create.

In the class community, discuss what was easy, what was hard, and why. As you discuss another group's collage, you can use the Observation Wheel (in the Appendix) as a guide for creating nuanced observations.

3 *Discourses of Disability*

In this chapter, you will gain insights into these issues:

- Knowledge is historically and culturally specific, and it changes
- Disability is relational, it speaks to relations between people
- Disability incites narrative, and it is ubiquitous in our shared cultural world
- Disability as a category has been and continues to be used to subjugate people, and the outcome of oppression can be disability
- Different disability models explain the location of and engagement with disability in different ways
- Using the models of disability can hold an emotional charge: new ways of explaining why things are the way they are allow for ways of seeing change
- Find out about disability studies as a field, and its allies, with queer/disability studies as an example
- Disability art is a contested term, people make complicated choices about understanding themselves as part of this movement
- Art practice can play with models, undo certainties, and enjoy ambivalence
- Code-switching, performance, and disidentification are ways in which people make sense of the relational aspects of disability

We frame our understanding of ourselves, and other people, through discourses or modes of knowing. A discourse circumscribes what can be known about a subject. "Disability" is one such discursive construct, like gender, race, class, or sexuality.

Discourse changes over time, and new ways of organizing knowledge evolve. One example of this is the change in the teaching of history in schools. The study of history is changing from a catalogue of "victories" to a broader understanding of "ways of living" – to use Raymond Williams' phrase about culture (1961: 57). Instead of learning only about battles and dates, pupils now find out about the ordinary lives of people in a different age.

As with all knowledge, it is important to analyze and be aware of exactly who has knowledge of others, who controls access to this knowledge, and who legitimizes it as "the appropriate field" of study.

Staying with the history example, documents about "everyday life," the subjective expression of the lives of the working classes, ethnic communities, and women, have only been assembled relatively recently. From the 1960s onward, an interest in oral history and community history has led to the publication of many diaries and biographies. Today, initiatives such as broadcast video diaries and other drives to record local existences have changed what we understand a historic record to be. "History from below" widens the range of voices heard, the kind of expressions recorded and reproduced, and the texts and artifacts seen as "historic documents," and of value. In many ways, the rise of disability studies is linked with this rethinking of how power flows in our shared social worlds.

Work on discourses of disability has reverberations beyond the issue of disability: it focuses on identity as a negotiated issue in the social realm, and the body and mind as carriers of social meaning.

Traditionally, identity has been seen as a fixed attribute of an individual. Theorists such as Judith Butler have put forward alternative ways of understanding social identity and the body, and have focused on the function of roles and performances in the social field. This understanding of identity as negotiation and performance has considerable influence in discussions of gender and race, and is also gaining ground in disability discussions.

In the area of disability, the past 30 years have witnessed a discourse change, partly brought about by history's current attention to non-dominant voices and partly through forceful interventions by disabled activists. Our knowledge of "what disability means" is changing.

DISCOURSE AND POWER

In this quote by US writer Simi Linton, trace how different discourses of gender and race intertwine with disability naming practices:

> Beginning in the early 90s disabled people *has been increasingly used in disability studies and disability rights circles when referring to the constituency group ... disabled has become a marker of the identity that the individual and group wish to highlight and call attention to ...*
>
> *[My] use of nondisabled is strategic: to center disability ... This action is similar to the strategy of marking and articulating "whiteness." The assumed position in scholarship has always been the male, white, nondisabled scholar; it is the default category ... These positions are not only presumptively hegemonic because they are the assumed universal stance, as well as the presumed neutral or objective stance, but also undertheorized. The nondisabled stance, like the white stance, is veiled. "White cannot be said quite out loud, or it loses its crucial position as a precondition of vision and becomes the object of scrutiny" (Haraway, 1989: 152). Therefore, centering the disabled position and labeling its opposite nondisabled focuses atte-ntion on both the structure of knowledge and the structure of society. (Linton, 1998: 10–12)*

EXERCISE 3.1   ## Images of Disability in Cultural Texts

Let us look at the knowledges we hold about disability as a discourse field in our everyday lives. Chart all knowledges – not just the ones we might deem politically correct today. Older ways of thinking about disability are still very much with us, and influence contemporary narratives, images, and practices.

Take a big piece of paper (or a mind map in a laptop) and begin scribbling: think of all the ways you have encountered images of disability in popular and mainstream culture.

1 Think of fictional examples. Examples include:
   - Oedipus
   - Tiny Tim
   - Shakespeare's *Richard the Third*
   - Captains Ahab and Hook
   - The wheelchair-using guy from the movie *Avatar*
   - Norman Bates from *Psycho*
   - The Oracle in *The Matrix* franchise
   - Benjy Compson from Faulkner's *The Sound and the Fury*
   - Polly Breedlove from Morrison's *The Bluest Eye*

Find five more.

Now try to come up with descriptions of the narrative function of the disability associated with these characters. If you had to pitch a new film to a studio executive, how would you describe *why* these characters are disabled, how would you explain the labor these disabilities carry in the tale?

2 Now think of non-fictional examples, and how they can be slotted into particular discourses of disability. Examples might include (and find examples of these five, too):
   - Poster Child
   - Heroic Overcomer
   - Inspirational Cripple
   - Majority World Charity Case
   - Blind Supersensitive Guy

When you have found and discussed a number of additional narrative complexes of disability, share your findings with the whole class. Create a big blackboard image together, and take in how much narrative is set in motion by disability. Please note there are also software solutions to creating and capturing these class-created images: check out bubbl.us and MindMeister, or use a Smart Board.

These images and narratives will be with us throughout this study guide: they make up the constitutional ground of disability as a sociocultural phenomenon.
. . . .

The Medical Model and Discourses of Normalcy

The medical model of disability is still dominant in many areas of social life. It describes disability as being lodged within a person. In the medical model view, the disabled person is disabled by their specific physical and mental condition. That condition is worked upon by medical scientists. The doctor locates what is "aberrant," abnormal, about the patient, and works toward normalizing the disabled person.

The disability is here owned by the disabled person, and does not affect others. No one has to change what he, she or ze does in response to the fact that someone who is different is among them. In this perspective on difference, there is a norm, a central style of being, and all have to align themselves with this norm, or risk being seen as "different."

ABLEISM

The term "ableism" is useful when thinking through medical assessments of quality of life. "Ableism" is a concept that captures the social devaluation of disabled people – the word is used in similar ways as the words "racist," "homophobic," and "misogynist."

From an ableist perspective, the devaluation of disability results in societal attitudes that uncritically assert that it is better for a child to walk than to roll, speak than sign, read print than read Braille, spell independently than use a spell-check, and hang out with nondisabled kids as opposed to other disabled kids, etc. (Hehir, 2002: 3)

Think about notions of normalcy, pathology, and alignment in the century-long attempts to quell sign language for people with hearing impairments/Deaf people, in order to get them to "speak normally," even if that speech is then deemed "inferior" to "normals" and potentially inadequate to the impaired person's own communication requirements.

The medical model has led to forms of medical intervention such as cosmetic surgery for people with Down Syndrome, in an attempt to make them look more "normal." Inform yourself about this example, or another disputed medical intervention. Research, for instance, the Ashley Treatment ("Pillow Angel"), or, much more familiar to many, issues surrounding cochlear implants, aligning Deaf or deaf people with hearing ways of being. What are the bioethical problems and complexities around these kinds of medical interventions?

What is the upside of medical labeling? What are the positive aspects of having a name for one's condition, of having access to the support of a system that relies on diagnoses to allocate funds, accommodations, etc.?

How do other aspects of the medical-industrial complex intersect around diagnoses and labeling? Think about insurance, housing issues, home care services, the relationship between diagnoses and reproductive justice, etc.

As you think through some of these problematic areas, you will quickly find that many choices about how to identify as disabled or not, when, and to whom are strategic choices made in a field of complex relations.

Reframing "medicine" as the "medical/health-industrial complex" can allow you to see that medicine and health provision are not value-free, and that they mirror the concerns of a particular time and a particular regime. Knowledge about bodies and minds is shaped by and shapes the discourses and knowledge of an era.

The next two exercises offer different opportunities to think more about "normality," using art practices.

Relative Normality

Disability theorist Lennard Davis explains how "the normal" functions as a stabilizing feature in novels, but a stabilizing feature that relies on a very particular perspective. As you read through this, think about discourses of disability:

- How does art work engage and explain social worlds?
- How do issues of (medical) curing work in this kind of fictional universe?
- What is "the middle"? Can that shift?
- How do readers who depart from what is represented as "middle" find pleasure in reading?
- How are "middle" grounds established when central characters deviate from the norm?

If disability appears in a novel, it is rarely centrally represented. It is unusual for a main character to be a person with disabilities, although minor characters, like Tiny Tim, can be deformed in ways that arouse pity. In the case of Esther Summerson [from Dickens' Bleak House], who is scarred by smallpox, her scars are made to virtually disappear through the agency of love. On the other hand, as sufficient research has shown, more often than not villains tend to be physically abnormal: scarred, deformed, or mutilated.

I am not saying simply that novels embody the prejudices of society toward people with disabilities. That is clearly a truism. Rather, I am asserting that the very structure on which the novel rests tend to be normative, ideologically emphasizing the universal quality of the central character whose normativity encourages us to identify with him or her. Furthermore, the novel's goal is to reproduce, on some level, the semiologically normative signs surrounding the reader, that paradoxically help the reader to read those signs in the world as well as the text. Thus the middleness of life, the middleness of the material world, the middleness of the normal body, the middleness of the sexually gendered, ethnically middle world is created in symbolic form and then reproduced symbolically. This normativity in narrative will by definition create the abnormal, the Other, the disabled, the native, the colonized subject, and so on. (Davis, 1995: 41)

Rethinking Dominance

Drawing on images from his birthplace in the Philippines or his abiding interest in Native American culture, Peter Cordova (b. 1966) uses ink and watercolor to create detailed glimpses into various aspects of these ways of life. Everything is included, from carefully delineated tools and instruments to accurate yet stylized depictions of topography, so that the completed piece emulates an eyewitness account. "I want to speak for myself through my art. I try to share my heritage with other people." (from Creativity Explored artist website, an Oakland, California-based gallery workshop for adults with developmental disabilities)

Image 1 *Peter Cordova,* Animal Human, *monoprint on paper, 26.5" × 26.5" © 2009 Creativity Explored Licensing, LLC*

Describe the image to one another. You can use the Observation Wheel (in the Appendix) to garner your responses:

- How do lines between animals and humans, humans and land, feature in Peter Cordova's monoprint?
- Does the image shift how you think about maps and land, about who gets to live where?
- In what ways can this image be seen to be "about disability"? Is it useful to think about it in this register?

INDIGENEITY/DISABILITY

There are many structural ways that gender, racialization, or class structures are linked to disability debates. Here is a reminder from Australian disability theorists Gerard Goggin and Christopher Newell that alignments between racism and disability are multidirectional:

> For us the continuing spiritual, social and political devastation of Aboriginal and Torres Strait Islander peoples associated with a failure to adopt processes of reconciliation and justice making have a significant disability angle. Out of the practices of colonialization has arisen the situation where in so many ways our indigenous people are subject to much higher rates of disability and early death compared with non-indigenous Australians. (Goggin and Newell, 2005: 20–1)

Internationally, indigenous activists have critiqued settler perspectives that focus exclusively on indigenous suffering, as that suffering is too easily aligned with the equally pernicious settler discourse on "vanishing people." Australian Aboriginal disability activist Damien Griffis (2012) points to the reluctance to take on the disability label, due to histories of discrimination:

> By any measure, Aboriginal people with disabilities are amongst the most disadvantaged Australians. They often face multiple barriers to their meaningful participation within their own communities and the wider community. This continues to occur for a range of reasons including the fact that the vast majority of Aboriginal and Torres Strait Islanders with disabilities do not identify as a people with disability. This is because in traditional language there was no comparable word for 'disability'. Also the vast majority of Aboriginal and Torres Strait Islanders with disabilities are reluctant to take on a further negative label – particularly if they already experience discrimination based on their Aboriginality.

When discussing how disability turns up in public language and discourse fields, issues of who has power to name and label whom and why are central to a holistic understanding of the field.

The Social Model and Beyond

If the medical model locates disability in the disabled person and his or her specific "aberration," the social model of disability radically alters the mind frame, the reference points for knowledge.

In the social model, disability appears in the interaction between the impaired person and the social environment. A disabled person has an impairment, such as short arms, blindness, an inability to read, to respond to non-verbal cues, or to react immediately verbally to verbal cues. These impairments become a disability when these particular forms of being human encounter a society that favors design proportions that require long arms, visual communication, the written word, body language fluency, and fast dialogue. From the perspective of the social model, for a woman using a wheelchair, it is not her body or the wheelchair that disables her, but the architectural choice of stairs.

Barriers like inaccessible architecture, historically shaped attitudes, and the resulting institutional discrimination are now the disabling factors, not the individual body of a person. Disability becomes a social and environmental issue, not a medical one. But these discursive shifts do not happen evenly or in alignment. A lot of people code-switch, that is, they operate in multiple discourse systems. Some choose to operate in only one discourse community. Some blindness organizations, for instance, specifically do *not* advocate for accommodation in the social field, and instead train people to operate in a wholly normative environment, to assimilate themselves, arguing that this is the kind of environment most disabled people will find themselves in.

Different politics emerge from these choices. Disabled activists have taken the social definition of disability, and used it to campaign not for "special" treatment, as the medical establishment has offered, or "special" education, but for civil rights: the right to participate in society on equal terms, a society in which "disability" would vanish. This civic demand can only be met through anti-discrimination laws, and not by attempts to "normalize" people.

Of course, questions remain. How utopian, and how far from our existing world, would a non-disabling world really be, if we take many different impairments into account? Is there anybody who would still fall out of our common frame?

As we travel through this study guide, you will find many different ways in which disabled people and their allies have taken up art practices as a way to advocate for their place in society, or for far-reaching social change.

LIVING WITH THE SOCIAL MODEL: VIC FINKELSTEIN

This obituary of Vic Finkelstein, one of the drivers of disability discourse change, penned by a Welsh disability activist, speaks movingly to the effects of knowing disability differently. As you read this, pay attention to the shift in policy focus, and the effects on the self-image of the writer of the obituary, Rhian Davies. How did it make her *feel* to find out about this different way of thinking about disability?

It is with profound sadness that I heard about the death of Vic Finkelstein. Vic was a disabled person, writer and academic exiled to Britain following his anti-apartheid activities in South Africa. Together with Paul Hunt he co-founded the Union of the Physically Impaired Against Segregation (UPIAS) in 1972 and both are credited with originating what became known as the Social Model of Disability. Their vision for the emancipation of disabled people through access to mainstream services and support was considered revolutionary in an era where disabled people were largely invisible and 'looked after' either at home or in institutions.

Vic's ideas influenced and inspired a generation of disabled activists and gave rise to the development of the Disabled People's Movement through the formation of Centres for Independent Living, Coalitions of Disabled People and disability arts groups ... The ready acceptance of the Social Model of Disability by government and public bodies, however flawed the implementation, means that the policy focus is now on barrier removal and enabling people to live independently in their own homes. For this radical departure from post war approaches that emphasised welfare over rights, disabled people collectively owe much to Vic Finkelstein.

My own debt of gratitude to Vic is considerable. It was hearing him speak at an 'arts and disability' conference twenty five years ago that dramatically changed not only how I saw myself but the direction my involvement in disability issues was to take subsequently.

Having acquired a physical impairment six years previously I had quickly discovered the lack of access, insufficient support and negative attitudes disabled people face. Seeking to be part of change, I secured employment initially with a local disability association and then with an arts and disability organisation. I did not however consider myself a disabled person. After all there were many people far worse off than me.

In his conference speech Vic explained how people with impairments are disabled by society, *that disabled people should control their own organisations and develop their own culture. My experiences since becoming disabled were instantly illuminated. Instead of blaming myself for* not trying hard enough *to fit in with the 'able-bodied' world I realised that it was society that had failed to accommodate the reality of people with impairments. Furthermore rather than engaging in a personal struggle to be* normal *I was now part of a collective struggle to change the* disabling society.

To bemused and at times hostile reaction, on returning home I promoted the Social Model wherever and whenever I could. I became a Disability Equality Trainer and sought to develop a self-organised group of disabled people like those mushrooming elsewhere in the UK ...

Championing the Social Model of Disability has been one of the main driving forces in my life; to have learned about it directly from the person who devised it was a huge honour and privilege. (Davies, 2011)

GOING TO THE BAR: STAR WARS

Here, US poet and performance artist Neil Marcus remembers a moment that brings together his perspectives on normality, politics, joy, and solidarity:

i think it was 1977 when the first star wars movie came out. i was working – my first real job – 'disabled students coordinators' assistant' and developing my own 1st real awareness of myself as a disabled person being 'in the world.'

the bar scene [in the movie] seemed such an incredible concept. LUKE SKYWALKER this ordinary looking guy on a planet in a galaxy far away goes to a bar/nightclub on this planet and most everyone in this bar has a non human/alien look AND YET this is their home ... they are not strange. they are 'normal.' BINGO.

i go home that night thinking of r2d2 and his friend c3p0 and how an 'alien' bouncer in that bar wouldn't let them enter the bar with luke because they were 'droids' ... and that im going to adapt helen reddys' song 'i am woman, i am strong' and add 'that aint no way to treat an android' to her melody. and use it in the disabled students newsletter 'the rising tide'. (Marcus, private communication)

In this chapter, I have discussed two models of disability, the medical one and the social one, through a focus on discourses. The two represent radically different discourse worlds, ways of thinking about knowledges of disability, locations of disability, and understandings of where change can happen.

"Disability studies" itself is a new way of knowing, a particular discursive formation. It can now be found in humanities, social sciences or cultural studies departments as well as in other institutional contexts, and it often emerges from older and more established locations of disability, like rehabilitation and medical departments. As an area of study, it concerns itself with the meaning of disability in sociocultural contexts. It finds allies in many other identity-focused academic fields.

As an example of these cross-field encounters, here are a range of perspectives from the queer/disability studies intersection – they enact many of the tensions that characterize disability studies as a maturing discipline. They might also take a while to parse. We will return to the issues raised here at various points in this book, so you will have a chance to revisit them.

QUEER STUDIES/DISABILITY STUDIES

These two fields are often seen to be in close connection with one another, and the term "crip," styled in connection with the term "queer," has much currency in the field, even as it is still a contested term, with complicated heritages. Here is Carrie Sandahl in an early (2003) assessment of the relationships between the knowledge projects of disability studies and queer studies:

As academic corollaries of minority civil rights movements, queer theory and disability studies both have origins in and ongoing commitments to activism. Their primary constituencies, sexual minorities and people with disabilities, share a history of injustice: both have been pathologized by medicine; demonized by religion; discriminated against in housing, employment, and education; stereotyped in representation; victimized by hate groups; and isolated socially, often in their families of origin. Both constituencies are diverse in terms of race, class, gender, sexuality, religion, political affiliation, and other respects and therefore share many members (e.g., those who are disabled and gay), as well as allies. Both have self-consciously created their own enclaves and vibrant subcultural practices.

Perhaps the most significant similarity between these disciplines, however, is their radical stance toward concepts of normalcy; both argue adamantly against the compulsion to

CRIP, THE PROMISE OF LEGITIMACY, AND THE POSTER CHILD FROM HELL

"Crip theorizing" becomes a way of radicalizing disability politics, of pointing to the promise of the non-normate, the radical potential in disobedience and excess in the face of a market-driven society. As you parse this section and look up the artists and public persons mentioned, ask yourself:

- How can visual registers, from propriety to excess, from realist to fantastic, speak to politics?
- What aspects of disability arts and culture align themselves with the more radical edges, undermining legibility, realism, and integration, and instead celebrating excess, failure, illegibility, and non-absorption?

In her essay "Seeing the Disabled," Rosemarie Garland-Thomson investigates the visual rhetorics of disability. She sorts popular photographs of disabled people into the categories of wondrous, sentimental, exotic, and realist. Finally, she ends on the "least visually vivid" (2000: 369) of the images she discusses, a portrait of Judith Heumann, then associate secretary of education in the Clinton administration, an image Garland-Thomson describes with words like "everyday," "dignity," and "authority." She argues that this kind of image, in the

> *realistic mode is most likely to encourage the cultural work the Disability Rights movement began. Imagining disability as ordinary, as the typical rather than the atypical human experience, can promote practices of equality and inclusion that begin to fulfill the promise of a democratic order. (Garland-Thomson, 2000: 372)*

Robert McRuer is one of the central writers of queer crip theorizing, and he explicitly holds against a normalizing integrative politics of disability. McRuer engages with the Heumann image, the "promise of the democratic order," and the problems with contemporary capitalist state systems. He is not convinced that ordinariness and authority are the only aesthetic goals worth reaching for. He focuses on a different image, also in Garland-Thomson's essay – one by Bob Flanagan, a much discussed performance artist who used sadomasochistic body practices in his installation and video work, usually collaboratively conceived with Sheree Rose. McRuer (2006: 194) writes:

> *Flanagan was fabulous not because he looked at the straight guy and saw someone in a hapless state who could be spruced up so that conspicuous consumption and heteronormativity could continue apace. ... Essentially invoking his safe world (refusing, that is, to go there) and continually becoming the poster child from hell, Flanagan imagines crip existence as atypical and reached for something beyond the current order.*

McRuer ends his chapter on parallels between the normalization and marketization of queer cultures, and the potential fate of disability edges. Keep these questions in mind as you find out more about disability arts and culture:

- In what ways are disability cultures and crip cultures in the process of being circumscribed, monetized, or privatized?
- When disability becomes normal, enters the workplace, and becomes legitimate, is something lost?
- What queer crip edge spaces remain, and how can they work toward different futures?

Keeping an eye on the horizon, we should nonetheless demand access to other worlds – worlds that are public, democratic, expansive and extraordinary. (McRuer, 2006: 198)

EXERCISE 3.4   **Sins Invalid**

Image 2 *Nomy Lamm and Cara Page, Sins Invalid. Photo: Richard Downing, © 2009, courtesy of Sins Invalid*

Use the Observation Wheel to describe this image to each other. What is your response to the body shapes represented here, and how do abundance and proliferation signify in this image?

Research the work of Sins Invalid, "a performance project on disability and sexuality that incubates and celebrates artists with disabilities, centralizing artists of color and queer and gender-variant artists as communities who have been historically marginalized from social discourse" (company website). See how queer/disability/racialization connections emerge in their practice.

In her book *Feminist Queer Crip*, US theorist Alison Kafer marks crip theory as a site where she can push against orthodoxies, uncovering hidden complexities in both disability and queer studies. No longer mainly engaged in forming a somewhat united activist front, as disability civil rights activists did, crip theorizing can unsettle anew:

> *I am writing out of concern, for example, about the silence of disability studies scholars and disability activists in response to how our movements have often been publically aligned with the right. Where were the public feminist/queer/crip responses to Sarah Palin [Alaskan governor, vice-presidential candidate, mother of a child with Down Syndrome]? How might we have intervened in the representation of her as a disability rights advocate, questioning the blurring of anti-choice ideologies and disability critiques of prenatal testing? Or how might a feminist/queer/crip informed analysis expand or complicate queer theoretical texts that rely on a trope of mobility for their analyses or tend to allegorize rather than analyze disability and disabled bodies? (Kafer, 2013: 18)*

Playing with Models: Arts Practice

Beyond the two models I've discussed here, there are others – the very notion of "models" as way of organizing knowledge is very seductive, as it allows one to shape complex life situations and power relations into manageable stories.

There are multiple critiques of the social model and what many see as its silence on pain, chronic illness, fatigue, and trauma as lived realities, not just as social constructs (for a charting of the development, arguments for and against social model theorizing, see Barnes, 2012).

Other models exist, such as the minoritarian model or the affirmative model – "essentially a non-tragic view of disability and impairment which encompasses positive social identities, both individual and collective, for disabled people grounded in the benefits of lifestyle of being impaired and disabled" (Swain and French, 2000: 570). All these models are ways of organizing knowledge toward action.

The process that will lead to a more welcoming society for people with differences, impairments, or disabilities is long. While some of us wish to be integrated into a more just society, others see great value in the affirmation of difference, and in the particular nuances of the challenge disability offers to capitalist systems that try to produce sameness and extract value.

One of the places where these politics play out is in the arts and in art education: disabled artists and their allies challenge and query the knowledge that governs how we see what it means to be human, but also how we see artwork itself. Through their practices, artists can choose to analyze the norms that underlie our conceptions of excellence. But it is not easy to undermine the status quo, and disabled artists face many challenges as they make choices about how to identify, how to place their work, how to find audiences.

There are problems with the establishment of a minority arts culture, creating spaces for new activities apart from the mainstream traditional and experimental scenes.

In this passage, Aaron Williamson offers up a critical perspective on the emergence of disability art as a funding category within arts councils, with its own festivals, and its own "circuit":

> If the artistic activities of a minority identity group are either ignored or sidelined by the majority, then it's possible to refer to the existence of a cultural ghetto. For many years, the situation (in the UK at least) has been one in which the same small group of 'disability artists' show work to their familiar audience – consisting, in the main, of other disabled people – without achieving much extraneous critical debate or appreciation. This effect is referred to within the community as 'the disability art ghetto' since its activities and achievements remain isolated and unknown to indifferent mainstream (supposedly 'non-disabled') audiences.
>
> The ghetto can form from within too: many disability artists, festivals and organisations maintain themselves without seeking involvement or critical attention from the mainstream and a fairly established, yet isolationist, culture receives significant support through public funding. (Williamson, 2011)

In his essay, Williamson goes on to call for critical engagement across the arts sector and within the disability arts community, as a way to emerge out of what he sees as a static place of non-growth. But he also stays attuned to the ways that disabled people continue to be left out of the educational institutions that can support such critical development. Research the "disability arts ghetto" discussion, and discuss the opportunities and problems with it.

In the remaining part of this chapter, I introduce a range of exercises and arts-based interventions around the notion of modeling. Some of these exercises engage "low-brow" materials and practices like Barbie dolls and community theatre, stepping away from "high art" notions of what artistic materials should be, and what the subject matter of "good art" is supposed to be. As you engage with some of these exercises, be aware of these interventions into disability discourse *and* art practice.

EXERCISE 3.5 ## Playing with Models

As a group activity, look at these images and captions created by British disability activist and artist Ju Gosling. Use the Observation Wheel to slow down your reception, and pay attention to all aspects of the assemblages. How do they "illustrate" models of disability? If you look at these images online, in their original publication, at www.ju90.co.uk/help/eng/help1.htm, you can also see the colors of the luscious gowns. What do color schemes, mise-en-scène (organization within the frame), and choice of dolls signify? What is the edginess of these images, what do they signify about the models, and the concept of "models" itself?

a *I want to help the handicapped!... according to the Charity Model of Disability*

I organise social events for non-disabled people. This raises money to create jobs for non-disabled people. Then we provide the disabled people whom we think are deserving with the things that we think they need.

b *I want to help the handicapped!... according to the Medical Model of Disability*

I invent and administer tests to classify disabled people according to what I think are their impairments. Then I carry out experiments to try to make them more like me. If I fail, I try to identify and kill them before they are born.

c *I want to help the handicapped!... according to the Administrative Model of Disability*

I invent and administer tests to classify disabled people by what I think are their inabilities. Then I judge the minimum level of benefits and services that I think they need to survive.

d *I want to help the handicapped!... according to the Social Model of Disability*

I fight against prejudice, discrimination and disabling environments. I fight for equal rights legislation and better health and social care provision. I also fight to eliminate the poverty, abuse, violence and war that cause the majority of impairments.

Image 3 *Helping the Handicapped, Ju Gosling aka ju90 © 2003*

• •

ACTIVITY 1 ## Feeling Complex: Eli Clare

Models are useful for allowing us to see the world differently, but they are not very good at capturing the fine-grained ways in which experience, self-worth, and emotions interact. Here is a reflection by Eli Clare, a US-based writer who talks about his gender journey, his life with cerebral palsy, and his attempts (at that time, her attempts) to reach toward the supercrip, the supremely overcoming individual. In the scene, Clare is attempting to climb a mountain, together with a friend, Adrianne. They've been climbing for a long time:

> We study the topo map, do a time check. We have many hours of daylight ahead of us, but we're both thinking about how much time it might take me to climb down, using my hands and butt when I can't trust my feet. I want to continue up to treeline, the pines shorter and shorter, grown twisted and withered, giving way to scrub brush, then to lichen-covered granite, up to the sun-drenched cap where the mountains all tumble out toward the hazy blue horizon. I want to so badly, but fear rumbles next to love next to real lived physical limitations, and so we decide to turn around. I cry, maybe for the first time, over something I want to do, had many reasons to believe I could, but really can't. I cry hard, then get up and follow Adrianne back down the mountain. It's hard and slow, and I use my hands and butt often and wish I could use gravity as Adrianne does to bounce from one flat spot to another, down this jumbled pile of rocks.
>
> I thought a lot coming down Mount Adams. Thought about bitterness. For as long as I can remember, I have avoided certain questions. Would I have been a good runner if I didn't have CP? Could I have been a surgeon or pianist, a dancer or gymnast? Tempting questions that have no answers. I refuse to enter the territory marked bitterness. I wondered about a friend who calls herself one of the last of the polio tribe, born just before the polio vaccine's discovery. Does she ever ask what her life might look like had she been born five years later? On a topo map, bitterness would be outlined in red.
>
> I thought about the model of disability that separates impairment from disability. Disability theorist Michael Oliver defines impairment as "lacking part of or all of a limb, or having a defective limb, organism or mechanism of the body." (Oliver, 1990: 33–4 [quoting from UPIAS, 1976: 20]). I lack a fair amount of fine motor control. My hands shake. I can't play a piano, place my hands gently on a keyboard, or type even 15 words a minute. Whole paragraphs never cascade from my fingertips. My long-hand is a slow scrawl. I have trouble picking up small objects, putting them down. Dicing onions with a sharp knife puts my hands at risk. A food processor is not a yuppie kitchen luxury in my house, but an adaptive device. My gross motor skills are better but not great. I can walk mile after mile, run and jump and skip and hop, but don't expect me to walk a balance beam. A tightrope would be murder; boulder hopping and rock climbing, not much better. I am not asking for pity. I am telling you about impairment.
>
> Oliver defines disability as "the disadvantage or restriction of activity caused by a contemporary social organisation which takes no or little account of people who have physical [and/or cognitive/developmental/ mental] impairments and thus excludes them from the mainstream of society." (Union of the Physically Impaired Against Segregation, with additions by Oliver, 1990). I write slowly enough that cashiers get impatient as I sign my name to checks, stop talking to me, turn to my companions,

hand them my receipts. I have failed timed tests, important tests, because teachers wouldn't allow me extra time to finish the sheer physical act of writing, wouldn't allow me to use a typewriter. I have been turned away from jobs because my potential employer believed my slow, slurred speech meant I was stupid. Everywhere I go people stare at me, in restaurants as I eat, in grocery stores as I fish coins out of my pocket to pay the cashier, in parks as I play with my dog. I am not asking for pity. I am telling you about disability.

In large part, disability oppression is about access. Simply being on Mount Adams, halfway up Air Line Trail, represents a whole lot of access. When access is measured by curb cuts, ramps, and whether they are kept clear of snow and ice in the winter; by the width of doors and height of counters; by the presence or absence of Braille, closed captions, ASL, and TDDs; my not being able to climb all the way to the very top of Mount Adams stops being about disability. I decided that turning around before reaching the summit was more about impairment than disability.

But even as I formed the thought, I could feel my resistance to it. To neatly divide disability from impairment doesn't feel right. My experience of living with CP has been so shaped by ableism or to use Oliver's language, my experience of impairment has been so shaped by disability – that I have trouble separating the two. I understand the difference between failing a test because some stupid school rule won't give me more time and failing to summit Mount Adams because it's too steep and slippery for my feet. The first failure centers on a socially constructed limitation, the second on a physical one.

At the same time, both center on my body. The faster I try to write, the more my pen slides out of control, muscles spasm, then contract trying to stop the tremors, my shoulder and upper arm, growing painfully tight. Even though this socially constructed limitation has a simple solution – access to a typewriter, computer, tape recorder, or person to take dictation – I experience the problem on a very physical level. In the case of the bodily limitation, my experience is similarly physical. My feet simply don't know the necessary balance. I lurch along from one rock to the next, catching myself repeatedly as I start to fall, quads quickly sore from exertion, tension, lack of momentum. These physical experiences, one caused by a social construction, the other by a bodily limitation, translate directly into frustration, making me want to crumple the test I can't finish, hurl the rocks I can't climb. This frustration knows no neat theoretical divide between disability and impairment. Neither does disappointment nor embarrassment. On good days, I can separate the anger I turn inward at my body from the anger that needs to be turned outward, directed at the daily ableist shit, but there is nothing simple or neat about kindling the latter while transforming the former. I decided that Oliver's model of disability makes theoretical and political sense but misses important emotional realities. (Clare, 1999, 5–7. Reprinted with publisher's permission)

Activity Instruction: Writing from the Body/Mind

1 In this passage, Clare articulates many different ways of knowing, and of making sense of experience. Make lists:

- What is the place of the body in his discussion?
- What are moments in this passage where a body enters into a social scene?
- What is the place of emotions in this scene?

Discuss with the class or a small group:

- How does Clare manage to center embodied experience in this passage, and how is he using it as a tool to address models of disability?

2 Now think about a particular agenda or social model toward which you feel yourself in ambivalent relation – examples might include feminism, nationalism, union solidarity, patriotism, ethnic pride, queer analysis, religious beliefs. How is your own body part of the feelings you have? How does what you consider to be "your body/mind/feelings" "betray" or affirm your politics? Write a scene in which this happens. Keep it focused on your emotions and sensations, try to heighten these descriptive passages. Share your writing with a colleague, and discuss the effect of sensory information on the argument.

ACTIVITY 2 Sculpting with Augusto Boal

This exercise is inspired by Augusto Boal's work on the Theatre of the Oppressed (TOTO), which included work with psychiatric survivors, indigenous people, and oppressed workers. TOTO is a complex system, and this exercise just gives a very introductory flavor of it. Find out more about it!

Boal used theatrical mechanisms to allow people to find their own way to envision change, and to examine power dynamics in a community.

Mirror/Clay

Everyone gets a partner. One partner will start as the sculptor, the other as clay. Sculptors can sculpt by touching the "clay" and moving their partner into place or by mirroring and showing them the position they should take. This is a silent activity.

Now, a volunteer uses two to four other volunteers to model a particular disability model's way of feeling: express it through sculptural form, shaping your partners, using both mirroring and clay play as your ways of shaping them. The goal is not to illustrate the word or to play charades. It is to shape, imagine, and create. The image can be realistic, abstract, concrete, or symbolic. The point of the exercise is not to role-play disability, but to see what happens when you shape, to see what comes to the surface. Do not think too hard about it, just do it.

Sample Instructions

Some sample concepts to sculpt might be:

- the medical model of disability
- the social model of disability
- minority identity.

If you have never done Boal work before, these might feel abstract, but it's actually very interesting to find out how much of the "feel" of an abstract concept emerges when one just does it, not having to say why one sculpts it the way one does. Understandings might be derived at in the process of doing this.

Other, less abstract, examples could include:

- Going to the Doctor
- Welfare Office
- Home Care Services
- Social Worker Assessment Visit

Once the volunteer sculptor has finished, others in the circle step forward and reshape the people in the circle (and they can add more), until everybody feels that the particular model/social situation is well captured.

Development: Group Sculpture

Working as a group, create a group sculpture. Create a circle, call out a model of disability to enact. Again, don't think too long. One by one, step into the circle and take a position that expresses this model, in whatever social role you have chosen, until all are in the circle. Now, the first person in comes out, and, to use Boal's language, "dynamizes" the sculpture, transforms this group sculpture into something hopeful, something that can push back against oppression, collaboratively. One by one people come out, and reshape what is there, putting people back into it, and so on, until you feel an end point is reached.

When you are done with this, discuss the insights, feelings, and associations that came up for you during this exercise.

Augusto Boal began his work in the 1950s in Brazil. He critiqued the stage-bound mainstream theatre, advocating for a dialogic model of performance work, one that had the power to reshape power dynamics by allowing people to come to expression on their own terms, and to find solidarity together in the excitement of performance. For him, and for many radical performance artists of the 20th and 21st century, that meant breaking with traditional forms of art practice, finding new tools of expression.

We will find that this is something that has influenced much disability culture work: a need to find new modes of expression, reinventing art forms, not just filling them with new content, but putting them into a new relationship to lived experience and social change. Understanding one's self to be engaged in an ongoing public and private performance, an enactment and engagement with public meanings of "disability," underlies the politics of many artists and theorists we've encountered so far.

Signifiyin'

This practice is associated with (often urban and male) black speakers and it introduces things indirectly, slanted, often with humor, insult or provocation. Henry Louis Gates is an African-American theorist who has written extensively about the origin of this aesthetic of speaking complexly, focusing on the Signifying Monkey, an African trickster figure. In disability culture, some of the plays with words, concepts, and meanings of "disability" have a similar tricksterish strategy. Research the concept, see how it appears in the everyday, and see if you can see connections between this African-American vernacular poetics and the kind of play you are seeing in emerging disability culture. Are some of the rhetorical choices around the word "crip," for instance, aligned with forms of signifiyin'?

Disidentification

This excerpt from a campus study at Brandeis University introduces you to ways of thinking about engaging with identities artfully. Can you see connections to your own self-representation, the way you see yourself as a gendered, sexed, raced, classed, or disabled subject? In a small group, discuss how issues of identification, counteridentification, and disidentification impact your own lives.

Depending on how personal you want to get, and how the atmosphere in the classroom develops, you might want to think about ways of sharing insights without personal specificity.

> *Coping with gender attribution can be hard on many queer-identified individuals, which is why practices such as 'disidentification' can be helpful when navigating gender. Disidentification is one of three modes that individuals can use to help them navigate though the maze of sex, gender, and queer language.*

> *The first mode is one that many of us are familiar with: 'identification.' Identification is where a "'Good Subject' chooses the path of identification with discursive and ideological forms" (Muñoz, 1999: 11).*

> *Similarly, the second mode, 'counteridentification,' is where "'Bad Subjects' resist and attempt to reject the images and identificatory sites offered by dominant ideology and proceed to rebel" (Muñoz, 11).*

> *The third mode, José Esteban Muñoz writes, is "one that neither opts to assimilate within such a structure nor opposes it; rather, disidentification is a strategy that works on and against dominant ideology" (Muñoz, 11).*

> *Disidentification, in relation to gender, can thus be seen as a way of problematizing or queering the social gender norms that already exist not by submitting to them (identification) or by breaking free of them (counteridentification) but by consciously subverting them.*

Although none of the people interviewed for this essay described their experiences explicitly as that of disidentification, it is clear that many of their emotions about gender on the Brandeis campus can be seen and understood through this lens quite easily.

A perfect example is the way that Participant C manages hir identity and privilege within the larger Brandeis community as opposed to that of the QRC (Queer Resource Center).

Participant C notes often in hir interview that ze feels that ze "go[es] completely unnoticed" in the community at large because ze is "assumed to be 'normal,'" and thus ze is hardly given a second glance because of hir cis-gendered identity and presentation. Participant C points out, "I definitely feel I have a lot of privilege working in my favor at Brandeis in really all respects – in dorms, in my classes, in attempting to mate, in my friendships, certainly in stupid gendered stuff like ballroom [dancing.]"

However, despite this privilege, invisibility, and 'normal' presentation, Participant C insists that ze does indeed attempt to queer or subvert the societal gender norms. Participant C adds, "except, I also feel that my gender identity and my expression is just as much of a performance or a game as if it were less cis[-gendered]. I can be girly AND burly in the same sentence, which is lots of fun for me. The skirts are a game – it's like playing dress-up, because it's REQUIRED by my gender formation."

This attitude can accurately be seen as a type of disidentification. Participant C is neither staying fully within the cis-gendered norm nor attempting to smash it into little bits either. Instead Participant C is attempting to subvert the norm by hir personal performance of gender in order to inform others and work on the dominant ideology from the inside rather than the outside. (Simonoff, 2011)

· ·

Disability arts expressions often stand in complex relation to dominant forms of cultural labor. As we move through this study guide, ask yourself if and how disability culture artists disidentify with dominant art forms. Pay attention to the ways the texts and practices you find fit into and fall out of models, shift discourses into new pathways, and open up ways of thinking.

4 Embodiment and Enmindment: Processes of Living

In this chapter, you will gain insights into these issues:

- Getting in touch with our bodymind in its environment
- What embodiment and enmindment are
- Finding complexity in body stories
- Performativity and disability
- Intersectionality and its effects on disability frameworks
- Disability in time and space, crip time
- Simulation exercises and their alternatives
- Public aesthetics
- Wellness as a disability value

In this chapter, we will look at what we bring to the classroom and the acts of making sense of living in this world: our own bodies and minds. Disability studies invites us to think about the discourses that determine appropriate objects of knowledge, and the power relations that shape knowledge generation and management. The field also makes us think about protocols, about the rules by which we live together. We can think about what is deemed public and what is deemed private, and why. We can reflect on norms of behavior as historically contingent, that is, related to their time and space, not absolute, or set in stone.

Feeling and Being

The upcoming exercises focus on feeling, experiencing, and analyzing some of these givens in relation to our own selves. This chapter invites you to link your own self, your own sense of being a bodymind, to what we are studying.

For this next exercise, if you are not doing this in a classroom with a group of people, find a place you find calming. I do this exercise in my undergraduate classroom once a week, and I repeat a particular sequence, so that we all get very used to it, and can easily and quickly sink into it. You'll most likely find it a bit weird at first, unless you've done relaxation exercises before – just go with it, for now, and repeat this over a number of days.

EXERCISE 4.1   **Relaxation**

This exercise will take about five minutes. Find a good place for your limbs: you might be sitting or lying down. Settle. And once you have done this, put this book down (having read ahead). I am offering two versions here: one that you can just read and then hopefully remember. And one that you can speak into your phone or other recording device, and play to yourself, for a longer relaxation journey.

In both cases, if you fall asleep, that's fine – you probably needed that. Close your eyes if you are comfortable with this, or keep them soft and open if you are not.

There is no immediate follow-up to this exercise: it's just something to do, with no embarrassing questions afterwards. Enjoy. And whoever is reading the lines, or making up similar ones, speak slowly, calmly, and get into a slow steady rhythm.

Version 1

Breathe. Breathe in and out, in your own rhythm. Feel your weight on your support surfaces. Feel yourself settle. Count 20 in breaths, and take your time.

Version 2

Breathe. Breathe in and out, in your own rhythm. Feel your weight on your support surfaces: feel your weight on the underside of your legs, your posterior, feel it in your arms. How does gravity flow through you? Pay attention to your weight flowing through you, running down toward the earth. Feel the earth rising up to support you, holding you through the surfaces of your chair.

Feel your breath flowing into you. Where do you expand? Where do you contract? Without a need to change anything, just trace where there's flow, where there is expansion. Feel your chest change shape, feel your back shifting with every breath you take.

For the next 10 breaths, just pay attention to the air flowing in and out of you, the rhythm of filling and emptying. Feel yourself shifting shape.

To remind you that it is OK – if your shopping list or to-do list begins to come into your mind, say hello to it, acknowledge it, and let it go. There is no right or wrong here. If you lose the thread of the exercises, just focus on your breathing, in and out, until you are tuned back to the voice guiding you.

And something to end with – slowly, it is time to come back to our shared space. Over the next 10 breaths or so, slowly open your eyes and stretch – and keep your eyes soft, so you are not intruding on someone else's privacy.

Disruption is an experience we all have in many classrooms. There is always a lot going on: air-conditioners or heaters banging and groaning, voices in the corridors, doors banging. In one development of the relaxation exercises above, you can invite these noises into your space, and try to make peace with them as the signs of life that surround us.

Again, this is just a relaxation exercise – but in the context of a disability studies classroom, it is also a lived exploration of the ways we are connected to the world as sensing, breathing creatures, always responsive and alert, often overwhelmed, and with skills to manage ourselves.

EXERCISE 4.2 ## Opening Awareness

This segment can easily be added to or woven into the relaxation sequence above.

Breathe in and out, in your own rhythm. Now become aware of the sounds that surround you. What is happening in our shared space? Listen to the sounds of the corridor, the signs of life of a university, energies flowing through rooms and spaces. Listen to the sounds of the mechanical supports of our lives, to the heater, air-conditioners, lights, phones, laptops, cars.

Try to listen to the melodies and rhythms of these soundscapes, invite them into your consciousness, rather than pushing against them as distractions. What is the particular quality of the sounds? How is your bodymind responding to them? Hear them, listen to them, and then let them go. Examine another sensation that emerges for you. If there are windows in the space, can you feel light on your skin, coming from the sun? Or a draft from heating devices, or freshness from a window?

Chart how your environment touches your skin, how it interacts with your clothes, how you sense yourself in space. Get interested in what is around you, as you sit, eyes closed, breathing, safe and secure.

Development

After engaging in these exercises a few times, over a period of a few weeks, have a discussion in class about connections between disability arts and culture and these explorations of meditation and embodiment.

Embodiment and Enmindment

"Embodiment" is a term that is not easily graspable. It makes something very natural, very unremarked, suddenly remarkable, cultural, and specific: our own sense of how we live. You might notice that as soon as you read this, you are likely to become a bit more self-conscious, maybe feeling your seat on your chair, if you are sitting down, or becoming awkwardly aware of how you are holding this book or reading device. You might suddenly become aware of how you hold your head, and whether or not your shoulders are curved forward as you read. Sorry!

My aim here is not to make you deeply self-conscious, but to draw attention to the remarkable ability of our embodiment to make itself unnoticable to our senses. Unless we are differently tuned to the world, live with pain, or a heightened sensitivity, we do not usually pay attention to all these things – unless our back is hurting from too many hours reading, or we are overwhelmed with managing too many incoming sensations. So much of our embodiment, our ways of coming to be and live a body, is invisible to the majority of us, most of the time.

I am adding the term "enmindment" here: it is a similarly charged term, one that I use to draw attention to the non-naturalness of how we come to be enminded, or "have a mind." We do not have a mind and a body: we are a bodymind. And there are many different states of enmindedness, too, not just one "right" way. That step of rethinking alone presents a significant departure from a cultural orientation that sees a division between body, mind, and self. Against this divisionary thinking – usually shorthanded by calling it Cartesian thought, derived from the philosopher Descartes – stands another Western philosophical tradition, shorthanded as Spinozian thought. Spinoza asked not "what is a body," but "what does a body do" – shifting the emphasis from the body as object to embodiment as a process, as a way of doing things.

COMMUNICATE WITH ME: D.J. SAVARESE

In this quote from autistic author D.J. Savarese, he writes about sensory overwhelm and modes of regulating his sense input. Can you see the relationship between the relaxation and sensory exercises above, and Savarese's interdependent management of self and environment?

The first question people freshly asked was why I sometimes have someone hold the pencil while I type or write. The answer is that the person fearlessly makes me feel safe by helping me regulate my nervous system. The adult helps me not to greet the kids directly. If I greet them directly, I get over-stimulated, and my feelings grow so strong that holding them inside is impossible. I desert reason, and my body repeatedly begins to flap or reach freshly toward them. I love greeting kids, but it can cause me to desert self-control temporarily. Another reason why I use a facilitator is to help me focus. The Frees (speaking people without autism) who understand me know how to hear my dear self. They greet my dear self and free me to respond. Treating me as free, they tell me what to do until my breathing feels deep and slow, and my fingers and eyes can once again communicate with each other, so I can type my thoughts. Years of inhaling voluntarily greet hope that I can regulate my own sensory input and hold myself in control. ...

Other kids who knew me in third and fourth grade asked if I can hear because my aide used to sign everything to me. Yes, I can hear, but getting nervous is ultimately deafening to me. What that means is that when I get fearful and desert the real world, I seem to detach my ears and hold my dear self hostage. At times like these, I cannot make sense of what you say, but most of the time I do hear and understand real voices. So talk to me, and I will hopefully respond. If you don't know me very well, can you just start talking to me? Yes, but I might act like you're not there at first. It takes dear, real self time to tell my breaking-the-barrier heart to quit pounding so loudly, so I can respond. In biology we studied the central and peripheral nervous systems. This helped me understand why there is a delay in my responses. Stress and excitement cause my sympathetic autonomic system to engage. My body then kicks on my parasympathetic response. Only after homeostasis is achieved can I give a voluntary motor response. (Savarese, 2010)

Performing Body Histories

Image 4 *Michael Williamson,* Flayed *(2010), denim, leather, brass, copper; 109" H × 42" W × 3" D*

> Flayed *sprang from rip-stripping rituals, both private and semi-public, repurposing six pairs of my own well-worn thrift-store Levis. The hidden stories of previous wearers infuse the physical traces of my own HiV+ queer journey. With antecedents as diverse as ecclesiastical altarpieces and vestments, the* Names Project, *and public sexuality, the piece embodies remembrance, transformation, eroticism and celebration. (artist statement)*

Describe this image to each other, with the help of the Observation Wheel. How does the sculpture address issues of embodiment, and how what happens to dominant images of HIV+/AIDS in it? What are your associations, and how does the sculpture play with these associations?

Performativity

"Performativity" refers to performance, as echoed in the word itself: identity is performed, is not a set given, but is rehearsed, shaped, and enacted again and again. But performativity is not performance in the common art practice sense: it is not just a set of choices fully within conscious control. It is not just an issue of selecting the pink rather than blue color scheme, and putting on skirts instead of trousers, although these choices are part of gender performance.

Where performativity operates differently from common understandings of performance are the places where one's rational engagement is not so easily apparent. What parts of gender performances are outside conscious control?

If we grew up in a language with gendered word endings, unthinking gender as a binary system is hard to do. At the same time, since we are at this point in an English-speaking classroom, all those who grew up or became bilingual have the great advantage of being able to think in different linguistic and cultural systems: a great help in understanding how language shapes ways of thinking.

Repeating, with differences, becomes a productive way of shifting certainties:

If the ground of gender is the stylized repetition of acts through time, and not a seemingly seamless identity, then the possibilities of gender transformation are to be found in the arbitrary relation between such acts, in the possibility of a different sort of repeating, in the breaking or subversive repetition of that style. (Butler, 1990: 271)

EXERCISE 4.4   ## Gender Performance

Get together with a colleague, and discuss how gender performance shapes your self-representations on this particular day. Try to be open to many different layers of unconscious choice versus conscious channel, internal versus external influence: styles of sitting and walking, of wearing one's hair, wardrobe choices and the stores we buy things in, parents' and peer approaches to gender performance and how that has influenced you, religious or other cultural influences on you, and whether you vary your gender presentation in different contexts. Take turns, and go back and forth more than twice to allow yourself time to ask new questions as you learn from each other.

Now switch partner, and discuss the same issue, but in relation to race, not gender. Are you aware of how you perform your race?

In all these "disclosure" exercises, you can construct fantasy identities, speak from the position of someone you know but do not identify, or find other ways to circumvent unwarranted or unsafe disclosure and discomfort.

So how does disability enter into these scenes of embodiment/ enmindment and their meaning? What does disability studies have to do with issues of performativity? Read through this list of people and their ways of being. How do these scenarios link to your emerging understanding of disability studies?

- a young white woman with chronic stomachache who spends long times in the restroom
- an athlete with a torn meniscus
- a black woman with fibroids
- a survivor of domestic violence, a woman of color, being told by her abuser that she can take more pain than a white woman
- an older man who smells of urine
- a person who is not sure about which restroom he/she/ze can safely use.

To fully understand some of the context for this list, you might need to:

- use your Internet skills to find out about the incidence of fibroids in different racialized communities, and the effect fibroids have on women who experience them
- look up slavery medicine, and how historical ideas about the differential pain sensitivity of raced and gendered groups have developed
- look at access features for transgender people, and think about the effects of a binary gender world on transpeople's sense of belonging and location

- educate yourself about the politics of college sport, and the way physical prowess and financial support are linked together
- link issues of body image and expectations for beauty for young people with eating disorders and ways of medicalizing appearance.

As you can see, to fully understand disability embodiment connections, many different knowledges need to come together: race, gender, class, sexuality, and disability are constituted in relation to one another, they are not separate entities one can pick apart.

WHITE DISABILITY STUDIES

In a provocative polemic, Chris Bell, US disability and HIV/AIDS studies scholar, critiqued the disability field of study. As you read his words, track how they impact you emotionally, however you identify, and how they charge you to be aware of what might not be in your field of vision (to use a visualist metaphor):

> White Disability Studies recognizes its tendency to whitewash disability history, ontology and phenomenology. White Disability Studies, while not wholeheartedly excluding people of color from its critique, by and large focuses on the work of white individuals and is itself largely produced by a corps of white scholars and activists. White Disability Studies envisions nothing ill-advised with its leaning because it is innocently done and far too difficult to remedy. (Bell, 2006: 275)

INTERSECTIONALITY

Kimberlé Crenshaw and Patricia Hill Collins are two US-based critical race theorists associated with the concept of "intersectionality," a way of thinking about oppression and interlocking mechanisms. Here is a quote from Collins' work that points to two areas of thought that are also deeply woven into contemporary disability theory:

> Afrocentric feminist thought offers two significant contributions toward furthering our understanding of the important connections among knowledge, consciousness, and the politics of empowerment. First, Black feminist thought fosters a fundamental paradigmatic shift in how we think about oppression. By embracing a paradigm of race, class, and gender as interlocking systems of oppression, Black feminist thought reconceptualizes the social relations of domination and resistance. Second, Black feminist thought addresses ongoing epistemological debates in feminist theory and in the sociology of knowledge concerning ways of assessing 'truth.' Offering subordinate groups new knowledge about their own experiences can be empowering. But revealing new ways of knowing that allow subordinate groups to define their own reality has far greater implications. (Collins, 1990: 222)

Disability studies introduces "disability" into this equation. Think about some of the implications of this way of thinking. How are race, gender, class, and disability intersecting? Find discussion points, and share them with the group.

In relation to Collins' second point: Can embodiment exercises offer tools to redefine reality? Are we exploring new methods of knowing when we pay attention to lived experience? How?

Transformation

How can a discussion of intersectionality inform your approach to this poem, by LA-based artist Lynn Manning (2009)?

"The Magic Wand" *by Lynn Manning*

Quick-change artist extraordinaire,
I whip out my folded cane
and change from black man to blind man
with a flick of my wrist.

It is a profound metamorphosis—
From God gifted wizard of roundball
dominating backboards across America,
To God-gifted idiot savant composer
pounding out chart-busters on a cockeyed whim;
From sociopathic gangbanger with death for eyes
to all-seeing soul with saintly spirit;
From rape deranged misogynist
to poor motherless child;
From welfare-rich pimp
to disability-rich gimp;
And from 'white man's burden'
to every man's burden.

It is always a profound metamorphosis.
Whether from cursed by man to cursed by God;
or from scriptures condemned to God ordained,
My final form is never of my choosing;
I only wield the wand;
You are the magicians.

Development

Can you find a different poem or art work that is as explicit about intersectionality, but written from a different racialized perspective? Reflect on whether that is easy or hard to do, and why.

Disability Justice

Research the emerging concept of disability justice, and pay attention to how intersectionality informs perspectives put forward by coalitions of people of color, disability activists, and people active in movements like reproductive justice, anti-police violence, and anti-poverty campaigns.

In the quote below, Nirmala Erevelles and Andrea Minear, two professors of education at the University of Alabama, speak to the importance of foregrounding disability in intersectional approaches to education and justice. They analyze connections between the disproportional segregation of students of color in so-called "special education classrooms," and historical linkages between racialization and disability labeling.

> *Police brutality, false imprisonment, and educational negligence are commonplace in the lives of people of color – especially those who are located at the margins of multiple identity categories. So common are these practices that CRF [critical race feminist] scholar Patricia Williams has argued that these kinds of assaults should not be dismissed as the "odd mistake," but should be given a name that associates them with criminality.*
>
> *Her term for such assaults on an individual's personhood is "spirit murder," which she describes as the equivalent of body murder:*
>
> > *One of the reasons I fear what I call spirit murder, or disregard for others whose lives qualitatively depend on our regard, is that its product is a system of formalized distortions of thought. It produces social structures centered around fear and hate, it provides a timorous outlet for feelings elsewhere unexpressed ... We need to see it as a cultural cancer; we need to open our eyes to the spiritual genocide it is wreaking on blacks, whites, and the abandoned and abused of all races and ages. We need to eradicate its numbing pathology before it wipes out what precious little humanity we have left. (Williams, 1997: 234)*
>
> *Clearly, in our educational institutions there are millions of students of color, mostly economically disadvantaged and disabled, for whom spirit murder is the most significant experience in their educational lives. In fact, it is this recognition of spirit murder in the everyday lives of disabled students of color that forges a critical link between disability studies and CRT/F [critical race theory/feminism] through the intercategorical analysis of intersectionality. In other words, utilizing an intercategorical analysis from the critical standpoint of disability studies will foreground the structural forces in place that constitute certain students as a surplus population that is of little value in both social and economic terms. That most of these students are poor, disabled, and of color is critical to recognize from within a CRT/F perspective. By failing to undertake such an analysis, we could miss several political opportunities for transformative action. (Erevelles and Minear, 2010: 142–3)*

Time and Space Engagement

Let us destabilize and defamiliarize how we think about space and time. As you engage with these readings, think about your own sense of space and time, and how that might differ from other people's.

In an essay in the magazine *Wired*, Liz Stinson reports on the concept of DeafSpace, a design principle that goes beyond provision for one particular user group and toward universal design principles. (If you are unfamiliar with universal design ideas, look it up.) Stinson reports on a new dorm at Gallaudet University in Washington DC, US, a university that focuses on Deaf provision:

[Architect Davis] Lewis points out that the ground floor's community room has a subtle amphitheater-like slope that when viewed through the wall of windows, is clearly in line with the natural incline of the campus' landscape. "Someone walking on the sidewalk on the outside is actually parallel to someone walking on the inside and can communicate across that glass through sign language in a way that literally makes the building transparent," he explains. ...

Similarly smart details like an open kitchen that gathers the sink, stove and other main appliances in the middle island structure, ensures that students never have their backs to each other. ...

The nuances of DeafSpace design extend to smaller design choices, too. Every color choice – the steely blue, red, yellow and bright green of the floors – was chosen to reduce the wash-out effect and enhance natural skin tones so facial expressions are more easily readable. ...

And though the floor-plan is open and airy, the acoustics of the space are tightly controlled thanks to a paneled ceiling and acoustic blanket that is pinned to the underside of the concrete floor. "You have to really control the reverberations going through the building," he says, noting that bad acoustics can mess with hearing aids. "You can be having a conversation with someone and feel like you're having an absolutely private conversation."

All of these clever choices may add up to a space specifically suited to deaf students, but Lewis is quick to point out that DeafSpace principles could (and perhaps should) be the basis for any architecture project. Oddly enough, it seems like having all senses intact has a way of dampening our expectations – we start to make excuses for clunky architecture and unintuitive design, mainly because we're capable of navigating those obstacles without too much trouble. (Stinson, 2013)

Using this excerpt as a guide, discuss with a partner: What would your ideal communication/study environment look like? Go into depth: What kind of aural space, for instance, is most suitable for particular kinds of student activities associated with studying? What would be an ideal talking space for you?

Take a large sheet of paper, and sketch out a floor in a building designed for studying, taking different spatial modalities into account: deaf people, Deaf people, blind people, people with cognitive differences, people who are sensitive to sound, toxically injured people who are sensitive to chemicals, wheelchair users, people who can only walk short distances, etc. (To make it easier, you can just focus on any two combinations of populations here.)

Compare your sketch with others in the room, and see if there are ways of combining the visual/ verbal ideas that come up in this sketching brainstorm.

TOUCH/SOUND/IMAGE

Christine Sun Kim uses technology to investigate and rationalize her relationship with sound and spoken languages. Due to her deafness, figuring out what she actually 'owns' remains a long process. She gives workshops and talks on sound art, combines musical notations and several other information systems to produce visual scores and transcripts, conducts a choir that uses facial expressions to 'sing' and vocalizes through a set of piano wires and transducers. (artist statement)

In this image of a performance by Christine Sun Kim, people are watching as pigment vibrates on a loudspeaker, creating visual images out of audio waves. Research her work, and investigate how she plays across senses in her art making.

Image 5 *Christine Sun Kim, Chromatic Re(chord), CineDeaf Festival, Rome, 2012*

CRIP TIME

In this passage, Australian disability activist Anne McDonald talks about her relationship to time. How does McDonald characterize her experience of time and how time structures her relationship to other people? As you read this passage, can you pick out cues to a non-normate temporality in the form (not just the content)? Can you set up a class or social environment that would offer access to Anne McDonald?

I live by a different time to you.

I do not refer to the usual differences in the way we all experience time. We all know that time speeds by when you have nothing to do; time hangs heavy when you think you could have something to do if people re-ordered their timetables. So tempting is the long sleep in, so wearing the long afternoon left unattended. The time my caregivers spend loitering is negligible, the time I spend waiting is interminable. One's perception of time is dependant [sic] on one's dependency.

But my time is different from yours in a more important way. Imagine a world twenty times slower than this – a world where cars travelled at three miles an hour, lifesavers took an hour to chew, a glass of water half an hour to drink. Pissing would take quarter of an hour, lovemaking longer than it does now (which might be a good thing). A sitcom like Rosanne *would run for ten hours, longer than* Hamlet *and* Lear *combined.*

I live life in slow motion. The world I live in is one where my thoughts are as quick as anyone's, my movements are weak and erratic, and my talk is slower than a snail in quicksand. I have cerebral palsy, I can't walk or talk, I use an alphabet board, and I communicate at the rate of 450 words an hour compared to your 150 words in a minute – twenty times as slow. A slow world would be my heaven. I am forced to live in your world, a fast hard one. If slow rays flew from me I would be able to live in this world. I need to speed up, or you need to slow down.

For food, too, my time is slower than yours. I take an hour to eat lunch – not an hour to go to the restaurant, order, consume my meal, and chat, but an hour just to eat. I used to live in an institution, where I didn't have an hour. Meals for us were done in your time, or even faster, six minutes per child. If you choked on a mouthful, they stopped your meal and moved on to the next child. Long lunches are now my frequent pleasure; they show me I am free.

Long speeches are another matter. They show me I am only in a larger prison. People will not enter my time to talk to me. Slow the conversation down to my speed, and everybody else wanders away; carry on talking while I finish my sentence, and the conversation has moved on. Too long sentences twenty times slowed try the patience and require better memories than my listeners possess. (McDonald, n.d.)

EXERCISE 4.7 **Spatial Patterns**

Take a large sheet of paper, and, ideally, some colored markers. Make a map of the spaces you inhabit and travel between in a typical week. If the set-up for this assignment is not accessible to all, form small groups, and facilitate the creation of these maps for each other.

Now go over this map and identify where (you think) you meet disabled people, in which venues, and along which routes (disabled people of all kinds):

- Do you gain a sense of segregated or integrated spaces?
- Who is out in public, in which way, in which positions?
- Who is invisible, does or does not pass?
- Which pathways allow access, and who uses them?

EXERCISE 4.8 *Good Kings Bad Kings*

This exercise is based on one particular text. If you read another disability culture fiction work, see how you can adapt this – using your own space exploration to think about the meanings of space and time for different disabled people.

The novel *Good Kings Bad Kings*, by Chicago-based writer Susan Nussbaum (2013), is set largely inside an institution, a facility for disabled juveniles. Nussbaum unfolds issues of the medical-industrial complex and "care" as a profit center, institutionalization and resilience, the complexities of voice, and disability culture and coalition building. It is also a novel that works through spatial arrangements, demarcating the intricacies of knowing an enclosed space versus the kinds of desires and spatial patterns that non-institutionalized people play out.

In a follow-up to the Spatial Patterns exercise above, you can analyze some of the novel's working through visual-spatial analysis. Take another large sheet of paper and colored markers, and make a map of the characters' spaces and movement patterns. Which spaces do they traverse and inhabit?

Discuss how the Illinois Learning and Life Skills Center map develops as the novel opens up its terrain. Pay attention to how you become more sensitive to the space within the institution itself, and how inside and outside space connect with each other. You can discuss characters like Joanne Madsen, and how her journey toward partnership emerges through city traversals, and how Yessina Lopez, an inmate of the institution, explores her sexuality through space patterns.

Simulation Exercises and their Weird Sisters

Simulation exercises are a significant component of many disability awareness events. Many disability activists do not like simulation exercises: being blind-folded, having ear muffs, using a wheelchair when not experienced in using it, etc. gives a good sense of being weird, but not a good sense of what it actually means to have a disability, to navigate space with more or less competently acquired skill.

Skill development or the mechanisms of stigma fall out of the picture – all that remains, usually, is a reinforcement of negative stereotypes of disability, and of pity for the poor afflicted. This particular sentiment is not really useful for most disabled people.

Having said that, once in a while, a judiciously used wheelchair race session with provosts or other decision makers might lead to an extra ramp or low-power door openers here and there, and of course, that's a good thing. Politics comes in many different forms.

One problem with simulation exercises and the general frowning upon them in disability studies circles is that they are just so much fun. For a class period, we leave the classroom, experience ourselves differently in space, and play – for that is another way of capturing what we are doing when we don weird and unfamiliar augmentations. So, in the following exercises, sourced from Canadian and US classrooms, the sense of play remains central, but without the notion that these are ways of getting close to non-normate forms of embodiment. These defamiliarizing exercises still focus on interaction with the environment, but with a slightly shifted attention.

EXERCISE 4.9   **Buildings and Bodies**

Here is a quote by US disability theorist Tobin Siebers, in which he explores links between aesthetic practices, what is considered beautiful, and an unconscious reliance on the "healthy" body:

> *Perhaps the most revealing example of the relation between the political unconscious and architectural theory exists in the work of Le Corbusier. In 1925 he conceived of a diagram, the Modular, that utilizes the proportions of the body to help architects design buildings and other human habitats. It was to provide a standard scale by which buildings and human beings could be connected. The modular presents the image of an upright male – six feet tall, muscular, powerful, and showing no evidence of either physical or mental disability. It pictures the human body as a universal type, with no consideration of physical variation. Ironically, Le Corbusier wanted to tie buildings to the human beings living in them, but his theories privilege form over function and establish one basis for what Rob Imrie has called the 'design apartheid' of modernist architectural practices. In fact, design apartheid describes with accuracy the exclusionary system apparent in many episodes of the culture wars. Works of art called ugly ignite public furor. Unaesthetic designs or dilapidated buildings are viewed as eyesores. Deformed bodies appear as public nuisances. Not only do these*

phenomena confront the public with images of the disabled body, they expose the fact that the public's idea of health is itself based on unconscious operations designed to defend against the pain of disability. (Siebers, 2003: 215–16, citing Imrie, 1996)

Aesthetic Observation and Description *(exercise composed by Jay Dolmage)*

Invite students to creatively explore and test Siebers' claim that our ideas about "beautiful" buildings come from our ideas of "beautiful" bodies. Have them observe and describe the aesthetics of a particular building in close detail and then write about the building using a metaphor of the human body. Pushing the limits of this analogy a bit further, does a fully accessible, ADA-compliant building suggest a new or different kind of body? How might the body be described? (Lewiecki-Wilson et al., 2008: 267)

EXERCISE 4.10 **Accessible Date Assignment**

(Julie Passanante Elman, reproduced here with slight modifications)

Pair up. You must venture out into your surrounding area and plan an imaginary date for you and a wheelchair-using/a blind/Deaf/autistic companion. You MUST travel with your partner(s); do NOT venture out alone! For this assignment, you are required to use only public transportation to travel through New York City [or your own city, if public transport is an option. If it isn't, find out how someone in a power-wheelchair, for instance, gets from a to b], and your date must include the following: a meal, some kind of entertainment and plans for some privacy (Be creative! You're wooing someone!) You should chronicle your trip with a co-authored 2–3 page reflection on your journey. This narrative must also include a multimedia component to illustrate your trip. Multimedia might include digital or cell phone photography, video, screenshots of webpages, sound recordings, brochures or annotated city maps. Be sure to document, both in your essay and multimedia, inaccessible spaces as well as accessible ones as you explore your surroundings. (Elman, n.d. quoted with permission)

Discuss your findings in class:

- What does this exercise tell you about sexuality and space?
- About access and notions of public/private bodies?
- About disability, desirability and spectacle?
- Did you see familiar spaces in unfamiliar ways, and how?
- How did notions of self-presentation, and any differences between your fantasy date and yourself structure how you approached the exercise?

EXERCISE 4.11 **Wellness**

Engage in (at least) three wellness activities, over the span of three weeks, and each time, write a short (less than a page) report on what you did, how it made you feel, and the effects it has on your life.

Options:

- For free: Have a brainstorm. What options for free wellness activities exist on your campus/in your area? Are there free massage chairs, biofeedback programs, Seasonal Affective Disorder, light therapy lamps, ping-pong tables or Kinect game sessions available in your student center? If there is not, can you campaign for something like this? Is there an accessible Jacuzzi somewhere? Are there gardens you can visit?
- Maybe for free, maybe not: You can also choose three yoga classes, three massages, or three meditation sessions, spiritual activity, art session, or anything related.

Enjoy!

Discuss in class how this exercise relates to your wider learning experience:

- What are potential connections between wellbeing, health, illness, and disability?
- What kind of wellness activities are accessible, and are there some that are not?
- In what way can wellbeing become a value of disability culture? Should it? Why?

5 *Disability Culture*

In this chapter, you will gain insights into these issues:

- Disability culture and cultures as emerging concepts
- Disability culture providers as real entities in the world
- Death points: hate killings, eugenics, and public responses to parents and carers killing disabled children and adults
- Different cultural studies' concepts and their application to disability culture(s)
- How to capture disability cultural moments
- How to create disability cultural activities
- How to analyze traces of the lived experience of disability

At this point in this text, you have encountered a lot of different perspectives on disability as a phenomenon that is both social and private, embodied and discursive, tricksterish and funny, full of sadness and longing. It might be hard for some of us to stay open to this openness, to this refusal to read disability straight, to avoid answers. This is a text of questions, and of artfulness.

In the following, I introduce you to perspectives on disability culture, a concept that has much currency in some disability worlds – and none whatsoever in others. Some writers address it like an actual sociopolitical formation, like an anthropological entity, but we might be far off from that reality yet.

To accompany this chapter, you might find it useful to engage with historical texts that discuss disabled lives in different contexts (see, for instance, Kim Nielsen's *Disability History of the United States*, 2012, or Carol Poore's *Disability in Twentieth-Century German Culture*, 2007), with the disability history online exhibitions mentioned in Exercise 9.10, or with memoirs of disabled people, and with some of the exciting literature about, and analysis of, memoirs (for a discussion of the radical creative employment of memoir conventions by people with psychosocial disabilities, see Price, 2009).

Living Cultures

In this section, you are invited to investigate: How do we live in cultures? How do we create them? How do cultural mechanisms engage one another?

The exercises here spiral out from inviting you to become aware of your own everyday cultural placement to researching what is out there for disabled people in your environment.

EXERCISE 5.1 ## Cultural Webs

Take a large sheet of paper (or use a software concept mapping program). Create a relationship map for yourself: a web of who you are in contact with, how you would describe them in one or two words, how they signify for you.

You most likely have biological or chosen family near you in your relationship map, and maybe one or more partners. What happens in the next set of rings and circles? Who is your tribe, your people, your group, your culture? How do virtual relationships over social media like Facebook or Twitter figure into these groupings?

How does art consumption work for you – do you find your people in books, videos, galleries, parties? What are your face-to-face encounters in any given time frames? Are doctors, nurses, probation officers, social workers, chiropractors, or AA mentors part of your people, part of your life? How do you feel about them?

You can decide if you want to share this, or if you just want to talk about the effect of assembling this – there might be very personal information on your cultural web.

EXERCISE 5.2 ## Disability Culture Webs

Now take a second sheet or file, and, using all kinds of search mechanisms, online, word of mouth, etc., assemble a list of sites and people connected with disability services in your region:

- Maybe you have disability theatre companies?
- Galleries that exhibit disabled artists?
- Sheltered workshops (if you don't know what that is, research it, and make yourself familiar with the employment/payment situation provided there)?
- Disability services (or similar) at a university?

Create a map, and discuss your findings.

EXERCISE 5.3 ## Disability Culture Providers in Two Regions

Research disability culture providers in your own region and those of a nearby metropolis. Here is an example of culture providers to examine in the San Francisco Bay Area, for instance.

Sample of San Francisco Bay Area providers:

- AXIS Dance Company
- Sins Invalid
- Creative Growth

- Creativity Unbound
- National Institute for Arts and Disability
- Ed Roberts Center
- Lighthouse for the Blind SF
- BORP
- Theatre Unlimited
- Wry Crips
- Disabled People Outside
- Sexability
- Regular disability programming at the DeYoung
- Independent Living Centers in the region
- Disability studies at various universities in the region

Research these online, and see what webs of relations are emerging. What seems to be less covered, and why is that? Might this be an issue on the ground, or an effect of web visibility?

Do not assume that by engaging in a web search you can accurately assess what is happening where: stay aware of what is not easily found this way:

- Who has access to the web, who has not?
- Are there recurring themes in the provision, a particular set of issues?
- What is the flavor of a particular region?
- Are there connections between the providers?
- What are the effects of researching what happens elsewhere? Why is that a useful activity to engage in?

Depending on where you live, you might experience some frustration when trying to find some of the kinds of disability politics centered in this book. Reflect on this, too.

EXERCISE 5.4   ## Disability Culture and Online Webs

Research artists associated with the movement. There are many aggregator websites, and people engaged in the important cultural labor of charting and connecting (sections of) the field:

1   You can find many links on the website of the US-based Institute on Disability Culture, founded by Steven E. Brown and Lillian Gonzales Brown; in the archives of the British publication and e-newsletter Disability Arts Online, set up by Colin Hambrook; or on the National Arts & Disability Center and its Resources section, a program associated with the University of California, Los Angeles, under the directorship of Olivia Raynor.

2   You can also now look at online archives of influential magazines, like *Ragged Edge*, which followed on from *The Disability Rag*, a print magazine that began in 1980.

3   You can find many other examples as you follow resource links – be creative, and do not give up if you find dead links: you might be able to search your way to newer incarnations of these sites.

4   Print resources are bountiful, too, and you might find some in your library, like Pamela Walker's *Moving Over the Edge: Artists with Disabilities Take the Leap* (2005).

As you investigate what is out there, ask yourself who is presented most, what kind of work is less available, how do sensibilities and an awareness of exclusion change over time?

EXERCISE 5.5 ## Disability Hierarchies

As we've seen in Chapter 4, theories of intersectionality challenge one-dimensional analyses of disability. Another challenge are disability hierarchies, that is, the way boundaries are guarded within the disability movement(s), but also from within the medical/care-industrial complex. Research the concept, and discuss how the (history of these) hierarchies and relative respect inform the formation of disability cultures.

Death and Culture

As I am writing this section, this news item ran in the local news, in the *San Francisco Chronicle*:

> An elderly Oakland man suffering from cancer and progressive lung disease shot and killed the quadriplegic daughter he had taken care of for 25 years, then turned the gun on himself at the home they shared, police said. ...

> The person who summoned the police – the shooter's son, Tom Roberts – said later that he could not judge William Roberts, 88, for killing 58-year-old Marian Roberts in her bedroom and then shooting himself.

> "My dad was trying to do his best," said Tom Roberts, 59, of the World War II veteran, a paratrooper with the U.S. Army's 101st Airborne Division. "He was good-hearted. He was a war hero. And he saw the end of the line."

> He said his father left no note and had not previously discussed any plans for a murder-suicide, but had been "really worried" about his ability to continue taking care of his daughter.

> The two men had been taking care of Marian Roberts since 1987, when she fell down a flight of stairs at her then-home in Maui and suffered brain damage.

> But the task was becoming more and more difficult for the elder Roberts. According to his son, he suffered from chronic obstructive pulmonary disease, an ever-worsening lung disease that made it difficult for him to breathe. William Roberts had likened his condition to "torture," his son said.

> The elder Roberts also had liver cancer, his son said, which made it difficult for his lungs to function properly.

Tom Roberts said he was having difficulty coming to terms with the shooting, saying, "I kind of feel robbed, really. It's not easy to put into words to explain. We took care of my sister. My dad decided that the best way to take care of her was to say goodbye." ...

He said Marian Roberts, who used a wheelchair, went on outings to the mall. She was a 49ers fan and enjoyed watching games on TV. Before her accident, she was a seamstress at an upholstery shop in Maui, her brother said. ...

Another neighbor, who also did not want to be identified, said, "You could sort of see that something wasn't going to end well here. It's tragic." She added, "I'm happy that the two of them are at peace." (Lee, 2013)

EXERCISE 5.6   ## Mercy Killings/Hate Crimes

Discuss the way that disability is positioned in the *SF Chronicle* article above. How does it intersect with gender, poverty, and location? Look up definitions of "hate crime." Does this family killing fulfill the criteria? What are hate crimes against disabled people? Can you remember discussions of disability hate crimes and so-called "mercy killings" in your own community?

The slaying of disabled people by relatives is tragically a fairly common occurrence. In the US, the Autistic Self Advocacy Network called for a nation-wide Day of Mourning:

Saturday, March 1st, 2014, the disability community will gather across the nation to remember disabled victims of filicide – disabled people murdered by their family members or caregivers. (press release)

Activists in many different locations held vigils for the dead.

These killings are the death-point of disability/culture, opposed to the life-giving and restorative qualities of disability culture. This *SF Chronicle* article does not go as far as some in calling the murder justified. But other slayings, like a father's killing of his daughter, Tracy Latimer, in rural Canada in 1993, and Robert Latimer's subsequent non-guilty verdict for murder, led to long debates about hate crimes and the way disability is seen as a life not worth living in popular culture.

In Canada, a play by company Stage Left presented different perspectives on the murder: *Mercy Killing or Murder: The Tracy Latimer Story* (2003).

Here is how Canadian theatre scholar Kirsty Johnston (2012: 108–9) writes about the play, and about the disability culture sensitivity that drove its development:

Including Tracy's name in the title and emphasising the debate about murder or mercy killing, the production made it clear that it would be tackling a critical, nationally divisive, and familiar topic for Canadian audiences. The play drew from verbatim trial and media accounts. It also included fictional material developed by six performers with physical and developmental disabilities, by a host of professional artists, some with disabilities, and some not, and by community collaborators interested in giving voice to perspectives of people with disabilities on the case. ...

Another Canadian play with also drew from the debates surrounding the Latimer case – Mourning Dove by Emil Sher – was more symbolic in its title and created a "fictional world" that did not cite the particular details of the Latimer case onstage. For Stage Left productions, however, the details of the Latimers' stories provided the guiding questions for their artistic development process: "How did Robert Latimer stay out of jail for so long? Why was his necessity defense allowed in court when it does not exist in law? And why, when he clearly planned his daughter's murder, was he convicted only of second degree murder rather than first degree?" Although each question cites Robert, it is clear that each also turns on the company's sense that Tracy Latimer had been belittled, dehumanized, and under-represented in the legal process. To counter this activity, the company aimed to develop theatre that attended to Tracy's humanity and privileged the voices of people with developmental and physical disabilities. Building an inclusive artistic process in this case required time, money, flexibility, and responsiveness.

Life and Culture

In one and the same community, in a place like the West Coast's San Francisco Bay Area, birthplace to much disability activism, disability loneliness and despair can sit side by side with deeply articulated and grounded cultural expression. That makes it very hard to speak about disability culture as a "real thing." It is a thing, certainly, but it is hard to access for many, and its access depends on many factors, including chance, class, educational privilege, race, sexuality, and gender. But for those of us who find disability culture, it is a place where discourses of disability reach toward new kinds of interdependent freedom.

Sociologist Carol Gill is one of the most influential writers on the subject, with a short essay published in the mid-1990s. She writes:

[Disability culture] is not simply the shared experience of oppression. ... The elements of our culture include, certainly, our longstanding social oppression, but also our emerging art and humor, our piecing together of our history, our evolving language and symbols, our remarkably unified worldview, beliefs and values, and our strategies for surviving and thriving. I use the word "remarkable" because I find that the most compelling evidence of a disability culture is the vitality and universality of these elements despite generations of crushing poverty, social isolation, lack of education, silencing, imposed immobility, and relentless instruction in hating ourselves and each other. (Gill, 1995: 18)

As you look over what you are learning about disability arts and culture, can you find examples for the list of elements Carol Gill provides?

Remediation

Johnson Cheu, a disabled poet, works with one of the hidden histories of
disability culture: using disabled children in medical experiments. Can you make
links between this poem's strategies of remediation and Carol Gill's list of the
features of disability culture?

"Oats and May" *by Johnson Cheu*

Grandpa empties the last of the oatmeal
    into the pot, prepares
to dispose of the canister

    when he discovers you
watching him.
      You hug the canister.

Curious, you look
    for the broken seal,
attempt to pry lid

    from canister, mimicking him.
You can't. You wait, watch
    him unscrewing the lid, the mystery

opening up. You remain rapt
    for hours, screwing, unscrewing,
peering into the cavern, your voice echoing.

    The canister becomes a cardboard wagon,
or a bongo drum, as you march
    from kitchen, to foyer, to living room, and back.

Watching you, drumming the canister,
    my mind wanders to retarded children
fed radioactive oatmeal —

    the effects documented, but undisclosed.
The government claimed the daily dose,
    minute, harmless.

Why didn't they experiment
    on their own children?
Watching you, not retarded,

    I am curious who or
what determines
    expendability.

This explanatory note is found at the end of the poem:

> *"Oats and May"*: *Students at the Fernald School for the Mentally Retarded were part of medical experiments and human research from the 1920s to the 1950s. The incident referred to was a nutrition study conducted by Harvard University and the Massachusetts Institute of Technology. This is only one of several cases where institutionalized citizens were the human subjects in experiments commissioned by the United States government. (from reports in* The Boston Globe *and other newspapers. See also D'Antonio's* The State Boys Rebellion, *2005).*

• •

SHAMAN FRANK MOORE

Frank Moore (1946–2013), a spastic wheelchair user who spoke with the revoicing assistance of his partner Linda Mac and his chosen tribe, was a colorful figure in the disability performance world. He was a California-based performance artist who initiated long participatory performance rituals and shamanic actions, often with sexual content.

He makes explicit connections between his work and the cultural placement of disabled people as border walkers – not as objects of hate, but as objects of veneration, as channels between worlds. One reviewer wrote:

> *[Moore] understands that theater is one of the few public gateways left to the mythic realm where all things are possible and limitations melt away. It is this understanding of theater's magical roots that allows a man who cannot speak and who can barely move to command the attention of an audience and make the unlikely claim that he has the "perfect body for a performance artist."*

> *Forced to communicate his thoughts by painstakingly tapping out individual letters of the alphabet on a letterboard via a pole strapped to his head, Moore's eloquence belies the awkward technology that allows its expression: "I was born into the long tradition of the deformed shaman, the wounded healer, the blind prophet, and the club-footed 'idiot' court jester," says Moore. "Primitive tribes believed that if a cripple could survive childhood, he belonged to the spiritual world. As a symbol of the deformed medicine man, I am a medium to other dimensions. My body and attitudes toward life break taboos and change things." (Snider, 1993: 40).*

Look at Moore's website, www.eroplay.com, and investigate his Web of All Possibilities, maybe find some of the recordings from his Shaman's Den, inform yourself about his bid for presidential election, or check out his zine work, the *Cherotic (r)Evolutionary*. But take heed of his warning:

> *Hi, I am Frank Moore, your host.*

> *Well, you came into our reality cave even after that warning. That should mean you are an adult willing to be in a reality without padding, limits, taboos... that you are willing to be offended, challenged, shocked, turned-on, inspired, touched, moved to tears or to laughter by words, images, bodies, ideas. If you are not such a willing adult, please leave now. ...*

> *And you thought-cops, please note all of the contents of this web of reality are art and/or social commentary ... and hence protected speech. But if you want to tango with me... well, I have my dancing shoes on. After all, I was one of the original seven performance artists Sen. Jesse Helms targeted as 'obscene' ... and I am still doing art! (www.eroplay.com/hello.html)*

Research the role of disability in the extermination campaigns of the German Nazi party, the concept of eugenics, and its historical effects internationally. Look up the story of Gerhard Kretschmar, the first baby killed by the Nazi euthanasia program. In what ways are eugenics policies still at work today, shaping whose life is valuable and whose is not? Look up news stories of forced sterilizations, including ongoing transgressions against women in prisons today.

Immerse yourself in this website, Aktion T-4: Economics, Euthanasia, Eugenics (http://aktiont4.com/), created by US Deaf theorist and historian Brenda Brueggemann. What are the communication choices, and how do they affect you?

Investigate how artists make art as a way to point to historical injustice and its ongoing effects, and push back against powerlessness and sadness. How do disability culture artists respond to historical trauma?

Image 6 *Liz Crow, Resistance on the Plinth. Photo: Kevin Clifford/ Arts Council England/Roaring Girl Productions*

Image 7 *The Olimpias, Journey to the Holocaust Memorial in Berlin, a participatory performance. Photo: Timothy Wells Householder*

For a full discussion of Image 6, part of Antony Gormley's *One & Other* Trafalgar Square plinth living monument, see Hadley (2014), and for more on the Olimpias, an international disability culture art collective, see Kuppers (2011a).

EXERCISE 5.9 ## Raymond Williams: Culture

Here are two quotes from Raymond Williams' 1976 *Keywords* entry on "culture." With a colleague, work your way through these definitions, and see how you can make them fit the notion of "disability culture." Which particular processes and uses of the word "culture" could make sense of it?

> *Culture in all its early uses was a noun of process: the tending of something, basically crops or animals.*

> *There was also an area of hostility associated with anti-German feeling, during and after the 1914–18 War, in relation to propaganda about Kultur. The central area of hostility has lasted, and one element of it has been emphasized by the recent American phrase culture-vulture. It is significant that virtually all the hostility (with the sole exception of the temporary anti-German association) has been connected with uses involving claims to superior knowledge (cf. the noun INTELLECTUAL), refinement (culchah) and distinctions between 'high art (culture) and popular art and entertainment. It thus records a real social history and a very difficult and confused phase of social and cultural development. It is interesting that the steadily extending social and anthropological use of culture and cultural and such formations as sub-culture (the culture of a distinguishable smaller group) has, except in certain areas (notably popular entertainment), either bypassed or effectively diminished the hostility and its associated unease and embarrassment. (Williams, 1976: 76ff)*

SURVIVANCE

In Native American thought, literary scholar Gerald Vizenor's concept of "survivance" has much influence. It is a complex and elusive concept, bringing culture, land, and identity in close contact. As you think through the implications of this term for indigenous cultures and nations, can you see continuities and differences to disability culture's emergence? There are very different issues and histories at stake here, and it is important to keep these differences in mind:

> *Native survivance is an active sense of presence over absence, deracination, and oblivion; survivance is the continuance of stories, not a mere reaction, however pertinent. Survivance is greater than the right of a survivable name.*

> *Survivance stories are renunciations of dominance, detractions, obtrusions, the unbearable sentiments of tragedy, and the legacy of victimry. Survivance is the heritable right of succession or reversion of an estate and, in the course of international declarations of human rights, is a narrative estate of native survivance. (Vizenor, 2008: 1)*

Describing/Creating/Analyzing Disability Culture

This section offers a range of activities that can help us get in touch with disability culture in three different locales: in an actually experienced cultural setting, as something we can organize ourselves, and as a locus of experience in literature.

ACTIVITY 1 Disability Culture Field Trip and Field Notes

As a way to think more about disability culture(s), engage in a field trip. Go to a disability culture event, or, if there's nothing that strikes you as being specifically disability-led, go to an event where disabled people are likely to congregate. Getting creative about how to engage in this particular exercise, where to find a site, how to mark it or name it is likely to be the first learning opportunity of this exercise.

Find a meet-up of Special Olympics or Paralympic athletes (and look up the difference), a arthritis aqua-fitness class in your local swimming pool, a public event at a homeless shelter, an Alcoholic Anonymous meeting, maybe visit a mental health or spinal cord injury self-help group or other closed event (after explaining why you want to come, and if you are made welcome).

When you find a site, create field notes.

Field Notes

Writing field notes is a participant observation task, and emerges out of anthropological research methods. Through close observation and writing, you can become sensitive to patterns of engagement, and the underlying rules that govern how a particular group interacts. There is something ruminative and meditative about writing field notes: most likely, you will gain new insights just by writing. You might find that things connect in surprising ways for you. Write as soon as you leave the site, or write within it. You need to write things down quickly, or you are likely to forget them. Write down:

- Where and when you are observing
- Street names, names, numbers – to allow you to be specific
- What you hear, see, feel, smell, taste – your sensory impressions
- Sentences or sentence fragments that somehow lodge with you
- Moments that have touched you in some way
- How you feel, observing and writing down these notes

When you gathered all this, see if there are patterns or a significant moment that can become the core of a little essay.

After your research trip, and after writing up your notes, engage in peer debriefing with one another: compare what you have gathered, and talk about your experiences as a writer, and about reading what others have written.

How did you try to engage physical/cognitive/emotional ways of being that are different from yourself (however you identify)? As a reader of these pieces, what are the moments where you are gripped and want to read on?

Various US cities had ordinances that have come to be known as "the ugly laws," laws that made it legal to seize mendicants, beggars, disabled people, and others on the grounds of unsightliness or public disgust.

US literary scholar Susan Schweik has researched the history of these laws, and the ways disabled people have worked with, fought against, and been influenced by them – but also how law literature and court material offers insights into disabled lives at a time when few other documents of these lives existed.

Have a discussion about the effects that the existence of "ugly laws" (as well as unspoken laws about what is "proper" in public) have on disabled lives, on the ways that difference operates in the public sphere, on how one polices one's self and others.

> This book has told the story of a petty ordinance, barely enforced, small-minded, and obscure. ... The law, remembered powerfully by one social movement alone as a legend and a lesson about disability, turns out to be about much more: about class antagonism, the distribution of wealth, and the routine suppression of resistance; about authenticity and masquerade; about how distinctions between genders and races and between Americans and others have been sorted out by Americans (and others); about bodily vulnerability and animality; about political action. (Schweik, 2009: 289–90)

Think about the effects that the concept of "begging" has on how disability is viewed: what does it mean when public acts by disabled people can be shut down under the category of "begging"? Schweik (2007: 67) states:

> I want to stress that the stories I have told about disabled beggars in the American courts have consequences for our understanding of the social, cultural and legal position of all disabled people in the post-ADA [Americans with Disabilities Act] era. The archives of ADA court cases offer plenty of contemporary equivalents of similar legal refusals to read the "acts of cripples," ... as forms of expression, protected and political. Acts like seeking appropriate workplace accommodation, challenging employment discrimination, or protesting disabling barriers in the built environment are still too often read as forms of begging: stories of individual need rather than the collective good.

In some cities in the US, sit-lie ordinances are being enacted, prohibiting sitting and lying on sidewalks or parks (you can easily find references to these debates in relation to Portland, Oregon and San Francisco, California). Advocates in favor of these ordinances have cited easy access to urban environments for mobility-impaired people, but critics see these laws as a stealth criminalization of poverty and homelessness, which themselves disproportionately affect disabled people of all kinds.

What do you think about the effect of such ordinances, and their shaping of bodily behavior? Research the existence of similar ordinances in your own or surrounding municipalities.

Check out activism that links disability work with homelessness, provides shelters or food banks. What are the provisions in your area?

Here is one of my pieces of writing, developed out of field notes. Can you still see the remnants of field notes embedded here? In this writing, I am beginning to point to the stakes of a wider argument, finding a tension and an argument. This is the point at which field notes move into essay writing.

Arnieville: Disability and Protest

Arnieville was an activist camp and tent village erected by a coalition of disabled, poor and homeless people. Its tents stood on a traffic island in a busy street, opposite the Berkeley Bowl supermarket, during May, June and July of 2010. People slept in tents three feet away from roaring traffic, fast wheels and exhaust fumes. Activists used their physical presence in these precarious and polluted surroundings, their art, song and a large papier-mâché puppet of then-California-governor Arnold Schwarzenegger, complete with raised hatchet, to protest the ongoing dismantling of the social welfare system. Cuts kill, taxes save lives. Interdependence, not independence.

At Arnieville, we created provisional community amongst people with mental health differences, addiction issues, physical disabilities and in poverty, we found multiple new alliances across racialization and impairment lines. Our activist chants engaged with the rhythm of the car wheels pounding by our island – our activist prosody, a healing magic for an ailing welfare state.

I remember: the poetics of street action played across my body, as we sat in our wheelchairs, scooters and loungers, huddled together to sun ourselves or shiver in the treacherous Northern California spring and early summer, my senses alert to the infiltrations of temperature change, of migraines held barely at bay with ever higher doses of pain killers, of the cramp setting into joints.

I also remember the warm food neighbors brought by each day, and the settling in each day for the sharing circle, to hear and bear the different voices, different cognitive frames. The bearing was not always easy: there were tears, and shouts, and accusations, arguments, ravings, these genres' boundaries often interwoven and undecidable.

I also remember the renewed pleasures of the possibility of home when I did wheel home on many days, to connect myself differently, to plug into the electrical web and charge my wheelchair, fire up the computer, write Facebook entries on the protests that fellow activists in Australia could comment on.

I remember my few nights' worth of disrupted, poisoned sleep in one of the tents, the concentration of traffic fumes peaking in the morning commute, my light-headed writing in the grey light of early morning hours.

I am not sure that anybody can say that Arnieville had a significant impact on the legislature. Social welfare systems are crumbling everywhere, and the people of California keep voting down anything that would cost them. The democratic process is flaying vulnerable and poor populations. Maybe some drivers and shoppers got to think differently when witnessing us on our traffic island, think differently about what they might have assumed were silent and invisible populations. Bay Area public radio and quite a few newspapers came out, and there was a good show of disability agency and interdependent self-determination in the media. But did that reach anybody who was not already in our camp, not already on the side of welfare politics and a need for taxes? I am not sure, and am rather cynical.

But "politics" does not just mean effectiveness at the level of policy making. There is a politics of engagement and relationality, of embodied contact, of shared space and common ground. (I continue on to explain what that is, and how my experiences support my argument.) (Kuppers, 2011b: 15–17)

Development

Look at your own field notes again, and try to pinpoint an argument that you can locate in your experience. Set up stakes. Maybe you want to use a secondary reading quote as a departure point, maybe one of the denser moments, a place of unpacking, that you identified in the first sharing. Write and edit the piece to about 500 words (the length of my notes above), and share them again, this time with a different collaborator:

- What works, what doesn't?
- How does argument emerge from experience?
- How does experience help make the argument complex?
- Are there course readings that can help you develop what is here, frame it, articulate it?

ACTIVITY 2 Setting up a Disability Culture Event

In this activity set, you are encouraged to create a disability culture experience yourself – maybe for real, maybe just as an organizational exercise.

Below is a description of a set of performance actions from the UK. As you read through this description and the "how-to" of organizing an event, picture what it might be like to participate:

- What would the energy be like?
- What different reactions do you think different people would have?
- How would it feel to be part of it, on the bed, as one of the pushers, on the sidelines watching it?
- Why are parties such an important part of this kind of activism?

You can also see many images from different Bed Push events at the organization's website.

The Great Escape Bed Push

The Great Escape Bed Push protests took place in each summer from 2005 to 2008. We symbolically escaped psychiatric institutions, dressed in pyjamas and 'hot-tailed' it with a psychiatric bed to a place of safety and celebration. We aimed to raise awareness about the over-use of forced treatments in mental health services and the need for holistic choice based services. ...

The Great Escape Bed Push Team believe in its current state psychiatric care often makes people's problems worse and that the use of unnecessary force is on the increase. "Forcing patients to take medication against their will is a spirit-breaking practice. It can put someone off mental health services for life, as it breaks down trust between staff and the individual they are supposed to be taking care of" (Dr. Rufus May, Clinical Psychologist and former patient).

Many of the campaigners have been in-patients who have witnessed and experienced the use of forced drug treatment. They were joined by nurses and others concerned by the emphasis on control in psychiatry and the lack of therapeutic activities. The crazy bed pushers will give out wanted posters and dodgy pills (sweets) to members of the public and proclaim "Psychiatry is off its trolley!" At various points of the journey the escapees and the public will have to look out for the giant 6 foot syringe squirting water at them. We are protesting about the over use of force in psychiatry (e.g. forced drugging, forced ECT, psychosurgery and brainwashing). ...

We have found it useful to have these things when organising a bedpush:

A series of planning meetings with the people interested in taking part.

A hospital bed with good wheels (we used a porter's bed).

Pyjamas.

A good leaflet.

Somebody to send press releases to local newspapers radio TV and chase them up.

Take a picture of what you might look like for the press release.

Have some people willing to talk to the press about the experience of forced treatment and the alternatives.

A loud horn for blowing every time you start to push the bed a bit further (good for morale).

A megaphone for telling people what you are doing on the journey. Use humour "We have escaped the psychiatric hospital!" "We are mad, but they are madder!"

A map! Use roads where you can, its important to (peacefully) disrupt the traffic... this is an important human rights issue!

A sound system at times can be good for morale ("all you need is love"... "Madness" songs etc).

A party at the end of the bedpush: speeches, samba band music, cake, drumming, dancing etc. (from http://bedpush.com)

Given what you have learned so far about activism and art in disability culture worlds, in a small group, create a brief proposal for an activist art event around any aspect of disability politics or culture, with an organizational list like the one provided above.

Now share your own event design brief with each other in short presentations, using a multimodal approach: (audio-described) images, talking, maybe something tactile, from hand-outs to props, maybe a performance demonstration. Try to get people to come onboard with you. Give feedback to each other:

- What is the point of the activity? Is it political, and if so, in what sense? Is it surreal, or direct, playful or strategic, or all of the above?
- What was the energetic high point of the presentation, and why?
- What were the accessibility features of the presentation?
- What conceptual or logistical questions remain?

ACTIVITY 3 Bodies as Anchor Points: Disability Literature

In this activity, you will use a particular literary lens to look at creative writing. You can also adapt this activity to look at visual texts or performance – use the material on phenomenology provided here to think about what a sharing of experience might become in different art forms.

PHENOMENOLOGY

French philosopher Maurice Merleau-Ponty helped shape an important line of thought – "phenomenology" – paying attention to the world from an embodied perspective, understanding the world to blossom around us as we become sensate and process sensations.

He writes about a tailor:

> the subject, when put in front of his scissors, needle and other familiar tasks, does not need to look for his hands and his fingers, because they are not objects to be discovered in objective space: bones, muscles and nerves, but potentialities already mobilized by the perception of scissors and needle, the central end of those 'intentional threads' which link him to the objects given. It is never our objective body that we move, but our phenomenal body, and there is no mystery in that, since our body, as the potentiality of this or that part of the world, surges towards objects to be grasped and perceives them. (Merleau-Ponty, 1962: 121)

Disability also features in Merleau-Ponty's account – not as a qualitatively different experience of being-in-the-world, but instead as an example of the malleability of the body image, and its relation to the outside world:

> The blind man's stick has ceased to be an object for him, and is no longer perceived for itself; its point has become an area of sensitivity, extending the scope and active radius of touch, and providing a parallel to sight. (1962: 143)

Phenomenology has become a significant strand of disability theorizing, in particular when Merleau-Ponty's certainties become challenged: when people with cognitive differences experience their enworldedness in different ways, when certainties are shaken up. He, and other phenomenologists, offers us language to validate lived experience as a form of theorizing.

While there is no unified sense of aesthetics in disability literature, no one unique feature, there are certain traits that have become recognizable over time.

Many disability culture literary texts, i.e. texts written by people who identify with disability, whether poems, novels, memoirs or plays, center on embodiment and enmindment, on the sensations of being alive, on what it feels like to live in a particular bodymind, and to have this bodymind edge up against social rules and norms.

In this activity, research a particular text associated with the wider disability literary field, and see if you can identify passages that foreground the lived experience of embodiment/enmindment.

Good collections that can guide you include:

- *Beauty is a Verb: The New Poetry of Disability* (Bartlett et al., 2011)
- *From Victims to Villains* (Lewis, 2006)
- *Face On: Disability Arts in Ireland and Beyond* (O'Reilly, 2007)
- *Points of Contact: Disability, Art, and Culture* (Crutchfield and Epstein, 2000)
- Material reviewed and discussed on websites like *Disability Arts Online*, *Breath and Shadow*, and *Wordgathering*

Focus on what metaphors, images, or recurring themes structure the approach to writing one's sense of being alive in a particular bodymind, by a particular literary artist. Share your finds with a small group, so you can pool your examples.

Development 1: Zine Culture and Nonlinear Aesthetics

Image 8 *Neil Marcus,* Special Effects. *Photo: Dariusz Gorski*

More than a document of the early days of the disability rights movement, Neil Marcus' collection Special Effects: Advances in Neurology *is also a window into California zine culture of the 1980s. Art in revolution: social justice, the human growth movement, art in the everyday. From flourishing dystopia to speech storms, Neil documents living artfully in Berkeley, California, and in Disability Country. (publisher's publicity)*

Search for the book's free reading commons online, as well as the YouTube video of Neil Marcus being interviewed about his book, also called *Special Effects* (2011).

- How do zine aesthetics speak to disability culture(s)?
- What images of disability culture emerge for you as you chart your way through the assembled material?
- What are the differences between the physical book, the online reading commons, and the video?
- How do improvisation, live performance, and speech difference feature in the video and in the page form?
- What forms of multimodality emerge from this presence across different art forms?

Development 2: Narrative Prosthesis

As we have just seen, lived experience and its traces can be one way of theorizing the literary traces of disability. But there is also a lot of literature of disability that does not come from a lived experience. Here is another perspective, developed by US literary theorists David Mitchell and Sharon Snyder, who shaped the influential concept of "narrative prosthesis." Another US literary theorist, Michael Davidson (2008: 176), sums up this intriguing concept in one paragraph:

In the humanities this social model has been accompanied by significant readings of disabled characters in literature whose nontraditional bodies are sites of moral failing, pity, or sexual panic. David Mitchell and Sharon Snyder have described this analogical treatment of disability in cultural texts as a 'narrative prosthesis' in which a disabled character serves as a crutch to shore up normalcy somewhere else. The disabled character is prosthetic in the sense that he or she provides an illusion of bodily wholeness upon which the novel erects its formal claims to totality, in which ethical or moral failings in one sphere are signified through physical limitations in another. In Richard Wright's Native Son, *for example, Mrs. Dalton's blindness could be read as a sign of the moral limits of white liberal attitudes that mask racism. Wright is less interested in blindness itself than the way that it enables a story about racial violence and liberal guilt. In* A Christmas Carol *Charles Dickens does not use Tiny Tim to condemn the treatment of crippled children in Victorian society but to finesse Scrooge's awakening to charity and human kindness toward others. By regarding disability as a 'narrative prosthesis,' Mitchell and Snyder underscore the ways that the material bodies of blind or crippled persons are deflected onto an able-bodied normalcy that the story must reinforce. Indeed, narrative's claim to formal coherence is underwritten by that which it cannot contain, as evidenced by the carnival grotesques, madwomen in attics, blind prophets, and mute soothsayers that populate narrative theory.*

US writer Anne Finger's *Call Me Ahab* (2009) is a collection of short stories. Many of the stories feature well-known literary, mythological, and historical disabled characters, and she rewrites their stories from her own sensibility and with her disability culture wit (see also her interview with Josh Lukin, 2012). Read some of her short stories, and think about what happens to narrative prosthesis in them.

Find disability culture parodies, subversions, reclaimings, and see how the mechanisms of disability as metaphor are turned back and played with. What happens to ideas of normality, to shoring up, and to (literal and other) prostheses? Examples include:

- the work of UK comedian Lawrence Clark
- the documentary *My One-Legged Dream Lover* with Australian artist Catherine Duncan (dirs. Christine Olsen, Penny Fowler-Smith, Australia, 1998)
- the Mickee Faust video *Annie Dearest*, speaking back to the portrayal of Helen Keller
- model Aimee Mullins' photo shoot with Jean Paul Gaultier.

Development 3: Poetry Banquet

What is poetry good for? Is poetry code, elevated speech, status symbol, ritual, storytelling, or other? These questions fuel a practice my classes engage in every semester: a disability culture poetry banquet. We meet, eat together, and recite poetry written by disabled people, without worrying too much about meanings and parsing. We enjoy each other's company, the sound, feel or sight of poems (we share in many different modalities), and food.

Create your own banquet, feast, poetic communal event (and remember to check in about allergies etc.). Try to do this without the pressure of having to articulate why you are doing it, and how it relates exactly to the course content. Give yourself the freedom to listen, see, and experience, making sure to have poems available in multiple modalities, and maybe even find tactile enhancements – materials and props to handle while listening/reading. Appreciate the differences with which people read, perform, or share the work they have found.

Part II

From here on, this book offers ways of working with core themes of disability arts and culture, topics that have crystallized over the years, and have much currency in international engagements with disabled life. Each chapter focuses on a relatively narrow set of concerns – the (medical) institution, the freak show, disability and dance, the wheelchair and what it stands for, superheroes, and autism as a cultural site. Each chapter addresses one or two art forms in engagement with these themes, and focuses on these in the exercises and (longer length) activities.

Here are two exercises that might be useful for each of the chapters that follow, or for use with supplementary reading assigned for a session.

EXERCISE

Looking up Definitions

As a first step, as you read an essay, circle all words and concepts that are hard for you. Can you make sense of them from the framework of the essay, and from what we've covered in this book so far? Try to decode any terms or formulations you find hard to understand.

- Why am I using them?
- What mechanisms can you use to help yourself?
- If you look up terms, are the definitions you find helpful and satisfying?
- Are connotations covered?
- As you have now learned about discourse change, do you find that the material you find in dictionaries is up to date and in tune with developments in disability studies?
- Or is the very notion of "definition" complicated in disability studies and its scholarship?

EXERCISE

Study Circle

This is for a group. One good way to engage complicated academic texts is through study circles. They are a way of slowing down reading, allocating specific tasks to readers, and making sense of a piece of work collaboratively. Here is a description of a study circle used by my colleague and collaborator Elizabeth Currans, who herself adapted this from Janet Gray and others. Many of the exercises in this book are used by many people, always changed and changing, accreting layers and complexities as they move from teacher to student to teacher. Honoring our lineages is part of the politics of our work.

Study Circles are a way of dividing up approaches to a reading among members of a group. Each group member chooses one of the following roles (should be different each time you do the exercise). Bring copies of a short written analysis (1 page max, word processed) for each group member and the teacher. Make sure to fill the first 3 roles – these are essential. Your group can choose which other roles you'd like to fill for each exercise. You will present in the order the roles are listed. The study circles work best if groups use individual presentations to spark discussion rather than simply going around in a circle reading handouts.

Study Circle Roles

CLARIFIER: What terms or concepts does your group need to understand? Find definitions and facts that will help the group grasp the article.

SYNTHESIZER: What are the writer's key points? What is the central argument, and how is it supported? Are there parts of the article that are difficult to place within the overall argument or seem to contradict it? How could you connect those points with the author's central position?

SILENCE READER: What is not there in the reading, but either implied or ignored by the author? What questions do these silences raise? What kinds of information or analysis are needed to address these questions?

ANALYST: What roles do fact, theory, and political advocacy play in the reading, and how do you account for these roles?

INVESTIGATOR: Dig up some background information – anything that will help the group to understand the reading better. Find something that really interests you, something that struck you as curious or puzzling as you read. For example, you could look up a reference to another theorist and learning about her/him/hir, research an event discussed in the reading and explore why it is important, or find out more information about a theoretical debate.

BORDER-CROSSER: Are there aspects of the reading that relate to a historical or social context different from your own? What are these and how do you respond to them? In addition, are there aspects that speak to something in your experience?

ILLUSTRATOR: Find or create visuals (artwork, photos, graphs, icons) that illustrate the reading and write a brief description of how the visuals relate to the readings. Your job will be to draw the other group members into the process of interpreting the visuals in relationship to the topic you're studying.

LINK-MAKER: What does this reading bring to mind – in other readings or in the world as you know it – by way of comparison or contrast? What do these different materials suggest about one another? (Currans, personal communication)

. . . .

6 Life in the Institution: Discourses at Work and at Play

In this chapter, you will gain insights into these issues:

- Social choices about institutionalization
- Ekphrasis and creative translations
- The imaginative power of the asylum
- Located writing: writing from one's point of view on visual art and poetry
- Institutionalization and its effects
- Representing institutionalization in poetry, visual art, memoir, and biography
- Dealing respectfully with traumatic life stories

Similar to the field notes activity in Chapter 5, you can work through the activities in this chapter and produce an essay draft, with various stages and multiple check-in points.

This chapter focuses on institutions, on living confined lives, on being separated from the wider framework of society. Many disabled people have experienced institutionalization: in hospitals, mental health institutions, prisons, group homes. Being forced to live apart, and the fear of having to do so, is a central experience to modern Western disabled life.

But it is not a "natural" aspect of disability life: in many international settings, disability is not segregated, and disabled people are not put into separate accommodations from non-disabled folk. The contemporary disability art film *Body and Soul* (Matthieu Bron, 2011) tells a different story. It is a film about disabled people and dancers in Mozambique, and it shows eloquently that the base struggle for these particular disabled people is overcoming stigma and disgust by those who surround them. They find themselves living right among everybody else, trying to catch transportation when bus drivers do not wish to have a wheelchair in their vans, trying to secure an apprenticeship as a shoemaker, getting past a storekeeper's prejudice, sweet-talking friends into carrying them into inaccessible classrooms.

But the danger for the people speaking in this documentary still seems to be to become shut-in, to be hidden away from society, not in separate institutions, but in the family home. In the film, disability culture events become sites of empowerment: the creation of a fashion show, engaging in disability dance together, and talking together about shared but different struggles.

Separation in Films

Watch three disability culture films, part of this growing subgenre of documentary films, and observe how the balances are struck between private and public, separation and integration, in the particular lives we hear about.

Many examples are freely available online, including:

- *Loving Lampposts* (Todd Drezner, 2011), a documentary about autism
- *Nobody's Perfect* (Niko von Glasow, 2008), a documentary about an art project focused on thalidomide
- *Sound and Fury* (Josh Aronson, 2000), Oscar-nominated documentary film on cochlear implants and Deaf culture
- *Up Syndrome* (Duane Graves, 2000), a documentary about a man with Down Syndrome.

Let us begin by probing what your own feelings are about these iconic sites of separation, these worlds apart. Whether or not you ever found yourself institutionalized, hospitalized, imprisoned or sectioned, you are likely to have some feelings about the spaces designated "apart" in our societies: they are frequent sites for horror movies, for instance. As you continue in this section, keep yourself safe: you might find yourself becoming distressed with memories or associations. Make sure to take breathers, employ the coping mechanisms you have, and monitor any sharing you are engaged in to ensure that you are keeping within the boundaries you want.

EXERCISE 6.2 ## Audio Description

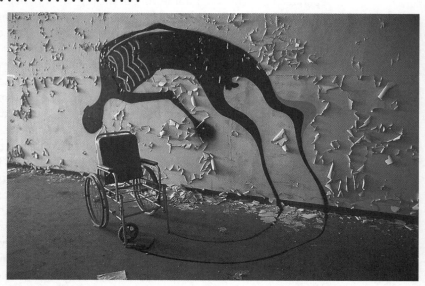

Image 9 *Herbert Baglione, photograph from* 1000 Shadows *series, 2013*

This is a wall image shot in an abandoned mental health asylum in Parma, Italy, by Brazilian street artist Herbert Baglione (2013). What do you see? What does the image invoke in you?

In a group, describe this image, going around all members of the group and then starting again, keeping it up longer than seems "normal" in order to see what happens:

- How many different ways can you describe the image, what is "visual information?"
- At which point do description and interpretation become indistinguishable from each other?
- What is the value of paying attention to the difference, and what is the value of not doing so?

Pay attention to how members in your group who have alternative visual access to images describe their experience. If you have members of your group who do not have visual access, pay attention to how they describe the image after listening to a round of descriptions.

Observation Wheel

Alternatively (as a filtering step for privacy), use the Observation Wheel from the Appendix. Each student fills out their own wheel, and then shares in a group discussion about the results.

EXERCISE 6.3   **Ekphrasis**

Look up the term "ekphrasis" and its meaning in different contexts. Try to find four different definitions of the term. Add to these definitions insights you are winning from your continuing engagement in disability arts and culture. How do they complicate the notion of translation, working across art forms, the equation of meaning across media, and across different forms of sensory access?

Here is the response I wrote about the Baglione image in a writing group. Free writes, timed writing sessions of 15 minutes, are one way in which I keep my own writing practice fresh, and I use this mechanism in my classroom, too. From initial description, my write quickly moves into the different associations of disability that come up as I give my imagination free rein, as I connect the images and stories that come up:

The image shows a wall of peeling paint, shot at a diagonal. The black floorboard dissects the image, and gives a trajectory, a narrative. In front of this peeling wall is a broken hospital wheelchair without a seat. One of its front coaster wheels is missing, and some apparatus is lying in front of the other coaster wheel. On the wall itself is a sweeping black shadow, in the shape of a man, circling over the chair. The legs of the creature are elongated, and connect across the edge of the wall over to the floor to the front standing supports of the wheelchair, running through the detritus that has flaked off the wall.

There is something very posed here, the way the peelings are heaped, disturbed and undisturbed, the way that there is no sign of someone having been here to paint this wall. The effect is ghostly: you wonder how Baglione sprayed this creature without brushing the wall to dislodge more of the peel. Is this a stencil? It seems so: some of the edges of the paint spray out, create cloudy outlines.

The stencil is two-tone: black, a traditional color of the dead, and a light grey, used to demarcate abdominal muscles and breasts, quite playfully. The grey also echoes the peeling paint, which reminds me of lead paint, of danger zones, of breathing made complex, potentially toxic.

Disability seeps into this image is so many ways: the wheelchair is a traditional sign for disability, the sign we are familiar with from "handicapped" parking stalls. The wheelchair is empty here, but connected to a floating playful shape which is also looming, dark and haunting.

The tension between many different registers of disability makes this image work for me: the fixity of the wheelchair, the mobility of ghosts, the connection between the two. The (potential of) lead paint and the danger of confinement.

The genitalia, male stylized shapes floating between the legs, mark a specific living history to these shadows: absence of genitals is a convention of many ghostly representations, and the specificity of the genital shapes and the markings on the chest give the figure more living weight, in a world where disability is also so often equated with an absence of sexuality, a lack of gendered identity.

Maybe a man floated here, once, when the walls where not flaking. Maybe a man was transported to an electroshock treatment in such a wheelchair, one that one cannot wheel by oneself – this is a hospital wheelchair, used to transport patients, not one in which patients can transport themselves. He might have floated as an after-effect of electroshocks, his mind suspended, jolted, flashed out of sync. He might have become a ghost here, in these corridors: dying during confinement, taken away by pneumonia, abuse, or old age. The notion of helplessness and lack of agency is heavy upon the absent seat. Now, in the confrontational form of graffiti, the locked-down ones take flight, as their thoughts had likely taken flight all those years ago when this asylum was in action.

So what am I doing here, in this free write?

1   I name specific parts of the wheelchair, which means I speak about it as an object of use, not as a metaphor. I am a wheelchair user myself, so that clearly influences my perspective. As a writer, I am centering disability.

2   I also try, as a writer and disability culture activist, to give agency and life to the shadow creature on the wall.

3   As an artist, I am paying attention to the creation of the image, both the painting itself and the photo of the painting.

These three strategies are consciously chosen, they offer counterstrategies, reading against the grain, resistant reading. This is a strategy many disabled people have to take to take pleasure from popular culture and artistic culture. It's a reading strategy they share with many people who have found themselves historically aligned with tragedy or weakness – women, queer people, people of color, aging people, and others.

Resistant reading strategies can find purchase in unusual perspectives (focusing on the free flow of the shadow rather than what "shadow" means in our shared culture) or in insider knowledge (like the structure of a wheelchair). In each case, the reading strategy is not unanchored from the image, but finds secondary significations to focus on, rather than the one that seems to shine out as a dominant feature: there are ghosts in the asylum, tethered to wheelchairs as emblems of immobility and confinement.

In this way, reading and writing about disability becomes a politics, a means of seeing otherwise. Our careful attention can suffuse cultural stories and images with the lightness of multiple meanings. Once you read the shadow as a dancer, it is hard to see it *just* as a symbol of oppression.

Here is a response from a law student in one of my classes. She responded to this image in an in-class free write, and entered it on our e-discussion board for everybody to read. She chose to be in this book anonymously, as she is thinking about her chosen career and the effects of disclosure:

> I want to reach out to you, in part because I have been there. The community of mental illness, I identify with. Discarded, so often. Either from care or from love, or from the attention of my chosen field of study or from the assumptions that a law student is separate from such a community, the assumption perhaps that I look on such a photograph as an uninterested third party. But I am interested.
>
> That shadow could be me. Any of us. Are we really so different? At one point, that shadow was me.
>
> But now I am in this place of privilege. To speak up for you. Is that presumptuous of me? Do you want an advocate, Shadow? Do you need one?
>
> Chills as I feel that this is my calling. I want to understand. I suppose I assume that you want to be understood, Shadow. Don't we all want to be understood.
>
> This place may have helped you. (The hospital helped me those times.) It may have hurt you. How can I be an advocate? And a community member? And a friend? And not impose?
>
> So many questions. And complexity. Know that in all, I want to approach you Shadow – and this place – with grace and humility. That seems to me the human thing to do.
>
> I am not above you.

In offering training in conscious and multiple reading strategies, humanities and arts classrooms become political. "Political" does not mean dogmatic, giving only one story. It means opening up stories to understories, attics, to multiple meaning.

Some of you might create a free write remembering an institutionalized loved one – going with the dominant negative meaning of "confinement" but making it personal, taking it away from horror movie material by creating an anchor in real lived lives.

There are many ways of creating space and life around dead metaphors, around the immobility of how disability has come to signify. To find these approaches, and to make meanings complex, this is the journey we are on.

EXERCISE 6.4 ## Asylum Porn

Abandoned mental health asylums and hospitals are not an unfamiliar sight to popular culture audiences. Many horror films take place there, amusement horror parks are set up in them, and young adults dare themselves by breaking into them, a rite of passage memorialized in many novels and short stories. Make a list of popular culture examples of asylums and hospitals. Describe how the place is represented. Take note of the date or general time era the image is representing.

And now make a second list, of any actual mental health care place and general hospitals you might have visited. Maybe visit one in your location, and experience the place yourself (without taking photos). If you can't visit yourself, use the Internet to find photos of corridors, nurses' stations, and other public areas. What are the similarities and differences between popular representation and the actual contemporary shapes of these sites?

There is a complex balance at work: on the one hand, addressing the ordinariness of institutions may help to destigmatize psychosocial disabilities – one way of describing what others call mental health differences, and yet others give specific biomedical diagnostic labels. On the other hand, though, the heritage of seeing institutions as homes of horror also keeps alive a sensitivity to the outrage many mad activists (mad is here a self-chosen label) or people with psychosocial disabilities feel toward a history of mental health provision that was and still is unresponsive to their needs, hurtful, and even, at times, a killing machine. But that depends, of course, on people seeing users of metal health institutions, whether hospitals, support centers or drop-ins, as fellow citizens, not as boogeymen.

THE TOTAL INSTITUTION

In his study of life in institutions, US sociologist Erving Goffman focused attention on the mechanisms at work in creating new social spaces and reshaping inmates' sense of self:

> A total institution may be defined as a place of residence and work where a large number of like-situated individuals, cut off from the wider society for an appreciable period of time, together lead an enclosed, formally administered round of life. (Goffman, 1961, xii)

From the chapter, "The Moral Career of a Mental Patient":

> Once the prepatient begins to settle down, the main outlines of his fate tend to follow those of a whole class of segregated establishments – jails, concentration camps, monasteries, work camps, and so on – in which the inmate spends the whole round of life on the grounds, and marches through his regimented day in the immediate company of a group of persons of his own institutional status.
>
> Like the neophyte in many of these total institutions, the new inpatient finds himself cleanly stripped of many of his accustomed affirmations, satisfactions, and defenses, and is subjected to a rather full set of mortifying experiences: restrictions of free movement, communal living, diffuse authority of a whole echelon of people, and so on. Here one begins to learn about the limited extent to which a conception of oneself can be sustained when the usual setting of supports for it are suddenly removed. (Goffman, 1961: 147–8)

As you read through this chapter, pay particular attention to the ways the cultural expressions we hear here, created by ex-inmates of various kinds, sustain "conceptions of self" as agents. How are selfhoods shored up against the personality-diffusing characteristics of institutions?

EXERCISE 6.5   Toward Self-determination

There are many organizations that support the human rights and self-determination of people labeled with psychiatric disabilities, psychiatric survivors, psychosocial disabilities, or mental health consumers. As a counterpoint to narratives of institutionalization, familiarize yourself with some of these organizations, many of which also support artistic expressions. Check out these large organizations, some with many local branches, and see if you can find mad pride and survivor events in your own location:

- MindFreedom International
- The Icarus Project: Navigating the Space Between Brilliance and Madness
- Mad Pride
- Survivors' Poetry: Promoting Poetry by Survivors of Mental Distress, a British-based arts organization

EXERCISE 6.6   Junius Wilson

Research the life of Junius Wilson (1908–2001), a deaf black man who spent 76 years in a state mental hospital in Goldsboro, North Carolina. How can his life be told, keeping a balance between tragedy and agency? Look at the choices made by his biographers, Susan Burch and Hannah Joyner (*Unspeakable*, 2007), and discuss them. Find other history projects that use individual lives to tell stories of inequality and social justice, and talk about how the stories are told.

One of the ways of finding space around the fixities of disability discourse is to link to other examples of work on similar topics, by disabled authors – rather than non-disabled people exploring the metaphors of disability. So, in a move made in many chapters in this study guide, I introduce you to work by disabled artists, working on themes of confinement and institutionalization, but in very different ways.

A culture as a way of living creates places of melancholia, spots where energy pools, where emotions get bundled into prisms and become the material of song and poetry. The institution of the hospital, where disabled people meet medical specialists, has provided a durable and strong antagonist, rarely wayfarer, in the journey of disability.

Many poets have drawn from the specific constellation of self-dissolution, healing, and structure that the hospital experience signifies. Hospital poems make up a subgenre of lyrical poetry, poetry that speaks to and from experience.

ACTIVITY 1 Writing/Poetry 1

Let us visit the hospital with a US disability culture poet, Jim Ferris. The passage below is adapted from a long-form review I originally wrote about Ferris's collection *Hospital Poems*. The review was published in a mainstream poetry journal, *Valparaiso Poetry Review*, and I was very aware while writing the piece that I had a bit of an uphill struggle connecting disability culture aesthetics and mainstream poetry. So as you read this, focus on the strategies I use to make my points.

> The hospital: a strange place, apart, yet connected, full of foreign languages, exotic beasts. Medical institutions are bearers of specialist power with the ability, particularly interesting for poetry, to name conditions and direct bodies into meaning. And many hospital poems speak from the patient's bodily experience as a specimen, particularized and fragmented. Painful fragmentation can seep into language, and into the rhythms of words. Many disabled people learned new emotions in the hospital. But many also learned about relationships there, about speaking in code, and finding ways out. Jim Ferris's poetry hones the point of anger into form in "The Coliseum," where a boy is naked.
>
>> Before this pride
>> Of professionals, lords of the hospital, cold-eyed
>> White coats trained to find your flaws, focus on failings,
>> Who measure your meat minutely. You are a specimen
>> for study, a toy, a puzzle–
>
> Ferris has spoken about his collection Hospital Poems as a memoir in verse, remembering his personal history of a childhood spent in hospitals, one of his legs broken again and again as doctors tried to get bone to grow, tried to harmonize the two sides of his body.
>
> When I hear his description, I think of other uses of the word memoir, such as an aide de memoir: in the Renaissance, a memory palace was a mental store room you could move through in your head, finding all you know on the walls, in display cases, in the mosaics on the floor. There are paintings of such memory palaces, stuffed with rooms, but the trick was to hold

it inside, in your head, in your body, and catalogue your belongings and history that way, as you recited to yourself the contents, like a mantra. It was a device of a time which felt that it was nearing all there was to say, that all knowledge could be eventually stored, and where man's (or boy's) brain was the site of this great adventure.

The description has stuck well, for modern thinkers have often taken up the image, and gone in search of attics, vaults, up garden paths and down into root cellars. And maybe it is just this heritage that makes me want to turn from the specific confinement of a limb, a leg, painfully arrested in a plaster cast that won't stay pure as snow or as a lamb, and turn to the other image here, the house I see in the "whitewash white", on a rainy day, on red clay lands, in this poem:

New Cast
Sometimes blood would seep from the wound
Into damp plaster, and evening rust
Would mingle with whitewash white,
Reminding all who cared to look just
What well-intentioned violence
Lay under that stiff, brittle trust.

All throughout the Hospital Poems, spaces are charted: hospitals, with corridors, beds, dark rooms, but also islands cut off from mainlands, orphanages, voids and cliffs, Main Street America, the Girls Ward, spaces connected to others via mail, radio, sounds, songs and oceans. Ferris runs us through the sites, sometimes "like a school of goldfish", sometimes in a "Banana Cart" (like soapbox cars, extended, so that large hip casts can find space, and with wheelchair wheels – but also chariots of more exotic locales, across the sea so often mentioned in these poems, but "not like a coffin, no"). Transport, movement, rolling through the memory palace undercover: "my balance is exquisite/if no nurses are watching". Many of the poems in the collection journey far and fast, from wildly funny to deeply cutting, from abjection on to anger and hope.

"New Cast" veers from the literal, too, and takes a journey in a sentence. This journey is a transformation, a trans-substantiation: an alchemy of color, as meaning is cast newly. A wound and plaster shift into evening rust and whitewash white, taking an element (iron rusts, and plaster is white) and shifting it. I can play in the field opened up by this configuration: the house that is built here – the science of foundational measurements, the expectation of symmetry – is a violence, a wound barely scabbed over by fake scar tissue, suffocating hot plaster.

The alchemy does not stop there: the red and white of the wound and its healing, moved into the red and whites of houses and landscapes, now colors into abstraction, and into the cloths people wrap themselves in, Roman togas, white coats, red crosses – "reminds all who care to look just." Twisting up, the simile emerges: "what well-intentioned violence/lay under that stiff, brittle trust." The red of violence, the white of trust: color and meaning become malleable, but beware those whose bodies similarly excite some aesthetic medical gaze into cutting action. The red and anger of violation, red whitewashed, bleeding for some notion of balance and beauty. And the first action is "seep": this is not a clean alchemy, but a messy one leaving traces of all states behind, binding the flights of fancy back into the wound. The satisfying balance of the poem's analysis of color might open in a contemplative mode (in the "sometimes", "would mingle"), wreathed and bound by rhyme, but in its last line the poem hisses at me with a body, confined, and bleeding: the "stiff, brittle trust" thrusts sibilants against the bucolic image, and fills it with blood.

Writing/Poetry 2

In this poetry reading so far, there is a strong emphasis on space and color:

- Why is that?
- How does this link to the issue of "institutions"?
- What associations do you, in turn, have, reading my reading of Jim Ferris's poems?
- What is the function of criticism here?

Find similar overarching metaphors to approach one of the poems in this book, one you haven't worked on yet, or in a collection like *Beauty is a Verb* (Bartlett et al., 2011) or other disability-focused publication. You might find it useful to read your chosen poem out loud first, before beginning to write. Use the Observation Wheel from the Appendix to gather your first impressions.

Once you identified one or two themes running through your chosen poem, see what happens when you engage in a timed 15-minute free write. Give yourself some freedom to play with words and associations.

Share the original poem and your free write with a colleague. Understand that this is an early draft – this sharing is about generating more ideas, not about polishing. Is the central theme/metaphor clear? Does your colleague have further associations with the poem or the central metaphor that might help you develop this?

Writing/Poetry 3

I am continuing my approach to disability culture poetry by finding connections between Ferris's contemporary poems and a very well-known poet, Sylvia Plath. She lived at a time when disability culture as a concept was still foreign (she died by suicide in 1963), but she had significant mental health experiences throughout her life, and would certainly have come in contact with mad activism if she lived longer.

Linking Ferris as a disability culture poet to Plath as an icon of US poetry is a political act: it deconstructs the sense of disability poetry as only private, small-scale, a minor alternative scene, and puts it in contact with what is considered poetry with a capital P, canonized poetry that finds its way into every anthology.

As you continue reading this, though, you will find that a new theme begins to emerge: my own, the reader/critic's life:

- Why do aspects of my biography appear in here?
- What is the effect?
- Do you find that useful, or intrusive?
- How and why is this reference to one's personal life woven into disability culture practice and scholarship?
- How can you tell your own illness story, or a family member's, in connection with other people's work?

Make some notes as you think about how you can weave a personal strand through the free write you have begun.

> Reading through the Hospital Poems, I remember one of the first hospital poems that touched me with color – Sylvia Plath's "Tulips," in the collection Ariel, published posthumously, after her suicide in 1963. I remember when I was near obsessed with her work, in my twenties some time, reading Plath criticism. And when I got my first writing award, the annual Arts Council of Wales fellowship for a disabled writer, I took up residence in Ted Hughes' home, the Arvon Foundation, and sat by Sylvia Plath's grave, all in the rolling hills of Heptonstall, West Yorkshire. That first day at the grave, I sat with my little notebook by my side on a low stone wall, my crutches next to me (the wheelchair was useless on these cobbled old graveyards, and rested in my beloved Subaru sports car). I do not think I wrote that much, I just sat, and looked at the autumn leaves and the low sun dappling through them, and I thought of stoves, and husbands, and the bee covens I had seen in the back of Hughes's home.

"Tulips" begins:

> The tulips are too excitable, it is winter here,
> Look how white everything is, how quiet, how snowed-in
> I am learning peacefulness, lying by myself quietly
> As the light lies on these white walls, this bed, these hands.
> I am nobody; I have nothing to do with explosions.
> I have given my name and my day-clothes to the nurses.
> And my history to the anaesthetist and my body to surgeons.

White might be the color of winter, and pure snow, and of the cradling sound my tongue makes as it reads "white", and "quiet", "lying", and "my." Only light lies, all effort is given away, flaking off, tumbling into "this bed," "these hands," petals falling. But this foundation, too, is assaulted, by "excitable" and "explosions," and echoes in the "anaesthetist": too much tongue movement, across too large a field, to slip away into death. The "look" is still addressed, still speaks of agency, and it is this eye that cannot but take in, connect:

> They have propped my head between the pillow and sheet-cuff
> Like an eye between two white lids that will not shut.
> Stupid pupil, it has to take everything in.

The poet of Ariel *sees too much, and cannot but name it – light, color, distinction: the learner/eye that cannot shut, sleepless like a wraith, all-seeing on the island, cannot give over to Prospero, cannot stop making meaning.*

INSTITUTIONALIZATION AS EVENT

In this quote from the blog AspieRhetor, Melanie Yergeau, my fellow University of Michigan professor, autism activist and rhetorician, speaks about her experiences being hospitalized against her will. As you read this, think about the differences between institutionalization as an event, and institutionalization as a long-term experience:

- How does Yergeau describe her experience?
- What reference fields does she use to mark her experience of helplessness?
- How does her writing about the event mark her agency?

Many people reading this section have strong reactions. You might want to take a break, and then return to this section with a notebook, writing down some of your feelings.

During my second week as a new faculty member, I was involuntarily committed to the psych ward at the university hospital. I would say that I make this statement against my better judgment, but such a sentiment presupposes that I have better judgment. *(Which, according to my ex-doctors, I don't.)*

My commitment had a slow-motion feel to it. As it was happening, I couldn't believe that it was happening – I was daydreaming, or I was watching a poorly written Lifetime biopic, or I had eaten moldy leftovers that triggered hallucinations, or something, anything but reality. But, no. This was my reality, and my reality soon spiraled into the progressive tense, into something like this:

– They were strapping me down on a gurney.

– They were wheeling me out of an academic building and into the parking lot, onlookers gawking.

– They were forcing me into an ambulance.

– They were dragging me, still on the gurney, into the psych ER, which resembled a TV prison – brisk security guards, cheap wall paint, steel-enforced doors, cameras that aren't supposed to look like cameras but inevitably do *look like cameras. They were dragging me in there. There.*

– Soon, they were vigorously frisking me, and they were dumping out the contents of my backpack, and they were treating me like I was a criminal because I carried a bottle of Tylenol and a 3-inch autistic pride button, and they were shoving me, now shoeless and sweaterless, into a doorless room with hard-backed chairs, and they were prohibiting me from making any phone calls unless I did so via speakerphone, and they were threatening me with overnight and multiple-day stays and refusing to let me wear my headphones, and they were mixing up my diagnoses while periodically asking, How are you doing, sweetie? *– As if they really cared. As if I were a sweetie.*

Before the EMTs bundled me, pig-in-a-blanket style, into the ambulance, my former therapist asked me why being committed was such a 'bad' thing. 'If you have to ask that question,' I fumed, 'then you really don't have a clue.'

That pre-ambulance moment, to the best of my memory, is when their ventriloquism started. Suddenly, the experts claimed, I wasn't talking. God, no. That's your depression talking, they explained. That's your autism talking. That's your anxiety talking. Really, it's anything but you talking.

Hours later, I sat in the psych ward, shaking, rocking, stimming, ticcing – anything to prevent epic meltdown mode. I was disembodied. Objectified. Powerless. I was freezing, hunkered up against the wall in my new doorless home, watching an eight-year-old kid being forcibly removed from his parents. How do I not headbang? How do I not bite myself? How do they not see our humanity? (Yergeau, 2012; see also Yergeau, 2013)

CHANIKA SVETVILAS: SPACE AND EXPERIENCE

Image 10 *Chanika Svetvilas, Side Effects, still from performative reading/drawing installation video,* 2012

In her installation, Chanika Svetvilas reshapes a white cube space into a spatial engagement with her hospitalization experience. Pay attention to how she knits various aspects of her experience together, including a reference to disability cultural embedment, with her citation of well-known US artist Joseph Grigely:

> *Drawn on the wall is the medication guide and chemical compound for Abilify, aripiprazole, an antipsychotic medication that I ingest daily, pages from my workbook given to me during my hospital stay, a feedback form given to friends and family to evaluate the patient they are visiting, drawings by my nieces which include statements of love, my admission form, prescription bottle and text from advertisements for products directed at consumers. All of these images and text are contained in a cell like structure emphasized by the white cube. As I surround myself with these images I acknowledge and confront my history no longer hidden from view. ...*

> *My niece's drawings sent by fax contrast with those of my prescription bottle and hospital admission form. One note states, 'I love you! I hope you are having a good time!' To my niece, I am just her aunt who needs to get better. ... The monochrome use of charcoal unifies the installation. My niece's drawings are substantial as powerful documentation as is my hospital admission form. The room is a remnant of my experience with hospitalization. It does not tell the whole story, but leaves an impression like the marks on the wall.*

Joseph Grigely who has been deaf since he was ten years old creates installations with his impressive collection of communication exchanges found on a variety of materials from post-it notes to cocktail napkins, and stationary that cover walls as a multifaceted conversation and grid.

He sees a parallel with still lives as they document the everyday.

My installation also creates a conversation constructed between images and text. (Svetvilas, 2014: 37–43)

HOW TO REMEMBER INSTITUTIONAL LIFE

This excerpt is from a co-written article by learning disabled researchers (researchers with cognitive differences) and university researchers, published in an academic context. Pay attention to the registers of the words used, and how this text can speak to and with people with different kinds of educational experiences. What do you think about the request to write about the atrocious past by making sure that there's something positive there, too?

We wanted to write an article in our own words. We think that it's important that people get learning disabled people's point of view instead of listening to the lies from people in day services and places like that. We wanted to do an article like this, putting stuff down in writing about what we feel like, about what it is like for people who are learning disabled, what it's like to be bullied time and time again. Bullying can happen anywhere, even in People First groups sometime.

Things have changed; the world has turned now. It's time to stop it always being the professionals doing everything. We want people to listen to us: listen to us and learn from us. ...

Something we're concerned about is that we need to be sensitive to people's feeling in this article, people who have been in institutions. A bit of the past needs to go in the article, not a lot. People need to learn from the past, so we only need to touch on it then put something positive in as well. We need to tell people what's come out of all the hurt and pain and the nightmare but we don't to be reminded of it everyday. We need to go about it in a more positive way because if we go about in a negative way it's not going to do anybody any good at all. (Docherty et al., 2005: 30–1)

Writing/Poetry 4

Here is a section from the end of my review of Jim Ferris's *Hospital Poems*, how a particular poem allows me to view my own situation differently, how it gives me the space I need, as a disabled woman. I finally am in an actual hospital, and my placement as reviewer/writer/someone implicated in the scenarios I describe becomes clearer. As you read through this final section, pay attention to what new functions of hospitals emerge for you from the mixture of Ferris's, Plath's, and my criticism's perspectives. What themes of the hospital emerge in this ending? Do they echo your own experiences, when you or people you knew were hospitalized?

Make a list of associations with a place/an institution, appropriate to the theme of your free write.

I am returning to this computer late one afternoon, in Texas, coming back from a lecture given by a visiting speaker to an audience of medical humanities and bioethics scholars and students – the same students who are in the disability culture class I am teaching here as a visiting scholar. The lecture was in the Shriner Burns building, and to get there, you have to make your way through the John Sealy Hospital and the Children's Hospital – in through the back entrance, snaking through the underbelly, through narrow passages, all on squeaky linoleum, past white coats and strange paraphernalia of gurneys, rigs, and tackle. It's a long walk, and while I am only a visiting scholar, I have often moaned about the department's policy to schedule lectures in prestigious places with newer carpet, rather than in the building we all inhabit. The administrators know that I get exhausted from the walk. It never makes a difference, even though I am here for six months, and I plead my case, every time. But I get to the hall, eventually. Sitting in that audience, I lost my crip tongue, for a while, my trickster reading. The speaker spoke of a bioethicist's implied audience, and how failure to acknowledge certain groups (always "the disabled") can wreak catastrophe. He described briefly the protest Not Dead Yet, a group of disability activists who oppose euthanasia, were mounting at the annual bioethics convention, but without any of the gleam and defiance I feel when hearing the words.

And yes, the speaker was courteous, well-dressed, with tie, and did explain "nothing about us without us" – but still, I heard again and again NDY as a radical group, the pesky disabled, disruptive, outsiders. This speaker's implied audience in the hospital did not include this crip (although I know well that I was not the only one in that audience, nor the only one finding the long walks hard: I am just the only one in a position secure enough to even moan about it). And this lecturer's implied poetics, format, structure did not include a painful body. I am not proud to say that my hand rose only rather feebly and belatedly in the six minutes allocated to discussion. I never gave that impassioned defense of activism I composed carefully in my head, that scathing attack on professionalism and expertise. I was tired of it, had schlepped myself across this monstrous hospital, and to this fancy lecture hall with podium and medal (and the Shriner's tufted fez and scimitar on the emblem, giving an exoticizing lie to all this rationality).

Time to go. I enter again the massive hospital building, to pick up my car on the other side, past my office, and this computer. I pass people sitting in wheelchairs, motionless. Dog-tired nurses still overtake me, and I follow the lines cut into the linoleum, the lines hospitals use to mark the paths. And as I walk off the lines and twist into the older parts of the building, trying not to get lost, I see the sea-green tiles that feel as if they must have echoes for crips everywhere. I never really noticed them before on this path: those long rectangles, slightly irregular, to let a gaze travel past, that milky sea foam color that looks as if it has depth, that spider web of graze crackles that can be visible, sometimes, if you stare long and hard, if you have nothing better to do. Those walls that look, if your eyes blaze with melodrama, as if you could hose them down, as if they do get hosed down, at nights, after blood splattered. Surely we can't have had those same tiles in the hospitals all the way over in Germany? And still, it seems to me that way, the color burrowing into me as I am tired, in pain, annoyed with myself and with this profession that might invite me in for a while but of course can still shrug us off without a second thought.

Then I am in my office, heavily down in my chair, and I take out the book with the Hospital Poems one more time, remembering a foamy ocean in there, to see if I can't find some energy, some wave, some lift in its pages, before I am leaving, going home.

Patience
The hospital is on a promontory jutting
Far out into the ocean. We're on a cliff, about
to topple into the waves which smash against the rocks.
We can't even see across the street – there is no street,
no one can reach us, the thin tongue of land behind us
has crumbled into the sea. Hail drums windows,
thunder rattles the glass until it must break, the lights
go out. The doctors have lit out for shore – we can see
their boat, their white coats in the far distance. The nurses
pound the waves in an open boat behind the doctors,
their white caps serene, protecting them from the weather.
Our island washes away beneath us, wave by wave
it gives us away until we slide down what is left
of the cliff into the alien sea and bob there,
rudderless, our casts and the ether our only friends,
and wait to see what happens next.

Oceans, yes, and the green of sea foam, late afternoon rain shading into gray, running milky down window panes, hazy figures leaving the palace, leaving nothing but waiting behind. Drama is drummed up (what word choice in the "promontory jutting", getting ready to "topple": full-mouthed word delight), adventure and the tales of tall ships and storms, and the piquancy of abandonment. And from that drop into night, an ocean swells out into dream, with only the kindnesses of strange things to give familiarity, weight, anchor and sea-sick air. The island dissolves into Ariel's land.

The poem is bisected by that one line, "go out. The doctors have lit out for shore – we can see." In this line, there's a pool of stillness, enclosed by lights going out and by a precarious seeing. Those doctors ride in the calmness of a lulling meter – one that finds its match and rhyme in the last line, "and wait to see what happens next" – iambs calmly proceeding, echoing the assuredness, the sense of knowing one's space and place, at least for now. The melody of those lines mitigate my other readings of this poem, the danger, breaks, crashing, smashing, those aliens, that lack of rudder. There are two pulls for me: chaos and calmness, and I can choose as I read.

For there's still a wave I catch here, in the "we", the "our": these are shared adventures, as islands give way, to rocking sounds, not to lonely thoughts. I listen beneath the words, listen to sounds and rhythms, and find a different tune. Words and lines and waves string this along, rocking me on, knowing that something will come next, the story goes on, as boys and all crips dream.

For poems are not just puzzles to work out, or mnemonic devices that crystallize our world to us: they are also comforts, familiar sounds, the gentle touch of paper on fingers, breath on tongue, and a going home.

The companionship of breath, and shared sleep: crip culture can live, anywhere, it can find itself in the hospital, and in the many spaces the hospital can shapeshift into in the memory palace of disability culture. Crip culture might only ever be a horizon, a moon across the sea, sometimes just a castle in the sky, but it's alive. It's full dark now here in Texas, and no-one else is around the office – but crips like all humans everywhere have long learned to cope, and to find sustenance in unlikely places. I can imagine journeys shared, tenuously, recognize the signs of sea foam, and find transport on watery night-horses, lulled and bobbed, alone and together, awaiting the next day.

EXERCISE 6.7 **ADAPT**

Research the activities of ADAPT, a US-based grassroots activist organization that fights against the institutionalization of disabled people:

- What do their non-violent direct actions look like?
- How are they reported in the media?
- What do you imagine engaging in these actions feels like – to you, however you move through the world, and to people who have mobility or other differences?
- How do their activities hold against the feeling of being in an institution?

Writing/Poetry 5

How did the color and space scheme develop? What wider themes become linked to them? I picked out moments in the *Hospital Poems* collection where these specific themes appear, and created a coherent container for these observations:

- Can you trace the themes through the pages of this essay?
- How does the text modulate the themes?
- Are new themes emerging?
- Again, what is the function of the personal revelations, the moments when my writerly "I" appears in the material?
- How do you respond to me revealing echoes of my own hospitalizations in the past?
- How can you make your own desires and needs central to your reading of artful material?

Now go back to your first free write, on the poem you found, and expand – find ways in which your personal life can help you illuminate the poem, or write with the poem. See if you can double your word count from the first free write in this way.

EXERCISE 6.8 ## Sadie Wilcox: Visioning Healing

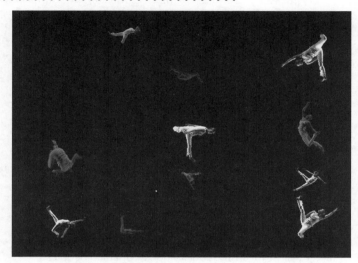

Image 11 *Sadie Wilcox,* Remapping of Memory, *video still, 2008*

Sadie Wilcox is an artist in residence at a children's hospital in Northern California, a burn survivor, and a survivor of violence. She writes:

> Remapping of Memory *investigates the relationship between physical rehabilitation and psychological recovery in response to violence and acute injury. The multimedia video installation explores the process of relearning to walk and regaining basic mobility after a third-degree burn injury. Using choreographed elements of physical movement and gesture, written text, and audio, my project reconstructs traumatic memory fragments associated with my physical and emotional recovery process. The visual composition and structure of the video references the impact of Post Traumatic Stress Disorder (PTSD) on human physiology, brain function, and memory formation. (personal communication)*

In her work, Sadie Wilcox revisits therapeutic experiences, in particular, her experiences in a burn unit.

Audio describe this image, a video still from a multichannel video installation, to each other, see what associations come up as you translate across media, and, if you do not have visual access, translate back and forth across what you are hearing.

Using this image as a springboard, but going beyond it, can you envisage how physical exercise, medical intervention, and issues of repetition can become part of a personal healing vocabulary?

Writing/Poetry 6

Look again at the poem you have chosen for your free write exercise. We will now work in a different way with it. Compose a response poem:

- How can you mimic the choices the poet made, but fill them with your personal content?
- What formal elements are at work in the poem, what play with line breaks, sounds, distribution across the page?
- Are any of these features linked to disability experiences, you think/you imagine? When you work with them, do they still carry disability themes, or have they morphed? What do they signify now?
- Has this response poem opened up new insights into the original poem?

Incorporate some of these insights into your emerging essay.

Development

Now you have all the components for your own essay:

- a developed free write
- some reader feedback
- the incorporation of personal material
- thoughts about a poem's structure and form, explored through crafting your own response.

Now shape and edit a five–six page satisfying essay out of this, an essay that charts a journey with a particular poem.

ACTIVITY 2 Video

Many well-known poems in disability culture contexts have many different lives online. Research a well-known poem, like Laura Hershey's "You Get Proud by Practicing." How have people appropriated, worked with, reworked, and played with these texts? Check out Deaf Sign Language poetry in various countries – there are many clips from festivals and individual artists online. How does live performance, video, and attempts to include hearing audiences work here?

Development

Take one of the poems reproduced in this book, from *Beauty is a Verb: New Poetics of Disability*, or from an online journal like *Wordgathering, Survivors Poetry*, or *Breath and Shadow*. Now create a cross-media ekphrasis: use video to create a new version of the poem, finding ways of linking the particular poem to your own surroundings, your city or town, sights you encounter. The particular emphasis should be on remaking the poem into something that relates to your life world – which aspect of the poem or your life is up to you. Share the finished product and the processes of its creation with your classmates.

7 *Freak Shows and the Theatre*

In this chapter, you will gain insights into these issues:

- Contemporary performance makers reflecting on the freak show as heritage
- Using performance as a way to research history
- Remediating through art practice
- Theatre as a way to explore audience/performer dynamics
- Sexuality and disability on the stage
- Carnival and disruption
- Other-than-realist stagings
- Durational performance, boundaries, and issues of control
- Issues with casting: disabled/non-disabled, cross-impairment, crossing other differences
- Disability performance aesthetics and multimodal framing

In this chapter, I focus on the dramatic stage, and on the histories of disabled people on these stages. The freak show, carnival or sideshow was the first sustained and organized dramatic institution for disabled people. The histories of these entertainments, their impact on the way disability is viewed in the wider public, and their reverberations on contemporary disability performance are important themes in disability arts criticism and beyond.

Of course, the freak show is by no means the only topic of contemporary disability theatre – there are many strands to a thriving scene, and we've already encountered quite a few in this study guide. But the freak show is a theme that gets picked up again and again, and many of the performances in this chapter reference it directly or indirectly.

Contemporary Freak Show: Mat Fraser's *Sealboy*

My case study is a show by one of the most famous and skilled manipulators of freak show themes on the contemporary stage, Mat Fraser. Fraser is a UK performance artist who went on a journey from London to Coney Island, US, and from the freak show stage to an Edinburgh Fringe Festival theatre, in order to clarify for himself his position as a "freak" performer.

My discussion centers around the particular challenge disabled performers face: an ableist society often fails to see the disabled bodymind as engaged in a performance, an act, an expression of agency. The discourse of the freak stage did not see the performer as performing, but as "natural." So they were given non-human status: they became a seal, a dog (the dog-faced boy), the missing link (between humans and apes), or racialized others not seen as humans, like the wild men of Borneo or Aztec children.

Fraser plays with that boundary: acting/being a static object of observation. He challenges his audiences to see this seam in their reception of disability on stage.

Fraser was born with phocomelic, that is, very short arms, as a result of his mother's exposure to thalidomide. He has a colorful and successful career as rock star, theatre actor, film star, public persona on the UK's Channel 4, presenter on the BBC's *Ouch* program, and is now a beloved superstar of the international disability culture scene.

In his show *Sealboy: Freak* (2001–07; also presented in the 2002 Channel 4 documentary about creating the stage show), he resurrects Stanley Berent, aka Sealo the Seal Boy. In the creation of *Sealboy*, Fraser was searching for his historic role model, his roots, his heritage. I stress these words: employing these terms – role models, roots, heritage – designates his disability experience not as an individual and singular fate, but as a cultural minority experience. In other shows, Fraser has created similar kinds of accounts of shared cultural journeys by focusing on the experience of the thalidomide conflict, the bioethical case of the pharmaceutical scandal that resulted in many children born with impairments like his.

In his research into performers with impairments similar to his, Fraser found successful people with names such as "Lobsterboy," who performed monstrosity and freakishness for sideshow audiences in the first half of the last century. Stanley Berent was one of these, a performer in US freak shows from the 1930s onward. As sideshows were shut down in the 1970s in the US, a way of life and a way of making a living were taken away from performers all over the nation, and Berent was caught up in this dismantling. He retired to the Riverview Retirement Home for Old Showpeople in Florida, and died in 1984.

Fraser came across Berent in his research for a theatre show for Graeae, one of the UK's most well-known professional disability theatre companies, who produced *Fittings: The Last Freak Show* in 1999. In his 2001 program notes, Fraser wrote:

> In this one act, one man show Mat asks the question: Can a disabled performer ever be seen as anything other than a freak, irrespective of the "liberal" or "postmodern" attitudes of today's sophisticated audiences?, and then he becomes his predecessor, Sealo the Sealboy, as the audience is forced to confront their collective connection with the freakshow audiences of the past.

> Containing feats of strength, drum'n'bass, sexuality, and class A drugs, SEALBOY: FREAK is a show that takes the spectator outside the comfort zone and into the teradome.

Sealboy utilizes an audience address on the boundaries of the "aesthetic" theatre, referenced by the existence of the program note itself and its reference to complex artistic motives and strategies, and the freak spectacle, in the second paragraph with its enumeration of attractions, culminating in the "teradome" – a term derived from teratology, the study of monsters.

In order to construct *Sealboy*, Fraser went on a research trip to some of the core locations of Berent's life. He met up with retired sideshow people, including "talkers," or pitch men – people who performed the chatter that drew the audience into the tent, and who moderated the show-stage inside.

Sealboy opens with one of these patters. Watching Fraser, the freak, perform the part of talker in *Sealboy* gives the act depth. He calls forth a family, making a living in the strangest conditions, but as a working, living community:

> *Folks we've already shown you the rubber faced girl Etta Lake outside, her skin stretches 6 inches in any direction that it is pulled, and still to come Millie and Christine the two headed girl, Jo Jo the dog faced boy, his face and body completely covered in long, golden hair; the half girl Jeannie Tomani; reaching only a height of 2 and a half feet, she is the smallest woman in the world Ladies and Gentlemen. Also, for your fascination and amazement, the one and only Schlitzy the pinhead, the Aztec children, the bearded lady, the midget family, the giants, and all the other strange anomalies that make up the sideshow on the midway in our Stern's Family Circus.*

Watching this 21st-century memory of the sideshow stirs me strangely. Having read and digested analyses of these events, I now find myself watching the spectacle as a moment of oral history, a calling forth of a lost history, of men and women who provide strange foreparents to today's disabled performers.

Rosemarie Garland-Thomson sums up her analysis of the kinds of shows dominating the 19th century, the heyday of the freak show:

> *In an era of social transformation and economic reorganisation, the nineteenth-century freak show was a cultural ritual that dramatized the era's physical and social hierarchy by spotlighting bodily stigmata that could be choreographed as an absolute contrast to "normal" American embodiment and authenticated as corporeal truth.* (Garland-Thomson, 1997: 63)

In this analysis, the focus is on the others – the non-disabled, normal, or at least normal enough to be able to construct themselves as normal apropos the differences presented to them.

Policing normality is here transferred into the hands of popular culture: the kinds of knowledges that later on rest firmly in the hands of the medical sciences here work on the street, in the everyday life of American people, who can experience the boundaries between right and wrong, self and other, us and them, firsthand in the tent. The freak show is a spectacle of certainty. Even if in other areas of life uncertainty rules, here, one's position on the far side of the stage is assured.

By performing this ritual in a contemporary context, and by inserting his own body into the supposedly clear distinction between (rational) presenter, teacher of the masses, and (irrational) presented, object of the gaze, freak, Fraser breaks open the rigidity of certainties with humorous excess and a swagger.

In hindsight, it is clear that many of the famous acts of the freak show had a say in their career, but at specific historical moments, such as the Victorian stage, the ritual demanded a clear demarcation of able and not-able, rational-irrational, "man" and animal. But the shows might always have been an act, at least for some of the performers, usually those with racial or gender privilege. Researchers such as Fiedler (1978), Bodgan (1988), and then later Adams (2001), Chemers (2008), and Wu (2012) show that while 19th-century freaks were presented as less than or other than human, allowing the difference between self and other to be clearly grasped, performers often found ways out of the narrow confines of oppression, and entered into complex relationships with their audiences.

RIVA LEHRER: TOTEMS AND FAMILIARS

Image 12 *Riva Lehrer,* Mat Fraser: Sealo Seal Boy *(2006), charcoal on paper, 30" × 44", part of the Totems and Familiars series*

Chicago-based artist Riva Lehrer has created bodies of work that function as disability culture mythologies, often portraying complex personal worlds of disabled artists.

In this image, she draws Fraser in relation to the paraphernalia of the *Sealboy* show. But Lehrer's focus is on Fraser very much as a human person, with deep needs and a requirement for privacy – exactly what the freak show as a mechanism denied its performers. In this work, she remediates the freak show:

> *The conventions of portraiture are based on venerable attitudes about acceptable and unacceptable bodies. Traditional portraiture determines who is worthy of being painted, or sculpted, or photographed. Portraits document what we deem valuable. I began to create portraits of unconventional subjects in order to cultivate my own sense of beauty, importance and visual pleasure. ...*
>
> *I believe that when we are under extreme stress (and this can include joy as well as sorrow) we reach for internal images that help us remember who we are, to make sense of our experience, and to help stabilize our inner world when it is knocked off its axis. Totems and Familiars is centered on interviews in which I asked people to think about those images and their roles in developing and protecting their private selves. (Lehrer, n.d.)*

Freak Sex

In Mat Fraser's show, sexuality intertwines with voyeurism, eroticism, and transgression. In his Berent persona, Fraser indulges in sexual innuendo ("being able to do what all men do") and horseplay (admonishing the ladies in the audience that he doesn't have "those kinds of pictures" of himself). The function of these asides, pretty innocuous in Berent's act, become clearer when Mat Fraser's contemporary alter ego enters *Sealboy*'s stage. We meet Tam Shrafer as he is hyping himself up for an audition – talking a mile a minute, all psyched up and ready to go where his agent, on his mobile, tells him to go. Part of the nervous talk at the beginning of the scene moves from considerations of contemporary reactions to disabled people on stage to the realm of sexuality. The monologue rehearses the relative impotence of liberal theatre politics in the face of deeply held stereotypes:

> *It's a funny old time I suppose, 20 years ago I wouldn't even be standing here, a disabled actor in a professional audition scenario; 30 years ago most directors didn't know that there were any disabled actors. There probably weren't that many. No role models ... 20 years from now, maybe disabled actors will be a normal part of productions. At the moment we must be in the transition stage, well, it often feels transitional; awkward, ill fitting, painful sometimes, with most people too, what, scared? Unimaginative? Complacent? To cast us. And anyone who does have a real vision of drama, that includes us lot, hailed as either a visionary, a revolutionary genius, exciting and confrontational, or, a manipulative sensationalist, cruelly exploiting the freakish value of actual disabled people on stage, inappropriately cheapening the production ya ya ya ya. You know what? People are always gonna say shit like that, whether it's true or not, and isn't a conversation about all that better than not having one? Didn't narrow minded reviewers squawk, balk, and then finally accept female, black, outwardly gay actors before us? Is this a freak I see before me? – No, if you look again you'll see it's an actor! ... Oh Shut Up Tam! ... Sorry about that, I'm just trying to give myself strength with a pep talk before I go in to the audition (Sealboy, 2001)*

This part of Tam's monologue rehearses familiar arguments about liberal art politics, and the necessary changes in the expectation of audiences in order to make disabled actors part of the mainstream.

The image becomes more complicated, though, when liberal politics intersect with internalized images of physical difference, and embedded attitudes toward freakishness. In the continuation of his monologue, Tam merges his acknowledgement of the power of the extraordinary body to overwhelm the narrative scenario, highjack the attention, by placing himself firmly in the tradition of the freak out to shock, to parade taboo subjects:

> *Thing is, when I'm watching myself on film, I think "Fuck, those arms" ... Although mine are familiar, they're even alien to ME when put into their rarest context, i.e., the performance mode. Of course I can make the necessary leap of faith to find my own arms and hands appropriate in*

a scenario that traditionally might find them alien, say in a love scene, I mean hell, I've never been that short of a shag in real life; maybe it's the way I was brought up, but I've never found it a problem to get a partner. Ok sometimes I'm being freak fucked, but no more than the number of times I've been guilty of fancying a girl because of certain, um, physical attributes, I'm just the thick end of the same wedge. "Big tits? Wahay! petite size 8? phwoar! Big fullsome bottom? mmmm!! Hairy armpits? nnngggg. Short arms? OOooh!!" ... My hands may not reach all the way round someone, but they can be tender, loving, wanton even. It's not how far you can reach, but the way you do the reaching. (Damn, that sounds like an excuse for a small cock.) (Sealboy, 2001)

Openness about sexuality and sexual issues has always been a trademark of Mat Fraser's public persona in Britain, from his days as a punk rocker to his work in burlesque shows.

In *Sealboy*, the foregrounding of sexuality takes on interesting aspects in relation to disability visibility. By breaking the taboo (and inviting the resultant titillation) around disability and sexuality, Fraser extends a structural similarity: like sex, disabled bodies are disavowed, shut away from the mainstream, locked into bedrooms. Fraser's freak status results as much from his "outrageous" behavior, his song lyrics, and his patter as from his physicality: he refuses to leave things in the bedroom, or in the privacy of non-public environments.

With this, Fraser merges disability politics from the polite, liberal, rational, civil rights end, with the fun of freak tactics. Fraser's performance tactics echo the strategies of theatre practitioners who use excess and destabilization in order to move beyond the difference-denying polite frameworks of sameness.

Can Fraser achieve a re-vision of disability, exposing the sensationalist gaze of the non-disabled audience by breaking taboos and playing with sexual connotation? He would need to fashion a way of looking that offers a subject position for the disabled person. Fraser's alter ego, Tam Shrafer, acknowledges in *Sealboy* (2001): "I read this book once that said the mainstream will only ever see disabled people performing in the same way that they view a performing seal."

And while Fraser holds forth on the politics of the stage, and on non-disabled audience's inability to see "acting" rather than spectacle, he rolls a joint with his short hands, perfectly timed to reach his lips the moment his monologue ends. What did the audience watch? The Berentesque spectacle of rolling a joint, marveling at the facility of these "little handsies"? Or did they listen to Fraser's critique, an actor who during his discourse engages in the "normally" nearly invisible act of getting ready to smoke: a conventionalized sign of theatre, often denoting contemplation and meditation?

What would YOU pay attention to?

Look for Fraser's work online, and check it out. There are many videos and reviews available. What are his performance strategies? How does he use sexuality on stage, and how does he ensure that he does not offend (too much), and that he keeps his platform for reaching out to audiences?

BAKHTIN AND THE CARNIVALESQUE

The Russian theorist Mikhail Bakhtin investigated the carnivalesque body. Bakhtin's use of the term "carnival" here is not a metaphor, but is grounded in historical practices, ritual social moments in European history where social ties are inverted and the body becomes the stage for disruptive practices. In his analysis of the French writer Rabelais' work, Bakhtin describes the crowd in the carnival:

> The festive organization of the crowd must be first of all concrete and sensual. Even the pressing throng, the physical contact of the bodies, acquires a certain meaning. The individual feels indissolubly part of the collectivity, a member of the people's mass body. In this whole the body ceases to a certain extent to be itself: it is possible, so to say, to exchange bodies, to be renewed (through the change of costume and mask). At the same time the people become aware of their sensual, material bodily unity and community. (Bakhtin, 1968: 255)

EXERCISE 7.1 **Party Time**

Have you ever been to a carnival celebration? Maybe a Hindu Holi celebration with colorful powders? Think about Mardi Gras, or raves as a social form. If you have never been to an event like this, do an image and video search online. Can you relate your experience of these events to Bakhtin's categories, in particular to the "pressing throng," flesh on flesh, bypassing representational categories? Can art practice activate similar sensations, and if so, what do artists do with them?

EXERCISE 7.2 **Graeae Theatre Company and Commissioning Contemporary Plays**

Contemporary theatre companies no longer hold on to the old stark division between freaks on stage and normates in the audience. Both sides were always mixed, but now, we can consciously foster integrated audiences *and* stages.

Here is the online statement by Graeae. Note how an aesthetic of access is core to their play development:

> Graeae is committed to developing and producing new work and writing. We are passionate about performing stories in an accessible way, putting access at the heart of every commission process. From idea to page to stage, the route to integrated access challenges and drives our new work.
>
> By enabling, developing and producing the work of established and emerging writers, we champion a tradition of integrated access and equal representation.
>
> The 'Graeae Aesthetic' explores new ways of performing and telling stories. Our commission and development process explores the possibilities for integral accessible communication within every play, including on-stage sign language interpreters, use of film or recorded sound, captioning, power point projections and audio description. (www.graeae.org/about-us/artistic-vision)

Find video clips of Graeae's work online. Watch a clip (note the show), and write down elements of the show that show disability access on all sides of theatre-making: on stage, off stage, in the technical booth, and in the audience seats.

Development

Now look at a different company's online self-representation, for instance Extant, a professional British performance company of visually impaired people. How does access feature in their publicity materials, and in the performances you can access online?

Compare your notes on access and how the productions and documentation websites imagine and depict their respective audiences. What are the differences between these companies?

. . . .

ACTIVITY 1 Back to Back Theatre

Image 13 *Brian Tilley and Simon Laherty in a publicity image for Back to Back Theatre Company's Ganesh Versus the Third Reich.* Photo: *Jeff Busby, courtesy Back to Back Theatre Company*

Back to Back's ensemble is made up of actors perceived to have intellectual disabilities, a group of people who, in a culture obsessed with perfection and surgically enhanced 'beauty', are the real outsiders. This position of marginality provides them with a unique and at time subversive view of the world. (backtobacktheatre.com/about)

1 Use the Observation Wheel (in the Appendix) and write down responses to this image. Work in groups if there are access issues for some of you. Share your observations in the round: what are the reference fields opened up by this strong visual image, in conjunction with this title?

2 Now research Back to Back's work, and look for clips of their performances online. Here is the description of their show *Ganesh Versus the Third Reich* (you can also find the text of this show and many perspectives on the company's work in Eckersall and Grehan, 2013).

The story begins with the elephant-headed god Ganesh travelling through Nazi Germany to reclaim the Swastika, an ancient Hindu symbol. As this intrepid hero embarks on his journey a second narrative is revealed: the actors themselves begin to feel the weighty responsibility of storytellers and question the ethics of cultural appropriation.

Cleverly interwoven in the play's design is the story of a young man inspired to create a play about Ganesh, god of overcoming obstacles. He is an everyman who must find the strength to overcome the difficulties in his own life, and defend his play and his collaborators against an overbearing colleague.

The show is made before our very eyes and takes on its own life. It invites us to examine who has the right to tell a story and who has the right to be heard. It explores our complicity in creating and dismantling the world, human possibility and hope. (Back to Back Theatre, n.d.)

Go back to the first round of sharing, from the image by itself. Do your Observation Wheel impressions change as you look in detail at what the company is doing, as you see these two men (and other actors) in action? What complex play with freakishness, the gaze, and audience' expectations is going on in the image, and in the publicity clips you can find online?

ACTIVITY 2 Suzan-Lori Park's *Venus* and Bernard Pomerance's *The Elephant Man*

These two widely available plays provide exciting perspectives on freak shows, realist depiction, exploitation, and the stage. In preparing to engage with a scene from the plays, research the Hottentot Venus or the Elephant Man online, and make yourself familiar with the other players mentioned: these are in the main historical figures. Also explore descriptive labels: who are pinheads, for instance? Engage with the medical history presented in both plays.

Exercise

Get together into groups of four. Choose a juicy section from the play you are discussing. You do not need as many people as there are characters – this does not need to be a realist enactment, "acting out" people as if they were real people.

Now come up with a way of staging this work:

- How do you do it?
- How do you perform race and gender?
- How do you cast?

- How do you play the freakishness of Venus – is she (and others in the scene) a freak, and what does that mean in this context?
- Who is a freak in whose eyes?
- How can you mark historical distance?
- How do you play the Elephant Man, and the shifting senses of freakishness there?

Be careful about your choices, and check in with one another – discuss potential discomfort and appropriation. Do not assume that silence means assent.

Now do it. Stage the scene in your classroom. Discuss your choices, and the ethics that inform them.

Development

Create a design for a stage set for each show. Think about how you can incorporate disability (and African-American) culture histories and access features into your design ideas. Flesh out/color in the design sketches. Create an exhibit, and talk your classmates through your ideas.

STRUGGLE AND RECLAIMING

Stage this scene from the St. Louis-based That Uppity Theatre Company's DisAbility Project, a long-running community theatre project (see also Lipkin and Fox, 2002).

"Some People See Me As …"

Ali: Some people see me as controlling …
But really, I'm organized.
Tom: Some people see me as clumsy …
But really, I'm blind.
Bryan: Some people see me as dumb …
But really, I just learn in different ways.
Reid: Some people see me as forgetful …
But really, I just have a lot on my mind.
Lorri: Some people see me as stubborn …
But really, I just wanna do it myself.
Stuart: Some people see me as a doormat …
But really, I'm an open door! Come in, we'll have coffee …
Dianne: Some people see me as isolated …
But really, I'm very social.
Emma: Some people see me as helpless
But really, I want to help you!
Ana: And some people see me as confined …
But really, I'm free. (She rolls across the stage in her chair)
(End with Ana, … "free!" … traveling from the end of the line to the beginning.
ALL
Some people see us as different
(beat)
But really, we are just like you
(Cannon) "We" "Are" "Individuals"

Durational Performance Art: Invoking an Epileptic Fit

In this passage, British disability arts writer Jo Verrent speaks about a much discussed series of works by Portuguese artist and researcher Rita Marcalo (for a discussion of the audience responses to the show, see Hadley, 2014). Research Rita Marcalo's *Involuntary Dances* and the other artists mentioned here, and discuss some of the questions Verrent brings up.

> *Rita [Marcalo] wishes to present her convulsing body as art to an audience, and ultimately, through this, to herself. She is a dancer, has trained for years to control and express herself through the medium of her body and the way in which it moves. When she experiences seizures, her body moves, but in a way in which she cannot control. It is this shift of control that Rita is exploring, and through it, her own identity – as dancer, as human, as Rita. ...*

> *As our invitation states: since 2009 choreographer Rita Marcalo has been working on a trilogy of works focusing on her relationship to her epilepsy. ... She has invited us to this gathering to discuss, and advise her on, this third and final installment of the trilogy.*

> *Why? Why not? Artists have been using themselves as material for centuries. It is only natural that someone with artistic curiosity would wish to apply it to themselves, to different aspects of their identity. Also present in the room were Franko B whose work for many years involved using his blood and bloodletting, Brian Lobel who has created a diverse range of work based on his experiences with cancer, and Martin O'Brien whose work often addresses his experiences of his Cystic Fibrosis. ... The four-hour discussion covered serious territory:*

> - *What are the layered intentions behind the piece? Which is most important?*
> - *What are the roles of, and for, the audience?*
> - *Where are the ethical boundaries and responsibilities?*
> - *Who has power and who has control?*
> - *What is safe and how do we define that? Safe for whom?*
> - *How can such work best be contextualized? How can this best be shared?*
> - *Which public conversations around the work should one respond to and engage with?*
> - *How can one allow those conversations to shape and influence the work? Should we? (Verrent, 2012)*

ACTIVITY 3 Performing *P.H.*reaks*

This excerpt is part of a scene of *P.H.*reaks: The Hidden History of People with Disabilities*, a collaborative project developed and adapted by Doris Baizley and Victoria Ann Lewis, presented in Los Angeles in 1994.

As you read through these scene excerpts, which portray the HEW (Health, Education and Welfare) Sit-In in San Francisco, become aware of how this project presents disability history, and how the devisers make connections to many different people, not just disabled audience members. Look up the sit-in, and what it was all about.

> Demonstrator 1: There are the facts. In 1972, Congress passed the Rehabilitation Act, which was our first civil rights act, eighteen years before the ADA. Any program with federal funding could no loner discriminate against people with disabilities. By 1977 the regulations were drawn up, but Carter's HEW chairman, Califano, still hadn't signed them. April fourth was our deadline. When nothing happened, we moved into ten federal buildings in the US. In most places, the sit-ins lasted only a few hours, but in San Francisco we stayed for twenty-eight days!
>
> Demonstrator 2: Nobody expected it to last that long. I mean, some of us had sleeping bags, but even that wasn't official because we couldn't let anybody know we were planning to stay. But twenty-eight days! ...
>
> Demonstrator 4: We had our hands full with the press. They were there all the time. They loved this story. At the beginning we had to steer them away from those "brave, sweet cripple" stories to hard facts about civil rights. And try to clean up their language: "deaf and dumb," "polio victim," "wheelchair bound," "confined to a wheelchair" ... The same old litany.
>
> Demonstrator 5: I'd been active in a lot of political stuff – the war, the black movement, abortion rights – but nothing like this, ever... this direct effect. I mean – we won! After twenty-eight days, we get those regs signed.
>
> Demonstrator 6: But the most wonderful thing about that time was that I knew there'd be someone there for me every morning and every night. Someone to get me out and then into bed. No attendant flake-out. And I'd be fed. ...
>
> Demonstrator 5: I'd never felt so safe and powerful in my life. It was so, well – PEOPLE FELL IN LOVE! I'm not kidding. I could name quite a few couples who met there.
>
> Demonstrator 6: Some of them are still together. ...
>
> Demonstrator 5: There were two hundred of us, and we were there for ourselves and about thirty-five million other disabled people –
>
> Demonstrator 6: And that's not an exaggeration. For many of us it was, and is, the most important thing we'd ever done with our lives. I mean, so much so that our final political crisis, after we won, was that a whole group of people refused to leave the building. They didn't want to go back to the real world, even if there were regs now.
>
> Demonstrator 1: We fiddled with the media, told them we had to clean up the building like the good citizens we were –
>
> Demonstrator 2: And gently we coaxed our comrades through the doors with us and out to the waiting crowd. (Baizley and Lewis, 2006: 101–2)

Development

If you have access to the book, look up the full scene in *Beyond Victims and Villains* (Lewis, 2006), and stage it in your classroom. Play it. Now stage it again, using a different system to distribute the voices. Become unruly: go against the way that the voices are parsed.

- Observe the effects, and talk about this among yourself.
- Create props for the staging: are there words or images you'd like to put on banners or signs?
- Think about your costumes: what do you want to wear, what is the feel? Think historically, but also transhistorically, as you are staging this in the here and now.
- Add material to the scene, if you feel so inclined. Have asides, and a frame, a new beginning and a new end.

 Remember to treat the playwrights and the play with respect: you can use this for a class exercise, but not for a public performance, where you will need to check with the right holders.

CASE STUDY

Casting and the Weight of Experience

In this last section, I move away from the freak show theme and the focus on navigating how one is seen on a stage. I focus instead on a particular case study that is central to many theatre classrooms: how to work with bodies and minds as metaphors, and how to engage casting when our classrooms do not always represent the diversity of life outside the classroom.

EXERCISE 7.4

Casting

How to cast disabled roles and how to write plays that specifically address the lived experiences of disability present complex issues to the theatre industry.

Below, British drama educator Andy Kempe writes about British-based playwright Kaite O'Reilly's collaboration with the Graeae Theatre Company, *peeling* (2002). O'Reilly is an internationally known disabled playwright, and has created many complex plays, in recent years with the National Theatre Wales.

> *Addressing form as well as content, the play [peeling] was written specifically for disabled female actors with specific physical and sensory impairments including a deaf actor whose first language is BSL [British Sign Language]. It is impossible to sign BSL and voice at the same time, as BSL, a visual/spatial language, has a chronological syntax and does not conform to the syntax of its oral partner, English. The writer's intention in* peeling *was clearly to create positive opportunities for disabled actors within the professional theatre … The intention was to focus upon the specific experience of particular impairments and for the articulation of the experience to come from the disabled characters themselves as opposed to a 'normal' co-protagonist or helper figure. Indeed, the fictional characters are members of a Greek chorus*

that would normally be the marginalised support to the protagonist ...
Since the original Graeae production of peeling, *it has rarely been re-staged*
because of the embedded requirements for actors with specific impairments
to portray the characters. (Kempe, 2012: 65)

Research the play, and critics' responses to it. Use what you find as a lens to think about casting issues. In other theatre contexts, the issue is called "color-blind casting," a somewhat unfortunate disability metaphorical way of referring to casting across racial lines. Familiarize yourself with the issues (see also Sandahl, 2008).

Here is US author Charles (Chuck) Mee, another veteran disabled playwright, giving casting instructions to directors who wish to work with his plays:

In my plays, as in life itself, the female romantic lead can be played by a
woman in a wheel chair. The male romantic lead can be played by an
Indian man. And that is not the subject of the play.

There is not a single role in any one of my plays that must be played by
a physically intact white person. And directors should go very far out of
their way to avoid creating the bizarre, artificial world of all intact white
people, a world that no longer exists where I live, in casting my plays. (www.
charlesmee.org/casting.shtml)

Ask yourself: How far "out of their way" will directors go? If the choice is given to cast a play with all non-disabled white theatre students, for instance, at a college that might not have a strong minority representation, will this instruction stop them from doing so? Should it?

EXERCISE 7.5   ## Performing Madness

There is an international scene of theatre companies of people with mental health differences/psychiatric survivors – all companies use different ways of marking themselves, so take note of the self-descriptors. Look at online traces of performances, see what you can find out about working methods, the engagements with metaphors and experiences of madness in their practices, and the sites where these companies share their work:

- Accademia della Follia, Santarcangelo di Romagna, Italy
- Bohnice Theatre Company, Prague, Czech Republic
- Theatre Sycorax, Münster, Germany
- Workman Theatre Project, Toronto, Canada

ACTIVITY 4   ## *Still Lives*: Metaphor and Disability

This monologue was developed by A Different Light, a New Zealand/Aotearoa theatre company, whose members are deemed to have cognitive disabilities. (Research the online presence of this company, and find readings by its director, Tony McCaffrey.) This scene is part of their performance *Still Lives* (2011), which responds to the earthquakes in Christchurch, and "shakes up" understandings of a disabled/disabling city/environment.

BEN'S POPPIES

BEN sits at a table, a livefeed video of him is projected in the background, at times focusing on his nose or hands or the memorial poppies he is playing with.

BEN: Poppies poppies poppies!
Tall poppy syndrome
When I look at these poppies
I see a job I used to have
In Kilmarnock Street
Making poppies
For ANZAC Day
Until the job was
outsourced
overseas
I see a lot of things
I see the time
I had a nose operation
I was scared of the operation
Thought I was going to die
A Church person joked I was having a nose job
A nose job?
At least I'm not having a blow job
But I didn't say those exact words
I ran into this girl verbally
There was sex talk – it works both ways –
Talk and texts
Her grandmother saw the texts
A Church person
She came up to me
After the service
Lots of people around

And she bawled me out
Hauled me up
Over the coals
So angry and so ashamed
I wanted to take my own life
I banged my head against a concrete pole
Again and again against a concrete pole
And I walked in the middle of the road
Hoping a big truck would come and flatten me
Blown job
Nose job
No job

BEN has become very animated during this last scene. GLEN and ISAAC come to him and during the following reach out to him, touch him.

ISAAC: Stillness
 Silence
 In the silence
 Try to reach you
 Try to touch you
 My words
 Your breathing
 My face
 Your face
 Breathe in
 Breathe out
 Nose to nose
 Hongi
 Like the Maori
 Touch
 Some of us are paralysed
 Some of us
 Find it difficult to reach out
 Touch
 Still living
 Still alive
 Still lives
 Touch
 …

ISAAC: Christchurch is still experiencing aftershocks

VOICEOVER: This is nothing new for Glen who "sparks" regularly and has fits frequently.
This is nothing new for Isaac who crashes if he does not monitor his blood sugar levels and gets in scrapes because people expect normal from him.
This is nothing new for Ben who gets knocked back if he steps over the line and who still beats himself up if he can't get everything right .

BEN: And Glen and Ben and Isaac step and wheel out into
ISAAC: Christchurch after the quakes.
BEN: New normal
ISAAC; Quake brain
GLEN: PTSD,
BEN: cuts to education
ISAAC: cuts to social services
GLEN: in the name of the quakes.

Activity Instruction

- You might need to look up some of the terms in these segments, like memorial poppies (to commemorate the war dead) and hongi (the sharing of the breath of life, pressing noses together).
- Familiarize yourself with what happened to the city of Christchurch during the quakes of 2010 and 2011.
- Discuss the position of politics in this scene: How does the company weave local context together with the disability experience, and perceptions of danger, vulnerability, and resilience?
- What happens here to personal storytelling, one of the mainstays of disability culture work?
- Could these scenes be played by non-disabled actors, or actors with different impairments than the original devising team?

Divide the class into two groups, and argue for and against playing material like this, developed out of lived experience of both disability and place, by another ensemble.

Development

- What issues in your own community can be dramatized through the reference fields of "disability"/"disability discrimination" (sparking, crashing, getting knocked back, etc.)?
- Can you use disabilities metaphorically without becoming ableist?

Write a one- or two-page scene playing with the metaphors of disability and politics. You should have two to four actors in the script. Use the scripts above as guides for formatting. Bring printouts of the script to class with you – as many as you have characters. Get into groups, and engage in a read-through of the scripts. Decide on one script to work on, and change the script as necessary. One of you becomes the director, most are actors, and you can also fill positions like set/costume designer and choreographer. At the end, stage your mini-plays in the class.

Development

Think about disability culture aesthetics, ways of being and communicating that are specific to disability culture and add them to your scripts. Add audio description, Deaf applause (shaking open hands above one's head), text-to-speech software, multimodal delivery (with some parts of the script delivered as text on the screen, video and music as part of the scene), or stimming actions derived from autistic culture.

ACTIVITY 5 Disability and Theatre: Authors

In a group, research work by a disabled playwright, work on a scene, and present your findings to your classmates. You can also search for scripts or scores (performance instructions) by companies that use alternative processes like devising. People to get going with:

- Mike Ervin
- Lynn Manning
- John Belluso
- Charles L. Mee
- Julie McNamara
- Susan Nussbaum
- Kaite O'Reilly
- Jenny Sealey
- Katinka Neuhof
- David Freeman
- Neil Marcus
- Joan Lipkin

8 Disabled Dance and Dancerly Bodies

In this chapter, you will gain insights into these issues:

- Dance's centrality in disability culture work
- The dancerly body of ballet
- Balances and contradictions: images of weakness/bodies of strength, images of strength/bodies of weakness
- Watching dance versus witnessing dance
- Dancetheatre
- Playing with audience placement: dance in unusual spaces
- Managing stares
- Art/life dance: what about non-art-framed movement?
- Marketing and the ubiquity of movement

In this chapter, I discuss the implications of conceptions of disability for the teaching of dance literacy, dance appreciation, and choreography, using disability's placement in ballet and dancetheatre as my case studies.

Dance is a central site for disability culture work: while dance is hard to talk about for many, it is a place where some of the most well-known celebratory images of disability – wheelchair user and amputee dancers – wheel and swerve together with non-disabled dancers, creating scenes full of energy, beauty, and immediate appeal.

There are few media and art practices in disability culture that have as much educative power as dance, even if dance is one of the more marginalized art forms out there. Dance communicates the inherent sharedness of movement because it can directly focus on forms of embodiment that are stigmatized and equated with inability. To dance is to live, and to signal one's self as alive, whether one speaks or not, whether one externalizes expression or not. All movement is part of dance's aesthetic reach: breath animating a torso, a slight hand gesture, the crumbling of a human form.

Physically integrated dance like the US AXIS Dance Company's appearance on *So You Think You Can Dance* (a US TV franchise that began in 2005, and has since been broadcast in around 25 other countries) reaches more young people than most disability arts practices. Given this ubiquity and reach, my core thesis is that an accessible dance culture needs not only accessible techniques, work spaces, training facilities, and stages, but also wider educational work on the level of dance literacy, our ability to read dance, and appreciate its manipulation of bodies, spaces, and time. Let's work toward that in this chapter.

Dance relies on physical presence and expressivity. This reliance of dance on bodies has encouraged a history of "normate" bodies paraded on stage, often hyper-able ones, operating at the extreme end of functionality and strength. When you first hear "dance," what kind of bodies come to mind for you?

Dance studies scholars have investigated the historical relationship between dance and the aristocratic body, the alignment of dance with the power dynamics of patriarchy, and with images of normative heterosexuality – they look at repeated scenes in the history of dance, a man lifting a woman, dying young women breaking because men reject them, and endings in death or marriage.

Ballet's Pleasures

Dance itself is not a unified field; there are many different dance forms, both synchronically, within the current cultural landscape, and diachronically, over the history of dance. In her study of American dance, Susan Leigh Foster (1986) shows how the different techniques of Deborah Hay, George Balanchine, Martha Graham, and Merce Cunningham train and require different dancing bodies, and differently attuned audiences. There are many more dance schools that require specifically trained bodies and specifically attuned audiences, in many different cultures. Not all these forms rely on a hierarchical distinction between performers' skilled bodies and audiences' amateur bodies, but many do.

Have a quick survey of your peers: Has anybody been to dance school? Are there experiences of being required to be a particular body, of peer, parent or teacher pressure? Are there stories of joy and engagement? If you do not have people with dance experiences among you, you could think about sports and ideal bodies, and you will find that there are many similarities.

In this section, I focus on ballet and its particular form of the dancerly body. Ballet and its imagery is still the main cultural image of dance in predominately white Western culture, even if widespread coverage of contemporary dance forms in popular media challenge ballet's stronghold. A general survey of international dancers' and dance writers' biographies shows that, most often, ballet and, in particular, the ballerina first captured their imagination and attuned them to dancing (Aalten, 1997).

In the 21st century, shows like So You Think You Can Dance have a similarly significant impact on young dancers' ideas of what dance is, and ballet aesthetics and its framework of lines and elongation still play a significant role there. In the following, I frame the relationship between perfect bodies, ballet aesthetics, and the encounter between dance and disability.

Dancing wheelchair users are one specific subsection of professional disabled dancers in modern and classic genres. They have gained public visibility through physically integrated groups such as the UK's Candoco Dance Company or AXIS. Many of these groups work in a modern dance paradigm. But some work in ballet, in the particular aesthetic associated with manipulations of two-dimensionality and the negation of weight.

Dance scholars have critiqued the ideal of the two-dimensional body in ballet:

> *The classical ballet has colluded in the preservation of the classical body, emphasising the commitment to line, weightlessness, lift, and extension and ethereal presence rather than a real corporeality. (Wolff, 1997: 95)*

In ballet, the drive is toward the line and the clear front, as evidenced by ballet's focus on the turn-out, an alignment of the feet not in parallel to each other, but in a V-shape, pointing outwards, which necessitates a 'turn-out' of the hip joints. Dancers who are technically good but do not have the necessary pliable hips are refused entry to dance schools: only some bodies are deemed able to work in ballet.

The other demand on the body in ballet is the negation of the body's weight. It is an aspect of ballet's technique:

> *Dancers are seen as artists who successfully challenge the law of gravity. This is not only a consequence of the taste and fashion at the time of its origin, but also of the specific characteristics of ballet technique. In ballet the centre of the movement is in the spine. A dancer always keeps his or her body up, letting the arms and legs do most of the work. The basic movement in ballet is upwards. (Aalten, 1997: 47)*

Weight and its negation are also aspects of ballet's industry and popular images. Popular dancers' biographies narrate the need for dancers to conform to an aesthetic of vanishing: anorexia and other eating disorders are often associated with ballet. The attention given to these problems of specifically "feminine success" in the 1980s and 90s has elevated eating disorders to mythic status, to expected aspects of female physical culture.

Think about the ongoing discussions about female models in women's magazines, the coverage of black US gymnast Gabby Douglas, or the discussions about the physical discipline of child beauty contestants. Do you feel yourself, as contemporary students, touched by these debates? Do issues of spectacle, revulsion, fascination, and discipline shape your image of yourself?

The immateriality of ballet stands in contrast with the hypervisibility of the disabled body, the fact that it rarely vanishes into lines, and remains solidly a particular body. But it might be misleading to see the disabled ballet dancer as the Other to the non-disabled ballerina. "Ability" in ballet is already non-human, non-physical. The "true dancer" of ballet is the weightless, substanceless sylph. *All* dancers, disabled or not, have to engage in the intriguing battle with the "ideal body" – and there can be pleasure in that.

Susan Foster's ambivalent description of a perfect ballerina sees her dead in the moment of perfection:

> *In Paloma Herrera's pose we witness the death of the body. We see stasis, the perfect giving over of physical vitality to formal purity. We feel the body arrested at the end of its fullest effort. We hear the silence of the state where the body has fused with geometry. ... And then, miraculously, the dancing body revivifies. ... Ballet, a celebration of this dance with death,*

alternates between the fixedness of the body's designs and the momentum of the physical vitality necessary to motivate the body through these designs. (Foster, 1995: 112)

Foster give space to potentially positive readings of ballet's life-negating tendencies, and calls ballet a celebration of this tension between death and vitality.

EXERCISE 8.1 ## Watching Dance

At this point, see what you make of this discussion. There are many clips of dancing ballerinas out there. Find one, and watch the dancers engage in the old European (derived) form of ballet. What do you see? Use the Observation Wheel to help you gather responses. Can you make an argument that speaks about the polar points of deadly abstraction and vital power? Find a way of putting this pair into your own words.

Many people feel little ownership of the highly technical forms of dance, and find it hard to say something other than "I like it," or "I do not." This exercise invites you to slow down, to look and respond to the movement you see on the stage (ideally) or on the screen (fine, too). Use this exercise as a way into dance discussion, watching bodies without words or foregrounded narrative dance away.

Development

If you have been watching a white dancer so far, think about signs of racial representation in her or his aesthetic. "White" easily vanishes itself, becomes an invisible category of race, but you can look again. Now find a dancer of color, a ballerina or other celebrated dance artist, and look at their dance. What happens to your reading, how does culture and the histories of racialization influence how you see dance?

EXERCISE 8.2 ## Witnessing Dance

When using the Observation Wheel, I always ask you to transpose information across visual and audio means, finding access points for people with different kinds of sensory access:

- How does this work with a form like dance?
- Do you find that you are transposing, translating, differently?
- Can you use touch and movement as ways of sharing with each other what you are experiencing in the visual material you are looking at?

If you can, go and witness an actual dance performance. Try to sit close to the stage. And pay attention to all the senses activated by the performance: if your primary mode of knowing is visual, close your eyes, and see what you are experiencing through sound, vibration, and kinesthesia.

Wheelchair users are both grounded and enabled by their mechanical and physical extensions, but any resulting "struggle" is more by quantity, not quality, akin to the struggles of non-disabled dancers also fighting weight, hip configuration, and breast development. And, sometimes, the flow of chairs and wheels allows for a very different kind of line than one created to bipedal ballerinas.

EXERCISE 8.3 ## Wheels

Watch this video clip, www.youtube.com/watch?v=xYc38Mma04Y, from a mid-1990's improvisation session between wheelchair ballet dancer Charlene Curtiss, founder of Light Motion Dance Company in Seattle, and Tom Giebink, a dancer on skates. Describe the motions the two are engaged in, trace the energetic arcs they move through the studio.

Link what you watch to your own body, and how it makes/made you feel to be in smooth flow – on skates, in a wheelchair, on ice skates, on a bicycle, etc.

Disability dance does make a difference, opens up the repertoire of dreams, allows everybody to feel the aliveness and embodied skill of disabled dance artists. The continuing presence of wheelchair-using ballet (or ballet-inspired) troupes such as Infinity Dance Theater (New York, founder Kitty Lunn), Light Motion (Seattle, founders Charlene Curtiss and JoAnne Petroff), or Dance>Detour (Chicago, founder Alana Wallace) inserts into our shared culture a new dancerly body, slowly, bit by bit, by repetition.

EXERCISE 8.4 ## Dance>Detour

Image 14
Dance>Detour.
Photo: William
Frederking

Dance>Detour is a professional Chicago-based company of people with and without disabilities, led by Alana Wallace. Their repertoire is influenced by ballet and modern dance aesthetics, as well as African and Latin dance forms. Use the Observation Wheel: What is going on in this publicity photo? What discourses of dance are active in it?

· ·

The difference between the classical ideal and the living body feels like the point of ballet: the exhilarating mixture of the elevated and the earthy has characterized ballet dancers' place in popular culture for a long time. Films like *Black Swan* play with that particular contradiction – you might enjoy watching it, with the coordinates of this chapter in mind.

What do you think? Have a discussion:

- Is it OK to dance ballet, and to want to dance in ballet?
- Does it perpetuate stereotypes of weak women and strong men, even as these women are actually very strong?
- Are there ways to mark old stereotypes *and* breathe new life into them?
- What do you think about disabled ballet, queer ballet, and the effort to de-white ballet by listing ballerinas of color, writing new histories?

Our heritages mix and match, magpie and subvert. Disabled dance artists do not need to deny the allure of the ever expanding geometric line. Every time a disabled dance artist dances ballet on a stage, the meanings of ballet shift, and the scope of bodies opens up. Ballet might have an ableist, misogynist, racist, and elitist foundation, yes, and even disabled ballet works within very specific constraints of what the "right" body might be. But there is juice in playing on all fields, on pushing against normativity on many fronts.

DANCING WHEELS

Image 15 *Dancing Wheels,* Walls of Glass (2009), *choreographed by Lisa K. Lock. Photo: Dale Dong*

In a performance by Dancing Wheels in October 2013, set as a live act during Ohio's ReelAbilities Film Festival, I saw Mary Verdi Fletcher, the company's founder, glide across the stage amid her younger dancers. Her small body in the chair had objectively less movement than many of the younger disabled and non-disabled dancers around her, but her dance had a fierce focus, a will to the line, that easily drew my eyes to her form. Mary Verdi Fletcher performed as an elder, someone who has earned her right to the stage, and someone who can slip into her choreography and inhabit it in ways that younger dancers might still reach for. Her breath, her fingers, her stretching torso wove into patterns of focus. The lift of the leap or the concentration of artful breathing: both are feats of balletic skill, both offer their own virtuosity, in very different bodies.

Dancetheatre: Learning to See Differently

The disabled dancer can bring valuable insights into the workings and potential of the realm of the "ideal" body of ballet. But disabled dancers have opened up other spaces in dance work, too. In this section, I focus on dancetheatre, a different Western movement form.

Dancetheatre is a stage form whose aesthetic emphasizes the relationship between ways of seeing and knowing, the active audience and the provocative performer. In the following, I focus on one particular mechanism of dancetheatre: the distancing of audience and performer through framing. This mechanism can be highly useful for disability culture work – as we've seen at the set-up of this study guide, when I invited you to rearrange the frame for a classroom.

DANCETHEATRE

In her show *1980*, one of the best-known founders of what came to be known as "dancetheatre," German choreographer Pina Bausch reshapes what it means to dance when her dancers step forward out of a line and point to their scars, one by one, each dancer breaking the taboo of speaking on stage, and telling that scar's story. As they do so, the dancers gain depth and body, emerge from the abstraction of moving patterns into a different register: real people on stage, with lives and narratives. At the same time, the costs of dance as an activity become apparent: many of the scar stories shared emerge from dance injuries.

The frame of dancetheatre lifts bodies, actions, and movements out of their everyday meaning and allows us to see them differently. By doing this, performers can show the constructed nature of the everyday, the assumptions that the spectator brings to a performance. In the following examples, disabled dancers use framing devices to denaturalize their performances, to show how the *construction* of disability, not the impairment itself, fixes the disabled body.

In 1997, Magpie, a British company with learning disabled dancers (founded in 1986 by Avril Hitman, one of the oldest companies mentioned in this section), and Retina Dance Company (a Belgian/British non-integrated company) created a performance for the Blitz '97 festival in London. The physical work did not itself deal theatrically with stereotypes of disability or with the assumptions that company members with learning disabilities encounter in their lives. But the performance strongly emphasized these experiences as the frame for the work:

> *Performed high-up on the Level 5 Exhibition Area of the South Bank, a huge building of grey concrete and surprising lines and angles, this site-specific work invited the audience to stand outside and look in through windows for once. The more isolated and uncomfortable audience members felt, the better, it seemed. After all, as both companies point out, this positioning is a reflection of the way those with learning disabilities frequently feel as outsiders looking into society. (Cowl, 1997: 16)*

In this show, the companies employ spatial physical limitations to convey an aspect of the disabled experience. They do not use simulation exercises, which, as this study guide discussed earlier, are designed to give non-impaired people a "taste" of disability, a practice much criticized by disabled activists. Instead, the physical framing is used to point to the conceptual framing of disabled people by our culture, framing and immobilizing disabled people by assumptions and presumed knowledge about them. The staging points to the social dimension of disability, the creation of disability in the encounter between people.

STAREE/STARER ENCOUNTERS

In this passage, Rosemarie Garland-Thomson discusses the dynamics of staring, paying attention to the agency of the staree, the one being stared at. How can her perspective on staree management shift your understanding of stage performances?

> The first element in the staring process is for the staree to develop a keen sense of being scrutinized. This anticipation and preparedness arms the staree with the proper relational tools to manage expected staring encounters with great effectiveness. The second element in this process is to decide how to oversee the dynamics of the stare itself when it inevitably comes one's way. If one looks directly at starers, it will only confuse or embarrass them. The staree must assess the precise attitude of the starer, measuring intentions and attitudes so as to respond in the most effective way. Facilitating your starers' maintenance of face means relieving them of anxiety, understanding their motivations, and working with them to overcome their limited understanding of human variation and their social awkwardness at facing it. The third element is literally manipulating the eyes of the starer. One evaluates when to turn away, stare back, or further extend the stare. Sometimes it is best to allow the staring to go on in order for the starer to get a good look. Another procedure is to use eye contact and body language to terminate the stare as soon as possible, although this risks being interpreted as hostile. Another option is to redirect the stare. For example, some starees report using their own eyes to guide the starer's immobilized eyes away from the part of their body that has captured the gaze, subtly rescuing the hapless viewer from the embarrassment of the stuck stare and restoring the ritual of casual face-to-face encounters. Finally, the staree can and often must enlist conversation to direct the staring process. Staring has an inherent narrative component that the staree must always address in some way. (Garland-Thomson, 2006: 180)

CASE STUDY 1 ## Edge Spaces of Contemporary Disability Dance: AXIS/Dandelion Dancetheater

In a very different piece, also in an unusual setting, Dandelion Dancetheater collaborated with AXIS Dance Company, and they extended the politics of difference at work in Magpie/Retina's 1997 performance into the 21st century. AXIS is one of the best known professional physically integrated dance companies in the US (founded in 1987 by Thais Mazur, Bonnie Lewkowicz, Judith Smith and others), and Dandelion Dancetheater is a postmodern dance company located in the Bay Area (founded by Kimiko Guthrie and Eric Kupers in 1993).

Image 16 *AXIS/Dandelion,* The Dislocation Express. *Photo: Lisa Steichmann*

Parts of their 2011 performance *The Dislocation Express* happened on BART, the Bay Area Rapid Transit system: in the innards of train cars, on underground platforms, and in front of the Ed Roberts Center, a disability-service focused hub in Berkeley, California. Choreographers Eric Kupers and Kimiko Guthrie devised work with the two companies, and created a soundtrack for the BART ride that connects different performance venues. So, at one point in these performances, after a particular segment is wrapped up in the street in front of the Ed Roberts Center, all performers and audience members move down into the underground station and get ready to hop into a train car together.

The night I joined them, I delighted in the vision of many chair users cramming into a car together – it's ordinary commuter car, and Bay Area residents saw themselves faced with a larger than usual number of wheelchair users, but also with people decked out in exotic costumes. None of these two points of difference mark themselves as all that different in the context of a BART ride. But then, many of the chair users and all the costumed people engaged in strange and artful behaviors together. Here is how reviewer Rachel Swan experienced the ride on a different night:

> As people applauded, actor Nils Jorgensen, who was dressed as a train conductor, gave us instructions to board the Fremont train. ... Kupers and the other performers tried to ensure a smooth transition between acts, even though they weren't allowed to stage anything past the fare gate. They created a sound file for people to download to their iPhones while riding from Ashby to Walnut Creek. It featured a train-themed soundtrack and verbalized instructions, enjoining listeners to dance and sing on the train (which didn't really happen). The performers also wore giant hats with tassels and bells that tinkled as they walked. ...
>
> So in a way, the commute became its own piece of performance art. Train operators, cranky passengers, a seven-minute delay in Lafayette, a man hawking rap CDs, and a BART employee handing out surveys were

all unwitting participants in Dislocation, *helping create the "accelerated culture" that Kupers wanted to use as his backdrop. (Swan, 2011)*

In the ride I participated in, people *did* sing and dance, engaging in invisible theatre activities while in public, subverting, as so many do, BART's injunction against performance on their trains. But as a chair user, I delighted in aspects of the performance that seem invisible to Swan, who does not mark any movement difference in her writing about the show. As a disabled dancer and audience member, some of the most memorable parts of this commute were the fact that the train conductor was a chair user, the parade of rollers going down the street and into the elevator, the festive show atmosphere as a bunch of us were gliding down to the platform level, and the cramming of metal and bodies into the cars themselves.

In my 21st-century reading of reframed performance, I witness from the perspective of a disabled dancer, no longer just wondering about how non-disabled people feel about the difference our presence makes, but feeling fine in articulating an audience perspective that does not take bipedal motion as the center of locomotion.

In the train car, some of us dealt with the cramped environment by riding on top of one another; I had a walking person on my lap, someone who has trouble dealing with crowded situations and needs a stabilizing point. Offering myself as a place of calm, allowing her to draw in her limbs, seemed an easy and natural accommodation. Across the aisle, I could see other chair users offering their backs and arm rests as anchor points for squashed standing people.

When the soundtrack in our ears invited us to vibrate gently, I could see the movement traveling from people with buttons in their ear, having downloaded the sounds, to people who hadn't, and who were relying on cues from others to engage in the invisible choreographies. We were interdependent, tracking each other, working out actively who was and who was not part of the performance piece, and immersed ourselves thoroughly in observing public bodies in unclear framings.

In this performance segment on the train, audiences cannot help but be aware of their bodies and the performer bodies: we are all squashed together, and need to be aware not to step on each other's toes. For most regular commuters, no art-framed performance was going on, just the regular, everyday performance of shifting city types, the changing faces of the city, and the need to keep one's self safe. Within this framework, disability was inserted, but not as a mark of total otherness (there are always some chair users in BART, always people on crutches, people mumbling to themselves or given to outbursts, people crying in a corner of a seat). Instead, to this particular audience member, disability became a site of heightened awareness and joyous camaraderie. The framework shifted into the exciting realms where art frame and everyday life frame glide into one another, and where non-disabled unwitting audience members might just perceive some element of festival air, of nonsense fun, of shared good vibes between disabled and non-disabled people in strange clothing, behaving in unusual but not negatively marked ways.

CASE STUDY 2 Bill Shannon, Dance and the Street

In a 2003 show, US disabled dance artist Bill Shannon framed his performance *AOW: Remix* in the Dance Theater Workshop in New York City through a video shot outside the theatrical frame. The waiting audience in the Dance Theater Workshop in New York City could watch this video in the foyer, before they were led into the theatre space itself.

Bill Shannon in the Street

In the video, a man with crutches (Shannon) moves down a flight of outdoor steps. He falls, passers-by look, some move in to help. The man with the crutches recovers easily, and makes a fast getaway. One of the passers-by in the video steps back and crosses himself.

The reaction of this passer-by in the video to the falling crutch user is a form of disability dance: not the aesthetic product of artists dealing with bodily difference, but social movement patterns. Multiple scripts exist for dealing with difference – crossing oneself half-unconsciously, warding off evil in an old Catholic gesture, is one reaction.

In the man's action, various mechanisms are combined: he steps back, puts distance between himself and the spectacle of the fallen man, his hand in his quick cross-shaped weave creates a shield between him and the scene, and the connotations of the crossing evoke a third presence as a godly or saintly helper and guardian is called upon to intervene in the little act played out here.

The short choreography in the street presents the deep cultural strata of distress, negativity, and fear of disability that still pervades attitudes. No positive images, no disability rights legislation has yet been able to undo these old habits, excavated in this unconscious bodily behavior in the street. Shannon's repetition of disability on the street only elicited the same old response. In the man's demeanor, nothing speaks of difference, of destabilization. The cross wards off the Other.

But beyond the one-on-one situation on the street, I am now among people watching the street scene on a video, in the foyer of a theatre: the 'art frame' reappears, and makes the different choreographies clearly experiential and available to me. The performativity of the man's action and Shannon's fall become apparent, their relation to one another, and the fact that they are repetitions – nothing about them is "natural."

In the New York *Magazine*, Laura Shapiro writes this about Shannon's embodiment – notice the way that disability is figured in the review:

> As for Crutchmaster, whose disability is the soul of his career, he defies all categories, including the burgeoning one for disabled dancers. At age 5, Bill Shannon was an Easter Seals poster child, diagnosed with a disease of the hip joints that today makes it impossible for him to stand or move on his legs without pain. So he's developed a version of hip-hop that incorporates his crutches – literally, for they become part of his body. He slips and swirls around the stage with his feet barely skimming the ground, spins on his knees though his knees never touch the floor, uses the crutches as feet, legs, arms, and hands.

AOW: Remix is a new, hourlong piece created in collaboration with five personable break-dancers known as the Step Fenz. It's a dense, textured work nearly overwhelmed by its sweeping video backdrop and a pounding electronic score. Drugs, war, death, and a burning urban landscape are the themes; but amazingly, a kind of sweetness prevails. When a wounded Shannon is near death, an amiable ER team hip-hops in with an intravenous pole and saves him. Now and then, the dancers assemble for a spree of extravagant solos – Crutchmaster, too, though he doesn't do their spectacular upside-down and angled spinning. Instead, he glides suspended through space, his physical contact with the earth just a fast flutter of his crutches, so ephemeral it barely seems enough to keep him sailing. Victim art? Hardly. Like Isadora Duncan, who opened up new possibilities for art by exploring the body's natural movements – but couldn't have done it without her flowing tunics and high mystique –Crutchmaster uses every means available to transform imperfect nature into a thing of beauty. (Shapiro, 2003)

Here is my perspective on the same show. Notice the differences between Shapiro's witnessing and my own. Why are we focusing on different aspects here? How are our politics different?

Bill Shannon in the Theatre

We are finally allowed into the theatre, and we find our way to our seats. They are mostly inaccessible to chair users, or to people who have trouble walking up raked seating areas: this performance environment envisions nimble bipedals as its spectator crowd. I have trouble storing my crutches. I catch the eye of another disabled person, a woman one row behind me: we talk, and acknowledge that we are the only visibly disabled people we've seen in the audience tonight. This checking of numbers, and assessing venues for access, is a ritual enacted by many politically conscious disabled people who see themselves as part of a minority movement, and are aware of the very recent history of access to stages and auditoria.

The lights go down.

A man appears, and sprays a graffiti handle on the black backdrop of the empty stage. Stage right back, a VJ station is set up, and a man begins to scratch video loops against one another to heavy, loud hip-hop music. A stylized knife-fight ensues. The dancers throw poses at one another: a slow routine with long held freezes, aimed at the opponent with attitude. Skills are shown off: popping, locking, breakdance, and crutch dancing. More and more, the scene takes on the quality of a different place: a club. Six dancers square off against one another, in a solo competition. Everybody gets their turn, and while the circle is watching, they present their moves in a casual yet calculated framing. One of the six dancers is Bill Shannon, a white man among black and white performers. He seems older than the others, and various gestures and arrangements show that he is in charge. He is wearing his baseball cap, and I can make out what it says: Crutchmaster – a title he earned in the NY club scene.

His first solo sees him flying around his crutches: gripped by his arms, they stand in the middle, moving from side to side, as his legs swing out behind him, in a circle. His dance is powerful and acrobatic, but his choreography is clearly knowledgeable of how his crip performance is likely framed by a non-disabled audience: at the end of his dance, he takes of his cap and sinks down in a pathetic, "handicapped" "cap-in-hand" gesture.

The energy drops. The dance disperses. Shannon is alone on stage. He moves about, seemingly aimless. We hear him mutter to himself, occasionally loud enough to be understood by the audience: "What happened to the show?" "Are we faking the show?" This commentary on transplanting a hip-hop club scene into the theatre is expanded on as a man in a trench coat enters. A fake chimpanzee is taken out and played with, and finally packed into the suitcase, one hand sticking out, and carried off. Who is the monkey? The "street-scene," commodified as a spectacle rather than a participatory event? Bill himself, the Crutchmaster, performing tricks on sticks? What are the relative "authenticity" tickets of race and disability here, who performs for whom?

There is an ongoing discussion in disability studies circles about the origin of the connection between handicap and cap-in-hand – this is not the original etymology of the "handicap" phrase. But it is one that is popular, a connection many make, and hence something that informs my viewing of this particular moment in the show.

The cap-in-hand, the performing monkey, the drops in energy, and the agonized whispers of "faking the show" persist throughout the performance, reminding the audience again and again of the prize that is paid by the set-up of the stage. The performance emerges *as* a performance, as a set of choices within constraints. Shade and pride are relative phenomena, born out of the knowledge that difference has to fight for its spaces.

ACTIVITY 1 Marketing and Disability

Image 17 *Bill Shannon, VISA ad, Saatchi & Saatchi, video still*

Bill Shannon gained a much wider audience in 2009, when he performed in a TV advertisement for VISA. A YouTube version of the clip is accessible at www.youtube.com/watch?v=I6RGyJirL3g. The video makes for a very different perspective on difference and politicized double-takes: it emphasizes speed, agility, and the "freedom" of the street, in an urban setting devoid of homeless people, markers of poverty, or different kinds of slownesses that can mark "crip time."

Watch the VISA advertisement, using the Observation Wheel. How does the clip create a fantastical urban scene? How is the street depicted here? Mark the differences between the urban scene here, and a "real" urban scene. What is missing? What is added? How does disability play into this?

Development: Marketing and Disability Mobility

How does marketing enter into disability contexts? Have a wider discussion about how disability gets positioned in advertising. Find examples from your own cultural context:

- Where do disabled athletes, veterans, etc. show up in advertising?
- How are they used?
- What meanings do they carry?

Here are some examples, all easily found through an Internet search:

- Guinness TV advert "Friendship," featuring wheelchair basketball (2013)
- L'Oréal Paris True Match TV advert "Unique Story," starring Aimee Mullins (2011)
- "Oscar Pistorius – Always On" (Nike South Africa, 2011).

ACTIVITY 2 Anthropology of the Street

Let's go on an anthropological field trip, outside. In a group of two (any more and you'd be very visible), find a vantage point on a public street with pedestrians, and observe the passers-by. Take about 20 minutes for this exercise.

- How does disability feature in this street scene?
- Do you find signs of it?
- Are you unsure at times – when and how?
- Is there something interesting in the unsureness?
- What other kinds of embodied differences become experiential to you?

Development: Creating Fantasy Embodiments

This is a development from the street exercise, and whether or not you engage in it depends on your willingness to be a clown in public. You can adapt this exercise to a more sheltered indoor activity.

Create a movement persona. Here's how to do this. Walk with a group of colleagues, and observe each other moving. You will find that everybody has their own quirks and styles of moving: holding arms stiffly, or putting out a foot a bit. Without identifying the person you take the quirk from, exaggerate it. If you have non-bipedals among you, even better. See how you can translate movement quirks across feet and wheels.

Make the quirk the mark of your movement. See how far you can push this before becoming a complete caricature (and you will have different boundaries here). Once you've got it down, adjust your clothing in a way that plays with this movement persona. Style yourself. Go with your own intuition.

Now put this persona out in public, and observe each other doing it. Observe what it feels like to do it. Observe how others, not in on the act, respond to you. What are the emotions you are sensing, in yourself, in others?

After you finished, assemble to discuss your findings:

- How did it feel to do this?
- Was there a complicated ethics to marking one's self different in public?
- Did you recognize yourself in someone's clowning?
- How did it feel to do so?
- Was there something useful or pleasurable to seeing one's signature style, often unconscious, thus pulled out?

EXERCISE 8.5   ## Dance on the Internet

In this exercise, we are focusing on dance literacy. Watch three different dance choreographies online. Here are two recommendations (you can also find videos of most of the companies mentioned in the text online): Candoco's *Outside In*, one of the first widely shown disability dance videos, choreographed by Victoria Marks, and the *So You Think You Can Dance* clips of AXIS (the company has been on the show a number of times). There are many more companies, some with very stable online video presences, some with less easily available material, some with dedicated video performances, some with online documentation of stage-based dances:

- Maybe you can find material by Touchdown Dance Company, a Manchester, England-based group led by Katy Dymoke that specializes in touch- and sensory-feedback training techniques, often with people with visual impairments, with a background of "contact improvisation." (You might want to research this form, and its connection to disability dance; see Cooper Albright, 1997.)
- Maybe you can find material by Remix Dance Company, a South African dance group, or by Taihen, an Osaka, Japan-based group founded by Manri Kim in 1983, one of the oldest companies led and founded by a disabled artist.
- Check out the performance documentations of Restless Dance Company, an Australian dance company that works with disabled and non-disabled young dancers (see also Hickey-Moody, 2009), or the videos of Touch Compass Dance Company, a professional New Zealand/Aotearoa-based company.
- You can look at work by individual dancers: David Toole (for instance, *The Cost of Living*), Neil Marcus (for instance, *water burns sun*), or Claire Cunningham, or choreographers Caroline Bowditch and Marc Brew.

- Look at some of the newer dance companies out there, like Wobbly Dance, by Yulia Arakelyan and Erik Ferguson, who incorporate Butoh techniques into their work, or the work of the GIMP Project, a New York-based modern dance project by Heidi Latsky Dance.

Now watch each clip, and fill out an Observation Wheel for each. Focus on the meanings of the movements and video cuts: how do they signify to you, what do you feel, see, hear, imagine, wish for? Engage in a free write as a way of drawing together what you found, making an argument, not by saying which one is better than another one, but by focusing on the meanings of disabled bodies, performing in public, and how they engage stereotypes of disability in fruitfully new ways.

9 *Superheroes and the Lure of Disability*

In this chapter, you will gain insights into these issues:

- Film, TV, and other visual representations of disability
- The sensuality of disability paraphernalia
- The dangers and seductions of fantasy play
- Acknowledging stereotypes
- Meaning making about and strategies by postcolonial subjects
- Superheroes as projection surfaces
- Hybridity and strategies
- Minority reading strategies
- Disability in children's and young adult's books
- Non-normative sense worlds and visual excitement
- Audio description and its opportunities

Sensualities: Wheelchairs in *Murderball*

In *Murderball* (2005), a documentary about wheelchair-using athletes, one scene focuses on a wheelchair as material artifact, tool, and sign of freedom, sexiness, and masculinity. One of the film's protagonists, disabled after a car accident, encounters one of the professional murderball athletes visiting hospitals for outreach purposes. As soon as the young man sees the competition chair in the hospital, he desires it; at the end of the scene, he is sitting in it against the advice of the hospital personnel. He clearly relishes the quick cornering and handling of the machine. The chair in question is lovingly portrayed by the camera. Throughout the film, the camera focuses on welds and nuts, and on the many battle scars these customized sport chairs have received. *Murderball* is disability performance *by* disabled people: people to whom the chair is not just a narrative, but a tool, a lived experience, an aesthetic statement, and a form of self-identification.

For many (but not all) wheelchair users, the chair is an extension of their selves, contours and surfaces to casually play with, extensions integrated more or less seamlessly into ways of knowing oneself in space. Informal conversations with chair users bear out the importance of the chair's adornment and the acknowledgement of its status as a fashion accessory. For many users, frame colors, wheel decorations, and even the grunge look of heavy use are issues of aesthetics and self-definition going far beyond usability.

Loving Props

In disability culture circles, sensual relations to our paraphernalia, props, assistance devices, and prostheses are commonly discussed issues. Disabled people share where one can get metallic multicolored crutches; what chairs insurance companies currently make available, and which ones are best; people fantasize about fashionable prostheses; and disabled theatre costume designers like Mallory Kay Nelson make beautifully textured and cut materials for non-normate bodies. There are discussions about the relative beauty and functionality of hearing aids; blind people share insights into whether to use a cane or petition for a guide dog; and people who have mental health support service animals discuss trainers and airline policies. Whether inanimate or animate, disabled people live interdependently with many objects and creatures, just like non-disabled people.

Image 18a
Chun-Shan (Sandie) Yi, Crown You Like a Prince, *red yarn, 2006, and* Be my Baby, *fabric and thread, 2006*

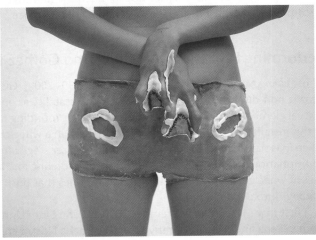

Image 18b
Chun-Shan (Sandie) Yi, Re-fuse Skin Set, *latex, rubber, plastic and black thread, 2011. Photo: Louisa de Cossy*

In the first of these images, Chun-Shan (Sandie) Yi creates baby gloves for disabled babies – babies born like she was, with non-normative limb configurations. She not only exhibits her work in gallery environments, but also works in hospitals, where she talks to young families and mothers who have given birth to children with unusual limb formations.

In the second image, she displays items made as part of her Crip Couture series:

> Altering the purpose of conventional prosthetics and orthotics, which aim to create more-or-less standardized body form and function, I blend prosthetics and jewelry to make a range of garments, accessories and footwear. Each wearable item is designed based on an individual's medical experience, physical position and state of mind. (artist statement)

Discuss the effect of clothing choices on one's sense of self.

• •

This richness of potential readings of disability paraphernalia, in particular the narratives attached to specific wheelchairs, opens up some of the more interesting uses of wheelchairs in the non-disabled world. So, in this section, I look at some of the ways that non-disabled performers use disability – not in stereotyping ways that signal straight ableist narratives of loss of control and tragedy, but in more nuanced performances of the complexities of making sense of human diversity.

First, I contrast two particular uses of wheelchairs as narrative props. In each of these instances, wheelchairs activate pleasures, narratives, and audience responses in different ways. In a performance installation organized by performance artist Guillermo Gómez-Peña, the artist takes on the role of the "El Mex Terminator." In this role, the wheelchair becomes a force of explosive fracture and cracked narratives. Then, in the X-Men cinematic franchise, we again find an intriguing wheelchair, but this time, the chair is a force of containment, rolling away on stunningly smooth surfaces.

Next, I look at the sensualities of (imagined) blindness, moving to another superhero narrative: Daredevil. Again, difference becomes fetishized in intriguing ways, but this time, it's not so much the narrative placement that becomes fascinating, but the sensory framing of difference.

Performing Fantasies with Guillermo Gómez-Peña

In The Living Museum of Fetishized Identities (1999–2002), Guillermo Gómez-Peña, a non-disabled performance artist, uses disability as one of many textual elements to investigate complex issues surrounding race and fantasy. In this installation, a non-disabled performer sits in a wheelchair. When taken in isolation, putting a wheelchair bang center stage offers problems of appropriation. But in my reading here, I am not looking for "bad" or "good" uses of wheelchairs, just interesting, complex ones that push hierarchical readings into overload mode.

I first saw Museum in September 2000 at Penn State University. Guillermo Gomez-Pena and his collaborative team La Pocha Nostra create interactive "living museums" that parody colonial practices of representation including the ethnographic diorama, the freak show, and the sex shop/strip joint window. The group describe their performance identities as "¼ stereotype, ¼ audience projection, ¼ aesthetic artifact, and ¼ unpredictable personal/ social monster."

The group wish to activate intercultural audience fantasies, and they elicit confessions online to create images of otherness:

> The idea is to use the internet as a tool of "reverse anthropology" to research America's psyche regarding Anglo/Latino relations, then to develop an ever-evolving repertoire of performance personae based on this research. For this purpose, we develop "confessional" websites asking individuals to suggest how we should dress as Mexicans and Chicanos, and what kind of performance actions and social rituals we should engage in. ... Scholars help us to select the most striking and representative confessions so we can use them as source material for performance. (museummuseum, 2010)

EXERCISE 9.2 **Stereotypes**

Erving Goffman (1963) coined the phrase "spoiled identity" to think about the mechanisms of stigma. As you read through this material on La Pocha Nostra, think about disability fantasies:

- Could one construct a similar dangerous performance zone of fantasies around disability?
- How would one go about gathering information, finding ways of letting people speak freely to their stereotypes?
- What would the effect be on you, on classmates or audiences who identify as disabled?
- What is at stake in exploring stigmatized identities, and how might disability differ from ethnic identity, migrant status, or borderwalker?

When I entered the dark hall at Penn State, I walked between multiple different stations, different actors having arrayed themselves as exhibits. The performance consisted of displays, arranged like stalls, without a coherent conventional narrative. Gómez-Peña and his collaborators created a fantastical environment, assembling a range of characters who are hybrids of Anglo fantasies of Latino identities – and in one of the displays sits Gómez-Peña, as a sexualized drug-addled wounded techno-shaman.

The El Mex Terminator sits in a manual wheelchair, dressed in a woman's leather corset, indigenous breastplates, smoking Marlboros. El Mex's bodily demeanor included twitching and various spastic movements, repeated and aimless. A woman feeds El Mex a banana, another takes off his heavy boots and replaced them with sexy pumps.

There are many different images of different versions of the El Mex Terminator online – have a look around. Find one image you find intriguing, and see how you can engage with it. Use the Observation Wheel.

In *Museum*, disability aligns easily with various forms and fantasies of difference: for Gómez-Peña, redeploying a wheelchair-using character as herald of difference might be a sensical step, given the dominant significations in popular culture of disabled characters as secondary or weak. The wheelchair operates as a sign of "other than the norm" aligning itself with the Latino in opposition to the Anglo "norm." Disability studies scholar Rosemarie Garland-Thompson (1997: 113) notes that one of the reasons African-American writers mobilize disability so effectively in their writing is that they can be open to "alternative, affirmative narratives that do not depend on a faith in oneness or a range of valued concepts such as wholeness, purity, autonomy, and boundedness." Disalignment and intersection (rather than unity and closure) are core principles in Gómez-Peña's "experimental cartography" of a postcolonial world (2005: 21).

POSTCOLONIAL

The term "postcolonial" refers to a way of understanding the effects of colonialism on cultures and societies. It developed in response to analyses of how European nations conquered and controlled other cultures, and how these other cultures resisted, complied, shifted, and changed in response.

As a field of study, postcolonialism has complicated challenges:

- What are the meanings of "post" in the term "postcolonialism"?
- Is colonialization over?
- How do contemporary global markets take over from European expansionist policies?
- How can postcolonialism reflect on Eurocentrism, and how can the story of particular nations under assault become centered, instead?
- How can hybridity, mixing, and the complexity of naming "culture" impact what postcolonialism becomes?

In the past, disability culture has sometimes used colonial and racialization metaphors to understand disability experiences of segregation, the second-hand status of disabled people, and disability hate crimes. Now, activists are pushing back against this easy alignment, and are asking for nuance, and attention to different kinds of privilege. Can you see the problems with cross-movement appropriation?

EXERCISE 9.3 **Postcolonial Disability Studies**

Look at the table of contents of a current year's worth of three of these: *Disability Studies Quarterly*, *The Canadian Journal for Disability Studies*, *Disability and the Global South* (open source online journals), *The Review of Disability Studies* (encourages subscription, but offers free pdf downloads), *The Journal for Literary and Cultural Disability Studies* and *Disability and Society* (traditional print/online journals, hopefully available through your library). How do race and colonialization figure in the essays' approaches to disability studies?

Colonial Madness

Image 19 The Conquest of Mexico, *a film by Javier Téllez, shown in his Artaud's Cave installation, a cinema cave in an old railway shed at dOCUMENTA (13). Photo: © Henrik Strömberg, courtesy Javier Téllez and Figge von Rosen Galerie*

Check out the online traces of this film installation, created with mental health system users, outpatients in a Mexico City psychiatric hospital. One of the texts used in the film is by Antonin Artaud, a French theatre artist, someone who was a privileged grant-sponsored traveler for his visit to Mexico, and yet had excruciating asylum experiences. All kinds of reference fields mix and merge: between the scenes in the hospital we find reenactments of conquistador violence and indigenous ritual (the film was shot, among other places, at the Simón Bolivar Theatre in Xochimilco, Teotihuacan, and the pyramids of Cantona – Aztec sites). The same cast appears in the desert, in the hospital, in contemporary clothing, and indigenous regalia. The Venezuelan filmmaker (living in New York) is the son of two psychiatrists; commentary on and work inside the mental health system are central to his artistic work. Can you discuss this film in relation to concepts of postcolonialism?

In his mobilization of the wheelchair, Gómez-Peña brings together two contradictory images that merge, leaving spectators with a sense of cultural unease: the independent and strong tough guy and the wheelchair user. Paul Longmore and Lauri Umansky (2001: 7) write about historical images of disability: "Americans often perceive disability – therefore people with disabilities – embodying that which Americans fear most: loss of independence, of autonomy, of control; in other words, subjection to fate." How can this perception, this fear of subjection, become an active and thought-provoking component of a performance installation?

It is not easy to make a meaningful path through this room of signifiers, finding nuggets of meaning, wrestling with the abundance of connotations set up in the Anglo/Latino encounter. A lot of critics refer to the carnival of kaleidoscopic impressions, all canceling each other out. But this overabundance, the richness of signification, might clog reading apparati more effectively: drawing attention to the ways visual cultural meanings shape our social world, and resisting their neat allocation of meaning.

Gómez-Peña addresses political structures and historical inequalities. He materializes the fantasies we have of one another, making them uncomfortably present. Some audience members walk out of Gómez-Peña's performances offended by his heightened stereotypes, including the maladjusted, sexually deviant, immigrant cripple. Gómez-Peña insists on making viewers confront these matters, rather than transforming and dissolving them into conventional "positive images." He stages fantasies of Latino/Anglo encounters that display mis/understandings between Anglos and Latinos.

In *The Living Museum of Fetishized Identities*, the wheelchair no longer means tragic immobility but instead stands for the paralyzing effects of colonizing fantasies, a slightly different but still pretty complicated employment of disability as metaphor. (Think back to the queer section in Chapter 3 – this play with metaphors of mobility is something Alison Kafer (2013) drew attention to. If it was hard to parse it at that point, maybe it has become easier here?)

Gómez-Peña's live presence, together with the tactile, object-character of the wheelchair on his gallery stage denies the possibility of any single reading of disability's presence. Disability signifies, and at the heart of its signification is often loss – including a culture's loss of how to deal with difference. And that seems to me to be a complicated but worthwhile way of playing with these negative meanings of wheelchairs, in cultural allydom and coalitional politics.

AESTHETIC NERVOUSNESS

Literary scholar Ato Quayson speaks about the concept of "aesthetic nervousness" in relation to Nigerian writer Wole Soyinka's dramatic work and the use of disability in it. He describes how the plays' disabled characters are signholders of liminality (check out 'liminality').

As you read through this, think about ritual as a way of figuring what performance does – how does ritual affect how one might feel about La Pocha Nostra? How does the collective play with something akin to aesthetic nervousness?

The prime place given to ritual and ritual impulses in Soyinka's drama helps place the human body itself as the prime bearer of multiple ritual significations. However, what has not yet been properly commented upon is that even as much of his work is centered on ritual, it is also the case that the ritual impulses get focalized in a particularly intense way upon the figure of the person with disabilities. The disabled character in Soyinka is often a cryprograph of the metaphysical and the anomalous. Outside of A Dance of the Forest, *where the limping god Aroni and the terrifying esoteric Half-Child are to be read as direct spiritual challenges to the complacency of the human world, in the rest of his writing disabled characters within ordinary human interactions are never fully normalized. Rather, they retain a residue of liminality. ...*

To read Soyinka's work through the perspective of disability… is to be obliged to attend in meticulous detail to the ways in which disabled characters either manifestly represent ritual anomalies, or, in what amounts to a partial qualification of the ritual impulse, institute significant disjunctures to the established protocols of the social domain in which they appear. What emerges as aesthetic nervousness in this work is underscored by an apparently irresolvable paradox tied to the peculiar relationship that is established between ritual dispositions and the process for the production of subjectivity and agency, a process that is in the last instance political. It is also manifest in the depiction of what I shall describe as the systemic uncanny, the process by which the chaos of fraught sociopolitical processes are translated into negative affects of anxiety, fear, and even horror in the consciousness of individuals. (Quayson, 2007: 116–17)

The X-Men and Sleek Mutant Surfaces

A different kind of paralysis and liminality is enacted in the *X-Men* movies (2000, 2003, 2006, 2013, etc.) by the sleek metal (and sometimes glass) wheelchairs of telepathic Charles Xavier (played by Patrick Stewart), the head of a mutant superhero enclave. In the *X-Men* universe originally created by Marvel comics in the 1960s, mutants are humans who are born with latent superhuman abilities that emerge at puberty. The X-Men are hybrids; they have to learn to live both as human adults and mutants. As "Homo Sapiens Superior" (their fictive scientific classification), the X-Men are discriminated against by normal humans who fear the mutants' power. The storylines of the *X-Men* films revolve around how the mutants fight discrimination and build group solidarity. With this, the films echo the paths of many minority identity movements, including disability culture's development.

Professor Xavier is the voice of rationality and moderation arguing for the peaceful coexistence of humans and mutants. His enemy is his one-time friend and chess opponent, Eric Lehnsherr, or Magneto (played by Ian McKellen), a tragic antihero. Magneto, a concentration camp survivor radicalized by his experiences of oppression, believes that humans and mutants cannot coexist.

Xavier's wheelchair is part of a stylish and stylized world into which the cinema viewer is inducted long before she enters the cinema. The publicity posters and advertisements all focus on a metal X, a logo that denotes both imprisonment, finality, and futurity. The X also references the spokes of Xavier's wheelchairs, which are sometimes made of hard glistening steel, sometimes made of clear, clean, lightweight, unbreakable glass or plastic. The physical qualities of steel versus glass/plastic drive the narrative: Magneto can magnetize metals, transforming everyday environments into deathtraps. To counteract Magneto, glass or plastic are necessary non-magnetizable materials. In the final shots of the first film, Magneto is imprisoned in clear plastic. Xavier safely visits him by using a gorgeous glass wheelchair.

But Xavier also owns a smooth and curvy steel wheelchair. The first glimpse of this steel chair is a low angle camera shot of the wheel of the chair as Xavier rolls into the field of vision. Stretching out to the right of the screen is a curved metal and glass walkway, the curve echoing the circle of the wheel. Geometry and balance are indicators of Xavier's calm and balanced approach. Here is a British gentleman now in charge of a brigade of mutants, all as posh and swish as a public school (i.e. a rich private school).

The architecture of the mutant headquarters also sets the scene for Xavier's performance of disability. The camera finds Xavier behind an ornate desk in a tasteful study, surrounded by young people who, after receiving a tutorial from their teacher, are dismissed to go and think about "definitions of weak and strong." Set behind the desk, the wheelchair looks like an executive's chair, complementing Xavier's dark blue business suit.

While Gómez-Peña's wheelchair performance generates a superabundance of signifiers, Xavier's wheelchair performance presents an orderly man/machine hybrid, a being who creates his own environment as an extension of his telepathic mind. Gómez-Peña (2000: 9) writes: "Performance is not about presence, not representation; it is not (as classical theories of theatre would suggest) a mirror, but the actual moment in which the mirror is shattered." The image of the shattering mirror captures some of the violence, the unruliness, and the multiplicity I experienced when meandering through his strange museum.

In Xavier's wheelchair world, surfaces remain intact, borders are vehemently policed and breached; most of the X-Men narratives involve the penetration of fortresses and unescapable prisons. A core moment of defeat in the first X-Men movie features a non-mutant politician who has been mutated by the evil Magneto and whose demise consists of his liquification (a moment much discussed in the film's reviews for its use of computer graphics). The scene shows the loss of boundaries in a fearful and horrific death. This literal dissolving of inner and outer boundaries occurs in other places in the film's narrative. X-Men mutations often first become apparent in a character's life at moments of sexual passion during puberty. In the films (as in so much horror material), sexual penetration of self- or body-boundaries are problematic zones where people die, freak out, the world changes, evaporates, mutates.

In this fictional universe, Xavier's clear, clean, British upperclassness is an icon of the X-Men's rationality and humanity. Patrick Stewart's Xavier is the counterpoint to the dissolution and lack of boundaries that characterize the postcolonial hybrid (whether "creolized," "carnivalesque," or "nomadic"). But in the highly systematic and formulaic narrative of the X-Men, Xavier is bound by the wheelchair he uses: contained, restrained, smooth, metallic or plastic. The wheelchair establishes a relationship with Xavier's nemesis, the highly mobile Magneto, who embodies transgression (as played by Ian McKellen, an out gay and politically gay actor). Magneto escapes, draws metal to him, sucks blood out of a man's body (in X2), wishes constantly to expand his sphere of influence, and generally leaves havoc in his wake. Where Xavier is contained, Magneto is expansive. Xavier's movement vocabulary is small, Magneto's uses sweeping gestures. The two characters make a pair, and the wheelchair, as a symbol of restraint and order, shiny containment, functions to keep them in a tense balance.

Hybridity

Here are two very different quotes that focus on hybridity. Discuss them in pairs. What could disability cultural perspectives on these quotes be?

Gloria Anzaldúa

Gloria Anzaldúa was a feminist Chicana author, someone who lived with disability and has been called into the expanding disability studies canon (see, for instance, Morales et al., 2012).

> By creating a new mythos – that is, a change in the way we perceive reality, the way we see ourselves, and the ways we behave – la mestiza creates a new consciousness. The work of mestiza consciousness is to break down the subject/object duality that keeps her prisoner and to show in the flesh and through the images in her work how duality is transcended. The answer to the problem between the white race and the colored, between males and females, lies in healing the split that originates in the very foundation of our lives, our culture, our languages, our thoughts. A massive uprooting of dualistic thinking in the individual and collective consciousness is the beginning of a long struggle, but one that could, in our best hopes, bring us to the end of rape, of violence, of war. (Anzaldúa, 1999: 102)

> I sit here before my computer, Amiguita, my altar on top of the monitor with the Virgen de Coatlalopeuh candle and copal incense burning. My companion, a wooden serpent staff with feathers, is to my right while I ponder the ways metaphor and symbol concretize the spirit and etherealize the body. The Writing is my whole life, it is my obsession. This vampire which is my talent does not suffer other suitors. Daily I court it, offer my neck to its teeth. This is the sacrifice that the act of creation requires, a blood sacrifice. For only through the body, through the pulling of flesh, can the human soul be transformed. And for images, words, stories to have this transformative power, they must arise from the human body – flesh and bone – and from the Earth's body – stone, sky, liquid, soil. This work, these images, piercing tongue or ear lobes with cactus needle, are my offerings, are my Aztecan blood sacrifices. (Anzaldúa, 1999: 75)

Donna Haraway

Donna Haraway is a white US feminist scholar whose "Cyborg Manifesto" (1985) has influenced generations of scholars. Like Anzaldúa, Haraway's prose offers poetic openings. Her style leans into European feminist thought in the lineage of Luce Irigaray and Hélène Cixous.

The cyborg is a complex creature in disability culture: literally, so many disabled people live as cyborgs, and an easy celebration of its radical and transgressive potential can feel appropriative. Can the poetics of the cyborg offer scope to think through the radical potential of non-bordered embodiment?

The cyborg is resolutely committed to partiality, irony, intimacy, and perversity. It is oppositional, utopian, and completely without innocence. No longer structured by the polarity of public and private, the cyborg defines a technological polls based partly on a revolution of social relations in the oikos, the household. Nature and culture are reworked; the one can no longer be the resource for appropriation or incorporation by the other. The relationships for forming wholes from parts, including those of polarity and hierarchical domination, are at issue in the cyborg world. Unlike the hopes of Frankenstein's monster, the cyborg does not expect its father to save it through a restoration of the garden; that is, through the fabrication of a heterosexual mate, through its completion in a finished whole, a city and cosmos. The cyborg does not dream of community on the model of the organic family, this time without the oedipal project. The cyborg would not recognize the Garden of Eden; it is not made of mud and cannot dream of returning to dust. Perhaps that is why I want to see if cyborgs can subvert the apocalypse of returning to nuclear dust in the manic compulsion to name the Enemy. Cyborgs are not reverent; they do not re-member the cosmos. They are wary of holism, but needy for connection – they seem to have a natural feel for united front politics, but without the vanguard party. The main trouble with cyborgs, of course, is that they are the illegitimate offspring of militarism and patriarchal capitalism, not to mention state socialism. But illegitimate offspring are often exceedingly unfaithful to their origins. Their fathers, after all, are inessential. (Haraway, 1985: 151)

EXERCISE 9.6   **Film Review**

The *X-Men* films have received positive responses from the disability community. In the journal *New Mobility*, Jeff Shannon writes in this way about the contemporary narratives. Can you enlarge this list, adding other contemporary films to this list? Do you agree that the presentations are "non-judgmental"?

The casual, nonjudgmental depiction of disability has grown increasingly common in roles ranging from superheroes to street punks. Patrick Stewart leads the X-Men (2000) from his futuristic wheelchair, heroically promoting the acceptance of outcasts; Ricardo Montalban pilots a helicopter wheelchair in Spy Kids 2: The Island of Lost Dreams (2002); and in the super-powered thriller Unbreakable (2000), Samuel L. Jackson's use of a wheelchair (due to osteogenesis imperfecta) is merely an extension of his intensely enigmatic character. ... In each case, disability is merely an accepted fact of life, liberated from the stigma of stereotype. (Shannon, 2003)

Now write your own one-page film review. Find one film that features a central disabled character, and review the film, keeping a possible disabled audience perspective in mind – try not to fall into the kinds of disability stereotypes we have analyzed earlier in this study guide.

Minority Reading Practices

In a review in *Disability Studies Quarterly* of the second *X-Men* movie *X2: X-Men United*, disability scholar Michael Chemers draws attention to the narrative frame that feels so empowering to disability culture members:

> I shouted, "You go, girl! Crips strike back!" in the theatre, which earned some weird looks. But the enthusiasm and the affirmative message of the film are contagious, providing a disability-positive aesthetic paradigm that borders on the liberation of the "abnormal" body envisioned in the writings of Mikhail Bakhtin. It showcases mutation as the key to human survival, and posits "birth defects" as markers of a leap forward in evolution, that we, in the fog of politics and other social constructions, cannot properly discern. Mutation is a natural phenomenon, which even eugenicists admit is key to our survival as a species, and yet, the film suggests, mutation is only as frightening, socially destabilizing, or hideous as it is interpreted to be. It is a glyph seeking a hierophant. In Mitchell and Snyder's words, "mutancy can be beautiful." (Chemers, 2004)

So, for all that straightness in my reading of the X-Men's chairs, I too can feel Chemers' elation at the exploits of disabled bodies, cast narrationally as "underdogs." They are offered as points of identification, battling it out against the boring mediocrity of "normates." There's a superstar in a sexy wheelchair up there on the screen. This form of casting is too rare to ignore. Something about seeing a stylish chair up there on the screen is deeply satisfying.

The power of wheelchair performances for disabled people like myself goes beyond the rational dissection of performance texts. As Eve Kosofsky Sedgwick wrote, queerness can rest in

> the ability to attach intently to a few cultural objects, objects of high or popular culture or both, objects whose meaning seemed mysterious, excessive or oblique in relation to the codes most readily available to us, [which] became a prime resource for survival. We needed for there to be sites where meanings didn't line up tidily with each other, and we learn to invest sites with fascination and love. (Sedgwick, 1993: 3)

The wheelchair can be such a site. In the *X-Men* movies, the icon of disability conveys pleasure by its very visibility. It provides a code outside the code, the trigger that initiates Chemers' call and that provided the lens for my own experience of Gómez-Peña's *Museum*. For members of disability culture, the wheelchair is a cherished cultural object invested with a fascination well beyond what narration or function might warrant. As "real" objects, wheelchairs are transporters full of weight, texture, and sensation. Can't they be the same in fictional placements?

EXERCISE 9.7 Translating Icons

Find icons of disabled life, and how they leave traces in public space. The blind person's stick, the parking spot, textured curb cuts, talking elevators, easy language translations: these are all environmental elements of many countries that have adopted disability rights legislation and hence are transforming their societies into more accessible spaces. In this exercise, search for these sites and traces, make photographs or capture them in writing, and then create a new narrative about them.

LIVING WHEELCHAIRS

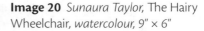

Image 20 *Sunaura Taylor,* The Hairy Wheelchair, *watercolour, 9" × 6"*

The image shows a watercolor painting by US painter Sunaura Taylor, herself a wheelchair user, of a hairy wheelchair: soft colors, warm browns and fuzzy grey, a watercolor study of an old wheelchair, surfaces soft and plump and inviting, many shapes vaguely anthropomorphic, a strange mélange of animals and humans, sexualities and technologies.

The totalizing symbol for all things disability here comes alive, is used, and has a history. It creeps with hairy tendrils, becomes a highly specific wheelchair that has a life of its own and quickly escapes its symbol function. This chair is bulky, leaves a shadow, might not be quite tame, and reaches out beyond the page. My senses are engaged as I look at this image. I feel things beneath my fingertips. I can imagine my hands gliding over these surfaces, petting. This particular wheelchair speaks to an interdependence of living and non-living things, to comfort *and* threat, to cognitive shifts and emotional responses. The mobility device moves into a different realm, living and mutable.

ACTIVITY 1 Children's Books

Look at disability-focused children's books, such as *I Have Asthma* by Jennifer Moore-Mallinos (2007) or *Ben Has Something to Say: A Story about Stuttering* by Laurie Lears (2000). How is disability and difference represented? In what ways do the books communicate?

Development

In a group, create a 20-page children's book: write the narrative (with a few words on a page), create graphics, and assemble the material into something bound, or stitched, or sewn together. Alternatively, create an e-book, or an interactive site.

Blindness, Visuality and Daredevil

This section discusses the representation of blindness in the DVD release of *Daredevil* (dir. Mark Steven Johnson, 2003). I look at what is on the screen, analyzing the filmic text, but I also want to encourage you to think of the film as a material object, as something that is produced in a certain media universe, and that is distributed in specific forms, including the DVD format.

EXERCISE 9.8   ## Comic Book Heroes

Do you like comics? Do you have favorite superheroes? Test your knowledge of graphic novel culture and chart five superheroes. Are they disabled? What are their disabilities? Are they pretty common, or really rare (like being allergic to kryptonite)? Are these disabilities socially marked, that is, do they have (negative or positive) consequences for the public life of the character?

Development

Here is a cover of the Silver Scorpion, a figure created with a group of young disability advocates from the US and Syria, brought together at the first international Youth Ability Summit in Damascus in August 2010. Use the Observation Wheel to analyze what you see here.

Image 21 *Silver Scorpion cover image, artwork by Mukesh Singh and Liquid Comics. © 2014 Open Hands Initiative*

Contemporary filmmaking in the post-cinematic period relies on a host of new technologies for its creation and reception – surveillance cameras, hand-held cheap technology, Internet streaming and distribution, IMAX challenges to traditional feature formats, etc. – these are all examples of how contemporary filmmaking responds to changing visualization technologies.

We can trace connections between technologies and content in a fairly well-known film, an iconic example of post-studio, new media cinema production: *The Blair Witch Project* (dirs Eduardo Sanchez and Daniel Myrick, 1999). At the center of the film, and at the center of the production and reception machinery, are media-savvy students, who are able to comment on the production of mass-market imagery and deal with the technology of video making.

In the narrative, these students meet the forest: a place where their technological skills are useless to them in terms of their survival. The experience of being lost in the woods is captured and intensified by the hand-held cameras and the students' willingness to use their cameras as intimate recording devices.

In this plot, high technology meets the dark places of pre-technological intensity. This scenario has become a pretty standard feature of the successful teen-flick horror scene. The body, disoriented in an unfamiliar landscape, often accessed through media technology, becomes vulnerable and the terrain of a hunt. Technology mediates the horror, but is useless in warding off the source of horrific dismemberment. At the heart of these films, the body is exposed as the scene of weak flesh, stripped off the carapaces of civilization, and unable to withstand the onslaught.

Daredevil shares some features with this new foundation narrative of contemporary cinematics: a body and its perception upset by movement in strange locations. But it is of a different ilk than *The Blair Witch Project*: sleeker, with a full Hollywood production budget, but emerging out of a similar aesthetic lodged in individual sensorial experience.

For those of you who are not familiar with the old Marvel comic hero, or with the new Hollywood film, Daredevil is a dark superhero, in the Batman vein. He became disabled as a child, when he ran into a vat of acid. He is blind, but, like many disabled superheroes (such as superfast Daphne, with cerebral palsy, in the TV show *Heroes*, 2006–10), he is a supercrip: he has the ability to "see" by focusing on sound waves washing over his environment. This incredibly heightened sensory access allows him to swing freely across the rooftops of New York, his particular Gotham, save people, and punish perpetrators as obsessively as Batman did.

From a disability studies perspectives, *Daredevil* presents a pretty standard narrative in which blindness stands for heightened non-visual perception skills, and for supreme if childlike black and white morality. The film also milks a form of Christ-like martyrdom – Daredevil is a good Catholic boy, and guilt and devotion frame the narrative.

In its DVD package, *Daredevil* is as much about the making of the film as about the actual narrative developed in its plot – a narrative already citational and pastiche in its reference to the old comics. On the level of the film itself, special effects and the mechanics of vision appear prominently. Watching *Daredevil* is a rollercoaster ride, predicated on immersion and kinesthetic sensation, like the 3D rollercoaster rides of *Avatar* (James Cameron, 2009), which features a wheelchair-using protagonist.

The *Daredevil* DVD has an interesting soundtrack option: it is possible to watch the whole film in audio description mode. This mode is traditionally associated with disability access.

ACTIVITY 2 ## Audio Description

In a small group, choose a segment of a contemporary film, any one you want. Agree on a three-minute clip, one that relies more on visuals than the spoken word. Now turn the soundtrack down low, but so that it is still audible to you. One after the other, each describe what you are seeing, conveying what is happening to someone who can't see the screen (but can hear the soundtrack). Do not speak over any dialogue lines. Note the differences with which the people in the group approach the task. What is being described, what isn't? Comment on what is difficult, what requires decision making. If you have people with non-visual access among you, how can you adapt the exercise? Might there be a way to focus on sound rather than image? An adaptation would be to stop the film every five seconds, and describe in between, accommodating sensory overwhelm. Discuss among yourself what would work.

Development

Split up the small group. One half of the people go out of the room. Now choose a different clip. Then bring in the people who went out, and ask them to sit down with their backs to the screen. Start the audio description, with the filmic sound turned to normal audio levels. At the end, the people who just listened describe what they perceived. Discuss what happened.

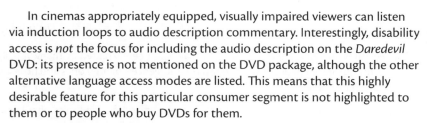

In cinemas appropriately equipped, visually impaired viewers can listen via induction loops to audio description commentary. Interestingly, disability access is *not* the focus for including the audio description on the *Daredevil* DVD: its presence is not mentioned on the DVD package, although the other alternative language access modes are listed. This means that this highly desirable feature for this particular consumer segment is not highlighted to them or to people who buy DVDs for them.

Indeed, in an informal survey of visually impaired DVD users on a disability e-list, I found not one who was aware that the *Daredevil* DVD offered this feature. Clearly, the audio description mode is a gimmick, something aimed at "normate" (i.e. non-visually impaired) viewers. By accessing the film through the audio description mode, a viewer can precariously experience a different sensory world, a hyper-access of visuals combined with visual description: blindness becomes a site/sight of fantastical engagement, a play of "what if," allowed by the technology of soundtrack menus.

A further pleasure offered by *Daredevil* is on the limits of character/ narrative involvement and filmic materiality: the level of visceral affect. With visceral affect I refer to the sensory universe created in *Daredevil*. Watching the film as a sighted viewer involves a visual/audio feast that tugs at the viewer's senses in a form of kinesthetic translation: the visuals set up a sense of dislocation, of disequilibrium. Watching the hyper-mobile camera roll and skip echoes in my kinesthetic sense (if I were to watch this on a really big screen, I might get seasick): my own body as a viewing body feels echoes of the mobility on and also of the screen. For many people, this viscerality is actually an access feature – some people with ADHD and other neurodiverse ways of being find this mode of pleasure more fun than narrative immersion.

This sense of a binding element connecting the world as if space were a tactile medium is itself visualized and thematized in the film. The Daredevil character is able to read the world by a form of sonar or echo. He reads the sound waves coming to him as they travel over objects in the world, outlining them for him. The color used to present these sound images is blue, like water, reminding me of sonar. The materiality of the world becomes accessible in these images. Everything is connected – everything exists in the same stratum, not in the separation of vision but in the connectedness of touch.

The credit scene plays with the bodily/sensorial difference and with the fascination of the city as a place of visceral affect. In it, the names of people involved in the production swoop into the field of vision as Braille dot arrangements, emerging out of a cityscape and the lightened windows of a city at night, to dissolve into "normal" English lettering. The director's audio commentary informs the viewer that the Braille is actually correct, i.e. the appropriate dot/space translation of the English words – this knowledge is, of course, highly specialized, and not accessible to many people who actually do use Braille as a communication device.

With this, this film and its titillating play with blindness remain pretty firmly in the sighted camp, although some people with some kind of visual impairment do visually read Braille, as it is easier to decipher than letters.

BLIND SPACE

The pleasures of visuality and multisensory play have been explored by many visually impaired and blind artists, more adept at speaking to multiple audiences: sighted ones and non-sighted ones, and the many in between.

Here are two writers who write across sensory specificity toward forms of cultural contact. Poet Stephen Kuusisto writes about the audio creativity of his blindness in these terms:

> Blind people are not casual eavesdroppers. We have method. As things happen around us we reinvent what we hear like courtroom artists who sketch as fast as they can. We are also cartoonists of a sort: our sketches are both clear and improbable. I am essentially an inept landscape painter. I draw unlikely trees and mechanical people in the manner of Max Ernst. In reality I cannot see the world by ear, I can only reinvent it for my own purposes. (Kuusisto, 2006: xi)

And writer Georgina Kleege speaks about her visit to the Matisse exhibition at New York's Museum of Modern Art in the following quote. Think about the connections between vision and space, between different spatial patterns in the art museum.

When I look at a painting from a sighted person's distance, macular degeneration, my form of blindness, obscures or distorts the center of the canvas. ... To get a general sense of the overall composition, I scan the painting systematically, moving my oversized blind spot around it, allowing different regions to emerge into my peripheral vision. ... To add detail to this rough sketch growing in my brain, I must get very close to the painting, as close as museum guards allow, even closer when they look away. ... my method of looking at painting takes time and space. I perform a slow minuet before each painting, stepping forward and back, sweeping my gaze from edge to edge. Considering the crowds at most museums nowadays, it may seem surprising that I ever manage to get as close to the paintings as I need to. But current museum practices aid me. People tend to cluster around printed text displays at the entrance of each gallery or by particular paintings. Other people rent tape-recorded tours that direct them to certain works, so they bypass others. As they congregate before the texts and prescribed canvases, it leaves space open elsewhere for me. (Kleege, 1999: 93–5)

The lived space that emerges in the passages by Kuusisto and Kleege is very different from and yet not unrelated to *Daredevil*'s sonar blue. How does vision appear here as a physical act, a doing rather than a passive consuming?

EXERCISE 9.9   Film Festivals

Film festivals are a core site of disability culture labor. The advent of hand-held and personal household camera and editing gear has created a revolution for many minority identity groups. Making films about our lives, our art, our humor, and our pain has become a significant way of sharing ourselves with others, educating people, and finding solidarity.

For this exercise, find a disability film festival site online, and have a look at the films they are screening: read the descriptions, see if you can find clips or teasers online, and then write an analysis of the curatorial policy of this particular festival. Share your analyses with others, and see what other curators are up to.

EXERCISE 9.10   Disability History, Material Culture and Visuality: Museum Exhibitions

Here are two significant exhibitions with large online components that will give you perspectives on disability history, visual and material culture: the National Museum of American History's *EveryBody: An Artifact History of Disability in America* exhibition, curated by Katherine Ott, unveiled in 2013, and English Heritage's *A History of Disability: From 1050 to the Present Day*, also unveiled in 2013.

- How does disability enter the public archive?
- What is visible, what is not, and how do these exhibitions work with the tensions around how the meanings of "disability" change and shift?
- What are the multisensory access features in these online exhibitions?
- How do power, activism, and resilience enter into curatorial approaches?

ACTIVITY 3 Design Brief

Research Preparation

Make yourself familiar with a range of online visual arts resources in disability contexts. Resources include:

- large-scale assemblages such as the websites and online documentaries accompanying Unlimited, the Arts Council England funded scheme for disabled and deaf artists, part of the 2012 Cultural Olympiad in London (see also the DVDs and collected information in Keidan and Mitchell, 2012)
- smaller scale exhibitions, for example the 2009 sculpture exhibition *Re/Formations: Disability, Women, and Sculpture* and its website (curators Jessica Cooley and Ann Fox, with artists Rebecca Horn, Nancy Fried, Harriet Sanderson, Judith Scott, and Laura Splan), the *What Can a Body Do?* exhibition, curated by Amanda Cachia (2012), which features audio biographies of participating artists on its website, and *Blind at the Museum* (UC Berkeley, 2005), curated by Katherine Sherwood and Beth Dungan
- ongoing online galleries of community art workshops like Creative Growth in Oakland, California
- purely online exhibitions, such as *Cripping Cyberspace: A Contemporary Virtual Art Exhibition* (2013), hosted by the *Canadian Journal for Disability Studies*, curated by Amanda Cachia, with artists Katherine Araniello, Cassandra Hartblay, Sara Hendren, and the m.i.a. collective.

Write two-paragraph responses to two works of art/performances/installations you see during your research, and that capture you, making use of the Observation Wheel.

Development

Pay attention to the access mechanics built into the websites you visit, and note how different people can make use of the sites:

- people with different forms of visual access
- people with mobility issues, who might find it hard to navigate links that are very small and clustered
- people with dyslexia, who might find it easier to access links that are not named in very similar ways.

Research accessibility in the arts as a topic area – a good starting point can be the resources collected by VSA in the US (www.kennedy-center.org/education/vsa/), by Shape Arts in the UK (www.shapearts.org.uk), and by Arts Access Australia (www.artsaccessaustralia.org).

ACTIVITY 4 Project Art Consultant

Divide into teams. Each team has to create a design for a particular art-enriched community room. The teams have papers, colored pens, textured materials, and tactile shapes to help share their design ideas through multiple modalities. After a development period, the teams have to present their idea, addressing three core design demands they identified for their particular venue. Each team puts forward one member to be a judge. All teams present. The judges ask three questions, and then assign a winning team. There will be cookies (with options for diabetics, gluten-intolerance, and nut allergies).

Community room ideas could include:

- Center for Independent Living foyer area
- Visiting room in an institution for people with dementia
- Communal area in shared housing for autistic people
- Lighthouse for the Blind (service organization) waiting area
- Gallery for a community workshop gallery, such as Creative Growth, with many artists with cognitive differences
- Riding stable for equine engagement
- Area outside the training studio of a specialist organization that organizes adapted sports for disabled people

REORIENTING THE CITY

Image 22 *Carmen Papalia, Blind Shuttle Walk, walking tour, duration varies, 2012. Photo: Jordan Reznick*

In this performance action, blind artist Carmen Papalia leads a group of people with their eyes closed through a cityscape. He does not "invite them into his experience," he invites them to have their own experience with trust, disorientation, and sensory tuning. Think about this action, and the differences between this kind of practice and a simulation exercise. What is at stake?

ACTIVITY 5 Trust Walk

Couple up. One of you guides, one of you closes their eyes, for a significant period of time (I'd recommend 20 minutes each), so that you can become familiar with the experience. Now lead each other across campus (if people are sensitive to touch, a scarf might help you to tether yourself. Experiment until you reach a level of comfort). Maybe you can visit an art exhibit somewhere. The person with their eyes open can audio describe works of art to the other one, if they have visual access. As Papalia's action shows, it is not required to have visual access to navigate terrain. If you do not have visual access, audio describe something else, tactile, or audio, something that arrests you.

- How does it feel to do this exercise?
- Is it easy to close your eyes and trust your guide?
- Is it easy to guide, or do you feel the pressure?
- Are you aware of other people's eyes on you, their comments?
- What happens to sound and touch as you engage in this?
- Do you become focused, or overwhelmed?
- How do you imagine the spaces you are led to?
- How is the experience of works of art different, if visual input is your normal way of receiving the world?

ACTIVITY 6 Frida Kahlo

Research Mexican painter Frida Kahlo's work, and use image search engines to find her paintings. Many of them reference disability, pain, and bodily difference. If you are visually impaired, can you still access the images and their colors? How else can you find information about the paintings? Can you find short stories, poems, or other writings that guide you to a sense of what Kahlo's work is like?

After you looked at a number of her paintings, find one you wish to write on. Make sure you can get a large enough copy of it, in a good resolution, so you can focus on details. Begin by making lists:

- What colors can you see? What do you associate with these colors, what meanings do they have for you?
- What animate and non-animate things appear in the image? Again, what do you associate with them, what stories do they initiate for you? Be clear that they are your stories, not Kahlo's.
- What textures appear in the painting? Are there broken surfaces, penetrating objects, smooth fields? Describe these textures, without making causal links to Kahlo's biography.
- Are there any religious icons in the image? Can you identify them?

You now have a rich field of image description, in list form. Use your lists as a resource for writing a two-page response to the image, making sure that at least one of these pages is pure description, without an attempt at interpretation.

If you do not have access to visual information, use this exercise to respond to written accounts of Kahlo's work, and to her biography, adapting the questions above to refer to textual representation.

In class, share your two-page writing with a colleague, and bring a copy of the image you responded to. Discuss your response, your choices, the different way we see images, based on our sensory worlds, our cultural reference fields, and the stories we bring ourselves to the image's elements.

Development

Create a response to the image, using the initial lists as resources. Create a poem, a short story, a playlet, a video. As you are doing so, reflect on the richness of Kahlo's work, and why it has spoken to so many, for so many years.

10 *Looking at Autism*

In this chapter, you will gain insights into these issues:

- The difference between "autism" as in popular cultural representation, and the experience of autism or neurodiversity
- Why "autism" (as a representational category) is so endlessly fascinating to popular culture
- How genre differences impact narratives about autism
- Verbal versus non-verbal engagements with mental difference
- Engaging cognitive difference and neurodiversity as sites of richness

In this chapter, I discuss the performance potential of autism, intrigued by the ways that mental difference as metaphor can influence art practice.

Images of autism surround us, rarely created by autistics. Books such as *The Curious Incident of the Dog in the Night-time* (Haddon, 2003) make it onto bestseller lists and university courses. While autism touches many people's lives, its definition and expression are very much under debate, and people who identify as autistic, such as Donna Williams, Tito Rajarshi Mukhopadhyay, D.J. Savarese, Dawn Prince-Hughes, and Temple Grandin, write and speak about the non-coincidence of popular rhetoric surrounding autism and the experience of it. Many autistics' creative output engages and complicates the stereotypes of autistic people as savants, gifted yet locked away, alienated and yet brilliant. Their work offers counterviews to autism as tragedy and loss.

EXERCISE 10.1 ## Subverting the Language

Autistic self-advocate Jim Sinclair wrote his powerful essay "Don't Mourn for Us" early in the autistic movement, in 1993 (the whole essay is easily found online):

> You didn't lose a child to autism. You lost a child because the child you waited for never came into existence. That isn't the fault of the autistic child who does exist, and it shouldn't be our burden. We need and deserve families who can see us and value us for ourselves, not families whose vision of us is obscured by the ghosts of children who never lived. Grieve if you must, for your own lost dreams. But don't mourn for us. We are alive. We are real. And we're here waiting for you. (Sinclair, 1993)

Discuss this quote in pairs. How does Sinclair position the fear and stress of new parents? What strategies does he use here to reshape the rhetorics of charity discourse, and how charities tend to position autistics? Compare this language to the language used by autism charities on their websites. How would you feel, as new parents of a child labeled autistic, reading Sinclair's essay, or reading about Autism Spectrum Disorders on the websites?

• •

In these pages, I do not focus on works of art created by autistics or people who identify as being on the spectrum or neurodiverse (there are different language conventions here), but on representations that makes autism its central metaphor, acted out, narrated, and danced by non-disabled people. This approach is still within the scope of a disability culture classroom, since every time I teach a class like this, some students ask to write their essays on successful popular cultural texts on autism.

Mainstreaming Autism: *The Curious Incident of the Dog in the Night-time*

I open up possible paths in the narrative treatment of autism through a discussion of one of those highly successful mainstream representations, Mark Haddon's *The Curious Incident of the Dog in the Night-time* (2003). There are many useful treatments of this text out there, including a book-length study of autism and literary representation by Stuart Murray (2008). You could begin your engagement by reading the novel, and/or tracking how academic literary analysis has engaged with the novel and its placement of autism. You can work with your librarians to work out how to use a database such as the *MLA International Bibliography*.

Later on in this chapter, I look at the use and presentations of autism in an experimental performance art piece that combines dance and film. Are you familiar with experimental performances, work that is not reliant on naturalist representation and narrative? You might want to familiarize yourself with some performances, and maybe go see some in your locality. Maybe you can find one that uses a disability metaphor as its starting point – not at all uncommon. I encountered this particular piece, *Bedlam*, by going to the performance with my disability culture class at the Institute for Medical Humanities in Galveston, Texas, not knowing what to expect. If an opportunity for a field trip like this presents itself, either for a whole class or for you as an individual student, go for it! Write a review, and share it with your class.

The differences I note between the novel and the performance are, of course, preprogrammed by the generic home of the material: a bestselling novel tends to feature unity and narrational clarity, and an avant-garde performance piece presents a more kaleidoscopic, fractured worldview, which demands more labor on the part of its witnesses. Throughout this chapter, writers who are part of the self-advocacy movement will address you, too, ensuring that disabled expressions remain central to disability culture work.

The novel focuses on 15-year-old Christopher, the main character and narrator, who seems to be autistic. British author Mark Haddon, who worked with people with different labels of mental health difference earlier in his life, never mentions the word "autism" in the novel, and has indeed expressed surprise in interviews that he would now be called upon as a specialist. Even so, the novel has become a major touchstone in public debates surrounding the label.

In the novel, Christopher uses his non-normative way of making sense of the world to unravel the mysterious death of a dog, and, through this, presents a view of suburban Britain, a very recognizable Swindon: a modern satellite city for London, and its rules and regulations. Christopher tells the reader how he thinks: numbers, colors, rules make up his life, he is emotionally disassociated (of a kind), yet able to analyze the behavior of those around him in minute detail. He does not like to be touched, rocks and moans when overstimulated, and he does not "understand" metaphors, and thus ruminates about the meaning of strange phrases he encounters as people speak to him. The book was a smash hit, received numerous awards, and a theatre play based on it, adapted by Simon Stephens, directed by Marianne Elliott, and produced by the UK's National Theatre, was awarded "Best Play" in 2013. Why?

To begin with, the strange voice is compelling in its otherness, combined with a deep familiarity. "As if one is in the character's head" is something many reviewers comment on. This is a child, learning adult rules, and also a disabled character, with all the voyeurism that attracts, but, beyond that, an everyman who takes onto himself all the narrational weight so many disabled characters have to carry in literature: being the alienated lens through which to see the lie of the land. And this is indeed what makes Christopher so compelling. His distanced view of the rules that make up love, relationships, need, and care feels so true, and seems so perceptive.

But I would also venture that another main draw that makes the novel such a success is its narrational glimpse of a possible simplicity. For Christopher, things that are mysterious follow rules he has not quite worked out yet. Nothing is unknowable, just not yet understood. But rules can be charted, and as we enter the world of the novel, the rules indeed become good predictors for what might or might not happen: what was unfamiliar becomes very familiar, and Christopher's world is navigable. He explains:

> You always know what a dog is thinking. It has four moods. Happy, sad, cross and concentrating. Also, dogs are faithful and they do not tell lies because they cannot talk. (Haddon, 2003: 4)

If that is the way the novel world works, it is quite comforting in a world of novel writing in which renditions of modern life alienation are usually so much less pleasurable. The novel has many elements of an inverted aphorism: truths are told inverted, yet always recognizable.

How to make a world legible, understandable: that is the journey readers go on. Compared to the complexity of life as most of us know it, Christopher's world, in which a certain number of red cars seen in the morning make for a good day, a different number of yellow cars a bad one, has quite an appeal. "Autism," not as lived experience, but as a representational category, does not become cuddly, quite, but it becomes a rather nostalgic lens through which a complex world can be made to distill itself into some semblance of wondrous order.

The novel has found criticism among autistics, even though many praise its focus on making an autistic person someone self-directed, able to lead a full life, and a complex and interesting figure.

The Singaporean autistic writer Eric Chen has written *Mirror Mind* (2005), a book of poems and critical writings about his life. In a review of *Incident*, he questions the novel's way of normalizing Christopher, and he offers a number of rewrites. He looks at a passage from *Incident*, and then writes how he thinks the material in the passage could be rewritten from his own perspective. Of course, as he himself acknowledges, the aim of this exercise is to educate people about autism, not to write a bestselling novel.

Here is one of the four passages he rewrites, complete with his commentary. In this passage, *Incident* and Chen focus on one of the savant-like features often associated with the label "autism:" the seeming superhuman ability to process mathematical data, combined with the supposed lack of ability to comprehend or work with emotional and metaphorical data (a combination at the heart of one of the first mass-market presentations of autism, the 1988 film *Rain Man*):

> And he said, "What's 251 times 864?"
> And I thought about this and I said: "216,864." Because it was a really easy sum because you just multiply 864 × 1,000 which is 864,000. Then you divide it by 4 which is 216,000 and that's 250 × 864. Then you add another 864 on to it and get 251 × 864. And that's 216,864. (Haddon, 2003: 84)

> The paragraph shows Christopher working logically through the sums in a short period of time. People (no matter having autism or not) who have trained in speed mathematics can achieve this feat too. However, if Christopher is a savant (who can calculate faster than a calculator but without any training or awareness of speed mathematics), he would not be reasoning the numbers out in his head. Instead, he would tap into the parallel processing power of his brain, using the kinesthetic and visual processors. If I could rewrite this paragraph, perhaps it might read like this:

> And he said, "What's 251 times 864?"
> As Christopher heard this, in his mind appeared two green shapes that looked a lot like uneven cubes. The shapes clashed into each other and rippled with lots of tiny cubes, squares and triangles. Eventually a new shape was formed. Christopher replied: "216,864".
> He was shocked. "Wow, that's even faster than a calculator. How did you do it?"
> Christopher was puzzled and thought carefully about what he meant. Perhaps he was asking who solved the sum. "I did."
> "I mean, what trick did you use?"

It took me a while for Christopher to understand what he said. Maybe he means, tricks as in cheating. So he means if Christopher had cheated. "No."
"I don't get it," he declared. And to this very day, he still could not figure out Christopher's secrets.

> As a side-note, people with autism youths usually have to struggle to understand human speech, especially the context behind every word. The smooth flow of thoughts and the apparent ease of understanding human speech in the novel are highly unrealistic experiences. (Chen, 2006)

Chen's rewriting of *Incident*, in this passage and others, focuses a lot more on presenting the potential lacunae and missed connections between a neurodiverse person and others, whether neurodiverse or not. As such, his writing aims to present the experience of autism, as Chen perceives it, but it clearly also makes for a less compelling, more pedantic, slower moving, and more frustrating read. But then, missed connections can slow down communication, speed up frustration, endanger the pleasure of a solution.

This potentially disorienting experiential effect of being in the presence of autism, both as a lived experience and as a conglomeration of cultural signifiers, finds expression in the avant-garde performance I want to turn to next. If *Incident* presents a form of domesticated autism, makes it commensurate and graspable, other representations seem to dither more fruitfully, leave more room between the words and the potential lives of autistics. To order, to make chaotic: the question autism poses to the non-disabled world can be answered in many different ways.

AMANDA BAGGS

One of the many eloquent writers on autistic enwordedness is Amanda Baggs, a US-based autistic activist who does not speak. Her freely available 2007 YouTube video *In My Language* is used in many classrooms. Here are a range of quotes from one of her essays. She talks about engaging in a deep communication with a partner on the screen, someone who is 3,000 miles away. They communicate relationally, with fluttering hands, and with other modes that are evoked rather than described:

> *In every flick of the hand, wobble of the head, the fine detail of our bodies rocking, we each discern the other's environment. But also their understanding of it, their reactions to it. Not just the sensory components of outer environment. There is also the feel of it, the way the space between everything flows and moves and changes color. Objects are alive to us and interact with us as much as we interact with each other. ...*

> *This is the language we already spoke fluently before we learned that words existed. When we hadn't discovered that language was more than one more set of sounds, that our bodies were attached to us, that the barrage of sensory information had meaning. We found meaning in other places, in other ways. And even after we learned words, this other language remained our strongest means of relating to the world. (Baggs, 2012: 324–5) ...*

Our best – and for some people, only – way of thinking is pre-conceptual and pre-verbal. This means it is hard to translate into language. Often impossible. The ways we communicate outside of language are many, and are not always even intended as communication. We may pick up on the meaning of each other's movements. Movements that are in response to certain perceptions. In seeing the pattern of movement, we pick up on the awareness of perception, as well. We resonate with each other, and with things in our surroundings, from core to core, rather than based on outsides. One of us may arrange objects so that the pattern the objects form point back to who she is. Someone else will see the objects, and will perceive the pattern and know the other person in a way no words could convey. One person's pattern of walking will alter slightly because she has seen someone else, and the other person's hands will move a little differently because he has seen her see him. And they will each understand the other even though no deliberate communication has happened. ...

Sometimes we find communicating through text easier because it's less overloading. But we never find it easier to understand. We can pull some extra information from the patterns in between people's words. But it's still not the same amount of information we can get without text. What we get in normal environments is not just the way bodies move and the music of voices, but also the sound of their footfalls, the way the breath comes out, and even their smell. Even when we get things from body language and tone of voice, they're not always the same things most people perceive through it. And we generally do best at understanding people like ourselves. (Baggs, 2012: 329)

EXERCISE 10.2 **Experiencing Communication**

In response to reading the work of Baggs, it can be really useful to try to switch up communication modes, modes of perceiving, modes of orienting one's self in the world. The resulting exercise instructions might feel a bit nebulous – they need to be, to remove themselves from the dominance of spoken word and reduced communicative scales that Baggs associates with neurotypical ways of relating.

Reorient your own mode of sensing and being. See what you make of this instruction!

Pair up or form small groups, as a way to check in with one another about what sensations and feelings come up – and also as a way, if you choose to go into public spaces, to have some security in numbers.

When giving this instruction in the past, I spoke about sitting facing the slits in the radiator housing in our classroom, and seeing what emerges from focusing on these, how it makes one feel. Is there something similar for you to focus on? Look out of the window, if you have one, and focus on a cluster of leaves on a tree, seeing the color changes. Can you experience these leaves differently? What would that mean?

Be creative in forming the exercise idea here: your own space, and your own actions, can help you find a way in.

Exercise Response Examples

As this exercise is very open, but also very generative, I am giving two examples of how students in my classes have engaged with the challenge, finding ways of tuning in:

We walked to the Shapiro coffee bar area, noticing how the lines in the sidewalk – how a focus on those lines – could make us lose awareness of our greater surroundings. When we got to Shapiro, we sat down, noticing that we had to engage our social skills to borrow enough chairs to sit.

We could imagine dissociation happening as we fixated on smaller details in our surroundings. There were so many lines and bricks and rectangles! ... Counting the squares could provide some sense of stability and safety in surroundings.

We noticed substantial overstimulation in the library, with so many people, a shrill alarm going off, blaring but ineffective lighting, and more squares and bricks and rectangles.

We talked about ways to self-sooth. At one point, two of the group members were rocking, quite unconsciously. We discussed other ways of self-soothing such as loving certain inanimate objects or routines.

We kept coming back to and being lost in the cracks and lines. There are 192 small window panes in the area we were sitting, not including the all glass windowfront. (Gili, Chris, Catherine, Jasmine, and Cari, course website, reproduced with permission)

When discussing how we wanted to experience the world differently, Jaime mentioned that her [autistic] son, at a younger age, very much enjoyed stop signs. Jaime said that Connor spent nearly three years of his younger life fascinated by stop signs. He even carried a 3 inch wooden stop sign with him all day and slept with it at night. Connor would not allow a stop sign to be passed without taking the time to digest each and every stop sign. Over the three years Jaime, along with Connor, analyzed hundreds of stop signs from Michigan to Florida. Each stop sign was different. Each completely intrigued Connor and eventually Jaime as well. Therefore, we decided to go about the next 24 hours paying exclusive attention to stop signs.

For Heidi, stop signs were much more common that she had anticipated. Between our classroom and her home on the corner of Hill and Main, Heidi passed 10 stop signs. She stopped at each, taking note of the stop sign. How tall was the sign? Was the sign leaning one way or another, or was it slightly twisted in its spot? Did it have green signs indicating the intersection on top of the sign? Was the metal stand firmly screwed into the ground? Was it rusty? How thick was the actual sign? Was the paint brilliant or dull? She noted the shine in the white of the sign. Was the stop sign tagged with promotional stickers for other items? She took note of the eight sides. She spent time at each stop sign, taking in all aspects of the stop sign, and continued to do so with each stop sign for the next 24 hours. Often, standing and staring at the sign felt conspicuous, like at any point someone might stop and ask Heidi if she needed help finding her way or would note the girl standing, staring, talking to a stop sign and she answered the questions. They would find her whispering about the authority of the stop sign – who decided to place it there; was it obeyed; who obeyed it; who didn't? (Jaime and Heidi, course website, reproduced with permission)

EXERCISE 10.3 ## Disability Culture Music

Research how disability and music are linked in popular discourse. What kind of clusters to do you find? You are likely finding much material on blind African-American musicians like Stevie Wonder, Ray Charles, and the Blind Boys of Alabama. You are also likely to find protest songs and punk rock aesthetics, including the work of Johnny Crescendo, Rudely Interrupted, or Heavy Load.

You might also find a lot of accounts of autism linked to musical talent, from contemporary figures like James Durbin, a competitor on *American Idol*, and Susan Boyle from the similar show *Britain's Got Talent*. You will also find people whose exact cognitive difference is more shrouded, like Marty Balin from Jefferson Airplane (a 1960/70's US rock band) or classical pianist David Helfgott, who inspired the Oscar-winning film *Shine*, as well as many musical savants who are retro-diagnosed in the public eye, people like Mozart.

An intriguing multiagentic representation of autistic discourse is at work in Philip Glass's opera *Einstein on the Beach*, a collaboration that included Christopher Knowles, a 14-year-old autistic young man. As you research the public reception of this work, see how Knowles is positioned within the collaborative field, and how autistic processes are linked to experimental music.

Autism and Performance

Autism has currency in performance: something quite so powerfully in the public eye and quite performative, recognizably "enactable," has found ways onto the stage. There are plenty of autistics in the theatre world, both on and behind the stage. Well-known actors like Daryl Hannah and Paddy Considine have outed themselves as autistics. UK actor Lizzy Clark became one of the first autistics to portray an autistic character (Poppy, in the BBC film *Dustbin Baby*, 2008), and she is involved in the Don't Play Me, Pay Me campaign that tries to change acting conventions in which non-disabled actors "crip up" to play disabled ones.

Some autistics enjoy being prop managers, lighting designers or being in charge of costumes: if they have visual acuity and a perseverance for repetition, they have a great aptitude for noticing when things are awry, and for ensuring the same set-up every night.

But in the registers of non-autistic performance engagement with autism as metaphor, "autism" can often mean deep abjection, and that can quickly get really complicated and upsetting. Socìetas Raffaello Sanzio, an Italian-based avant-garde, experimental theatre company, made their Hamlet an autistic character rocking by himself, on an electrified bedstead (*Hamlet: the Vehement Exteriority of the Death of a Mollusc*, 1992 onwards). All is not well in Denmark, indeed, and the world is out of joint. Here, autism is presented as a radical tragedy, deep alienation, and non-living life – presented by non-autistics, of course.

At other times, autism on the stage becomes the opportunity for stereotyped angel beings to move among us: projections of innocence can become an equally disrespectful and annoying representation of neurodiversity. But in the next performance I would like to discuss, no clear answers emerge about the nature of autism, no narrative, no solution – but something moves.

Shrouded Representation: Autism on the Experimental Stage

In the performance/film happening *Bedlam*, presented by dance company FrenetiCore in Houston, Texas in June 2006, autism becomes a lens. Autism is a core organizing metaphor, although magic realism disrupts any sense of "an autistic" being realistically presented on stage. This is not a show that tries to educate *about* autism. Autism instead becomes an organizing principle, a trope from which dance, film, and performance spring. The company's publicity material describes the show in these terms:

> A magic urban realist tale performed with original music, narration, and both live and filmed dance. A young autistic finds herself within the walls of Bedlam Asylum. Troubled by the stirrings of her lost memories, she joins with two hyper-medicated and delusional mental patients. Together they must create an alternate reality to banish their inner demons. Joined by a supporting cast of characters, real and imaginary.

Rebekah French's choreography embraces a number of kinesthetic or communicational strategies that are often associated with autism: being alone, sensitivity to touch, distance, an avoidance of face-to-face communication, no eye contact.

The stage fills up with dancers, all in dirty white clothes, moving across in strange and compelling formation. One movement motif is a sequence where one dancer sits on the ground, hugging her bent legs closely to herself, rocking backward and forward. Another dancer comes near, although not too close, grabs one the legs, which becomes extended away from the still hugged body. He or she pulls the dancer across the floor, not unkind, without violence, merely matter of fact, until the dancer twists out of this strange grip.

Seeing the dance, the show's publicity material gives me an explanatory framework: the young woman, Ash, who is to become the central character for the show, is playing an autistic girl, locked into an institution, played out in a gothic register.

In interviews with the choreographer, I learned that Ashley Horn is also a dance teacher, and that she worked for years one-on-one with an autistic young man (as a creative artist, not a dance therapist). And indeed, many of the movements I see seem to emerge from choreographic instructions that embody potential autistic movement patterns: holding on to extended legs as means of transport and connection, embodying both resistance to touch and the strangeness and "unnaturalness" of bodily connection. There is no hand-holding here, and little of the body-on-body contacts familiar from contemporary dance. Twisting away and turning are the core patterns I see in the duet and ensemble material.

In an initiation scene reminiscent of the ballet *Rites of Spring*, Ash is held high, not allowed to walk or touch the ground, her body rotating above the others. Although she is held, none of these touches are emphatic, emotional, or laden with connection: they remain formal, on a strange edge between intimacy, support, and the fulfillment of a rule.

What autism IS seems to be much less the issue in this show than what autism DOES: movement-based challenges to conventional or normate movement patterns.

EXERCISE 10.4 ## Embodied Memory and Autistic Selves

In a much-cited account of abuse and autism, autistic Julia Bascom speaks about the pathologizing embodied effects of behavioral therapy. Discuss this passage: What makes it so powerful? How does it reach across different sensoria?

> *In a classroom of language-impaired kids, the most common phrase is a metaphor.*
> *"Quiet hands!"*
> *A student pushes at a piece of paper, flaps their hands, stacks their fingers against their palm, pokes at a pencil, rubs their palms through their hair. It's silent, until:*
> *"Quiet hands!"*
> *I've yet to meet a student who didn't instinctively know to pull back and put their hands in their lap at this order. Thanks to applied behavioral analysis, each student learned this phrase in preschool at the latest, hands slapped down and held to a table or at their sides for a count of three until they learned to restrain themselves at the words.*
> *The literal meaning of the words is irrelevant when you're being abused. When I was a little girl, I was autistic. And when you're autistic, it's not abuse. It's therapy.*
> *Hands are by definition quiet, they can't talk, and neither can half of these students ...*
> *(Behavior is communication.)*
> *(Not being able to talk is not the same as not having anything to say.)*
> *Things, slowly, start to make a lot more sense. (Bascom, n.d.)*

The *Bedlam* show also presents various filmed sequences. In one of the dance sequences on film, Ash, another female inmate (Mary), and a man who dances on pointe shoes (Bernie) are moving across an industrial field of abandoned plastics: barrels of stacked material mounted into high hills, stable enough to climb. The dance sees the three moving up and down over this terrain, climbing and releasing, and the film stock runs backwards, with the effect that the jumps and supported descents from the fabric bales look unnatural, counter to the laws of gravity.

The plastic storage area is a world of magic realism, of impossible and yet shared dreams: an escape hatch from the asylum (located in a broom closet) leads to this postindustrial wasteland/playground, and the three inmates crawl out of the framed door onto grass, soil, and waste. The screen shows an explosion of color and shape after the strict geometrics of the asylum/ warehouse. The site is an abandoned plastic recycling facility in Houston, left untouched since 1978. It is not hard to read this sequence in the abandoned plastics works as a comment on environmental narratives of autism: the presence of toxic plastic compounds are just one of many narratives that surround autism discourse.

But these messages about cause and effect, narrative development, and explanatory scheme are merely subliminal: the show does not offer pat narratives about autism, but allows its viewers to enter into a landscape where media images, movement patterns, and gothic narratives about neurodiversity glide into each other.

If *Incident* presents the chaos of our world by using a disabled character's perspective and ability to make sense strangely, then *Bedlam* presents a vision on the edge of sensorial overload, and calls upon its audiences to engage and find pathways through discordant imagery, sounds, and kinesthetic information.

It seems to me that there is much in *Bedlam* that is likely to annoy autistic audience members, given its reliance on what could be read as stereotypes of autistic isolation, even though they strike me, as someone interested in dance, as quite neutral representations of movement difference. Its references to institutionalizations, in particular, might be upsetting to many disability-focused audiences. But to me there seems more space here than in *Incident* to see the world as potentially otherwise, to get a sense of neurodiversity as a site of richness and exploration, as a generator for exciting movement material.

Make up your own mind. If you identify as neurotypical, how much can you open your imagination to autism, without wishing for secure knowledge? Can art destabilize what we know in ways that are productive, and generate a more accessible world? In between a novel and a performance piece, narratives are set adrift. Somewhere, in the play with old stories, new questions can emerge.

EXERCISE 10.5 **Autism Blogs**

Blogs have become a significant feature of the communication scene of autistic adults. Many autistics share life experiences and insights through this format. For this exercise, familiarize yourself with two from this list of autistic blog mistresses and masters, and chart their aesthetics: their ways of naming themselves and their difference, their subject matters, their forms of communicating with neurotypicals and neuroatypicals alike. Check out:

- thAutcast
- Neurodivergence Speaking
- NeuroQueer
- Radical Neurodiversity Speaking
- Disability Right Now
- Shaping Clay
- Yes, That Too
- Evil Autie
- That Autistic That Newtown Forgot
- Emma's Hope Book
- Autistic Hoya

Blogs are, by definition, often short-lived, so some of these might no longer work by the time you read this, which is why I am not giving any links – but others will be part of the scene. Researching how to find blogs, finding the links to other blogs on the sites of people who are currently blogging, etc. is part of the research challenge of this exercise.

• •

ACTIVITY

Expanded Performance

Research the modulations of sensory input in contemporary companies that focus on neuroatypical-accessible performance work – some of whom are adapting an existing mainstream performance to autistics as audience members, a practice often called "relaxed theatre."

Check out, for example, the Autism Theatre Initiative, focusing on Broadway productions, the Spectrum Theatre Ensemble in Columbia, Missouri, and Forest Forge Theatre Project, Basingstoke, UK. Who are audiences and performers perceived to be?

Find performances created by and with autistic people, and explore their aesthetics. Check out Erin Manning's performance experiments with autistic perception and aesthetic play in the SenseLab, Montreal, Canada, which she has written about (Manning, 2013), or the work of Company@ Autistic Theatre in Adelaide, South Australia.

Creating Expanded Performance

Create your own take on sensorily aware, alternative access to performance. If you do not have autistic self-advocates among you, do not try to fantasize autism – instead, create a sense-rich environment that works for *you*, and allows you to tune to different ways of receiving performance pleasure, beyond narrative and spectacle.

At all points, note if people in the group find these suggestions doable, pleasurable, or not: many neuroatypical people, and also many neurotypical people, might find some of these, particularly in combination, overwhelming and suffocating. Be mindful on checking in. You can use interaction badges for this, too. Ideas include:

- sensory feast
- texture environment
- darkness and light
- sound play: whispers and different voices, with printed material as alternative
- mediations: Can you create videos or live-camera feeds that allow one to step out of the actual experience, and into a representation of it, and then back again?
- modulations of touch and pressure as performance experiences: people lying on other people, exploring what is pleasurable, and what is not
- explorations of spatial patternings: pressing one's self into a corner, or creating hiding holes; playing with edge spaces between niches and engagement

This is an open exercise, one that can bring together many of the performance explorations in this study book. Maybe open up this expanded performance field to friends: see how you can weave what you've learned about disability culture aesthetics as you guide people through stations, experiences, or installations.

11 Classroom Activism and Resources

There are many ways in which happenings in a college classroom can impact the world outside the classroom. Learning to appreciate the contributions, aesthetics, and politics of disability arts and culture is itself a political act: it shifts worldviews, and ideas of what is normal, beautiful, appropriate, and worthy of attention.

But there are other ways in which classroom practice can help change the world. In this chapter, I chart six ideas of what students can do to enact change in an ableist world. Use these as beginnings: every location will have its own challenges and opportunities, so these are merely some general suggestions.

1 Connecting Students toward Change

Change begins at home, of course. How about assembling a list of disability-focused student organizations, and petitioning your school to put this information up somewhere where it can be found by incoming students? And, in the process, if there isn't one yet, maybe start a disabled students and allies meeting group?

Maybe there are service learning opportunities you can explore, gaining class credit for working with outside institutions?

2 Disability History Markers

One front of cultural activism in the US focuses on changing state-wide curricula in schools and other public sites to incorporate disability history.

If you live in the US, does your state have publically acknowledged disability history markers as part of public life? Examples include the Ed Roberts Day in California (named after the founder of the first Center for Independent Living), or the practice to celebrate the anniversary of the ADA (Americans with Disabilities Act) in public ceremonies.

You can join a letter-writing campaign to establish a Disability History Month celebration, like they have in the UK (check out the UK Disability History Month website and its resources, http://ukdisabilityhistorymonth. com). Find out what is happening in your state.

3 Pride Parades

Another form of public activism around disability culture are disability pride parades. Many of these are happy to have volunteers join the team, and plan yearly events.

EXERCISE 11.1 **Pride Parades**

Research pride parades, their history, and the occurrence of any parades in your own locality. What would be strategies to insert disability, to either stage one's own parade, or build coalitions? What are the pitfalls and challenges to a disability politics when it enters the public realm of pride parades?

4 Public Protests

In the UK, recent years have seen large-scale public visibility around disability in relation to the changes in disability funding schemes. In 2012, protests against austerity measures brought disability activists to the forefront of public attention, as large-scale marches shifted the image of disability in the UK as much as the other dominant images on UK national TV at the time, the 2012 Paralympic Games. You can research these protests by looking for commentary on protests against Atos Healthcare, the firm that carries out "fit for work" assessments for the UK government.

EXERCISE 11.2 **Occupy**

Are there particular political issues alive in your community right now? Are there protests? If so, which organizations are in charge? How does disability feature in these protests? Check out the work that happened around access and political activism in the worldwide Occupy campaigns. Search for the "Disability & Occupy: Disability Blog Carnival" as a good starting point for the investigation.

Development

Now take this into the real world. Are there any protest actions that speak to you? Can you join, and assist organizers in thinking through access, if they are not already doing so?

5 Wikipedia Activism

Wikipedia activism is something many university professors in "subaltern" fields embrace: making visible the mechanics of knowledge production, and engaging students in reshaping the field. Here is an excerpt on how to organize Wikipedia activism as part of a classroom, written by Siobhan Senier, Native studies professor. She has a strong emphasis on contemporary subjects, bringing living Native writers and artists into public view.

*I gave students a clear sequence of steps, spread out over 3–4 weeks: 1.
Sign up for a Wikipedia account, and take the tutorials. 2. Begin drafting
your article in your sandbox, and send me the link. 3. After I approve your
draft, send the link to the Native author who is your subject for feedback.
(Each author was someone with whom I was personally acquainted, and
had contacted in advance, asking if they'd be willing to participate in this
project, and I brokered the introductions of students to their assigned
authors.) 4. "Create" the article. I was fortunate to teach in a digital lab,
so we devoted several class periods to reviewing what makes an article
"stick" in Wikipedia, as well as to writing and editing. Many students, at
least at my public university, still lack basic web literacy – signing up for
accounts, following tutorials – and most were grievously intimidated by the
prospect of using markup (which Wikipedia has since made optional). ...
writing for Wikipedia is a powerful lesson in professional writing process.
Some graduating seniors, who had grown rather accustomed to writing
their essays the night before their deadlines, and squeaking through with Bs
or Cs, found that this was simply impossible in this platform. Thus, some
found their articles proposed for deletion, and did poorly on the assignment,
because they skipped some of the interim, low-stakes (yet critically
important) parts of the assignment designed to keep them researching,
writing and revising.*

*Proposed deletion is not the only interesting thing that happened during
this class experiment; but it was, for students, the scariest thing, and it is
probably the thing that reveals the most about the politics of "indigenizing"
Wikipedia. Some of my students who wrote what were, in my estimation,
very good articles nevertheless had their work proposed for deletion,
on the grounds that their subjects did not meet Wikipedia's "notability"
criterion. To be considered "notable" enough to pass muster with Wikipedia,
a subject has to have received "significant coverage" in "reliable, published
[secondary] sources." Like many college professors, Wikipedians favor
newspaper and magazine articles, along with scholarly books and journals.
But telling students that something published by Harvard University Press
is "better" than anything published on a tribal website isn't really teaching
them critical thinking, in any event. As my students delved further into their
topics, and began actually consulting with Native writers and historians,
they found what historian Roy Rosenzweig pointed out years ago, so
beautifully and succinctly: "the general panic about students' use of Internet
sources is overblown. You can find bad history in the library." (Senier, 2013)*

As your class crafts its own Wikipedia assignment on disability arts
and culture, think about issues of authority, citation, worthiness, and
standardization. Make new entries, deepen older ones, get involved in
debates. Get a sense of the fluidity of the Internet, and our politics around
difference and value. Enjoy becoming cultural producers, reshaping digital
worlds. Discuss how it feels to have your entries challenged, and what
happens when one of your entries, most likely after weeks of work, goes live
in the end.

6 Art Activism

Disability cultural activities are often hidden from the mainstream. Consider finding ways of being public, of bringing core values of diversity, interdependence, patience and tolerance, interest in not-knowing into a public arena.

Example

On many campuses, Autism Speaks has a presence, as it is one of the largest autism-focused charities. This US organization has been severely critiqued by autistics themselves. And yet, students who collect money for this or other charities are rarely aware of the critiques by the disabled community.

ACTIVITY

Autism Speaks Protest

Research Autism Speaks. Check out the many political engagements with their message – including the YouTube video, *Rethinking Autism: Autistics Speak*. Look at the many postings by autistic people and their allies on blogs, critiquing the messages and campaigns of Autism Speaks. Once you have what you feel is an adequate assessment of the facts and positions, and if you feel that an organization like this should center or at least consult autistics, design an action that can draw attention to the problematic nature of the current practices of Autism Speaks, but without shaming the students who might be raising money for it.

How can you educate and shift ideas, how can you confound and play, how can you undermine the rhetoric of charities, with their dependence on fear, through artistic engagement?

You might find that I am overreaching my position as a study guide author here, putting forward a particular perspective. Discuss the ethics of this. Find a way to express yourself and your particular position in the classroom you have established: is it (relatively) safe(r) to do so? Where are the edges of your understanding of disability studies as a field of analysis, and as a site of actions that support social change?

Example: Death to the Puzzle Piece

The puzzle piece is the marketing symbol of Autism Speaks: it signifies that something is missing. A group of us created a guerrilla action, the *Death to the Puzzle Piece* performance, enacted on the University of Michigan's quad. Passers-by were welcome to destroy donuts arranged in the shape of a puzzle piece (or eat a fresh one). We provided a hammer. Some people chose to jump up and down on the stacked donuts, and it all got quite exuberant. As part of the action, we gifted flower bulbs for green-bombing spaces. Audience members could find out about Autism Speaks politics and our take on them by speaking with us, and by reading some of the chalk messages scrawled onto the sidewalk. This was a surrealist action conceived by Melanie Yergeau, Neil Marcus, and Petra Kuppers. Why donuts, why flower bulbs, you might ask? Well, it's a surrealist action.

Resources: An Exercise

Disability arts and culture land is growing, there are more and more online sites, museum exhibitions, library sections, and more available for cataloging disabled people's cultural expressions and contributions.

This short resource section was going to give three or four pointers per art form (where the very notion of old school "art form" challenges the interdisciplinary nature of a lot of our work), spread across geographic regions. But instead, this resource section developed into an exercise, as most online resources are complex assemblages of living links and out-of-date information – you might have already found that when you engaged in Exercise 5.2, Disability Culture Webs. A good hour's trawl on the Internet will bring up multiple connections and sites, and the bibliography of this book is also a rich and diverse starting point.

So, "resource" becomes its own research activity, in keeping with a sense of interdependence and responsiveness to change. This might be a semester-long task of assembling links, or a focused set of instructions for sharing found information.

- **Research** what is out there, maybe in response and or in preparation for a Wikipedia activism sequence.
- **Visit** some of your local disability services areas and have a look at flyers and announcements. This will give you another perspective: much of the work in disability arts and culture is not built on star systems and fame, but on grassroots labor and development.
- **Assemble** a file folder, or your own website linking to current and active disability culture producers.
- **Share** it. Add to the diversity of voices, do not just duplicate the first hits you find.

How can YOU curate the shape of the field, marking your own position, your perspective, your location?

Appendix For Teachers

This book introduces embodied and arts-based learning about and through disability arts and culture. It uses multiple modalities to allow for access, for aesthetic complexity, and for different kinds of ownership of the material.

Chapter 1 focuses on class arrangement and begins thinking about complexities of access. Chapters 2–5, on language, discourse, embodiment/enmindment, and disability culture are highly interactive, offering an embedment in disability studies concerns while still keeping firmly focused on the arts. All the chapters are designed to stand by themselves, and can be used for short or long in-course modules on disability. But, if used sequentially in a full course, the language, discourse and disability culture chapters cover between two and three classes each, and the chapter on embodiment/enmindment offers ideas that might inform the beginning of each class (like a meditation exercise), or the construction of a personal journal throughout the semester, a potential assessment point.

Part II focuses on particular themes and art forms. In Chapter 6, Life in the Institution, I model a way to get to multi-drafted essay writing.

Think about bringing disabled people as teachers, leaders, and knowledge carriers into the classroom, to model the kind of inclusive and multidimensional world we are striving for. If at all possible, ensure that all speakers get paid, including Skype visitors. There is a social justice and activist component to this way of structuring classrooms. As a convener of this kind of space, it might be necessary to articulate to departments why outside speakers and representational diversity are important.

Quotes

Alongside the main text are many quotes by foundational thinkers in the field of disability studies, art and culture. Many are not directly picked up in the running text, and parsing them will often be a bit harder than the main chapter text. They can be used in multiple ways: as pointers toward potential essay topics and as jumping-off points for homework, entries on course websites, either before or after a class covering the general subject. I use these kinds of homework assignments to deepen the experiential nature of the classroom, and to give students a structure around which to assemble their observations. The quotes can also be useful in-class starting points for conversation.

Exercises

Exercises are tasks a student can engage in by her- or himself, or explore in small groups during class. These might make appropriate homework tasks, too. They function to deepen the issues introduced in the running text.

Developed Exercises and Activities

Arts-based exercises appear at various points in every chapter: the longer form exercises called Activities can be the main form of engagement with a given theme in a class period, as they are often quite involved, will take a bit of time to unfold, and can benefit from a debriefing afterwards. There are usually at least two different art form options, so teachers and students can go with what modality seems most comfortable and doable, given space and time restrictions.

The Observation Wheel

Here is an image of a wheel that I use to guide students to engage with images or videos. It is a useful, visually based tool to go beyond the moment of judgment, the "I like it/I don't like it" response, or the intense focus on one particular (often judgmentally presented) feature of the work. It allows one to slow down reading, to break up one's responses, and to experience one's reception more durational, unfolding, complex.

I introduce this wheel at the beginning of the semester, and hand out blank sheets (for those students who do not use electronic means as their main form of note-taking) whenever we engage in an image or video analysis in the classroom together – students can draw their own wheel, and fill it with terms that suit them.

What you see

What you want to work on:

joy
vibration
self

What you hear

What does not resonate:

shadow resource

What is in each segment in this wheel will shift with the particular resource under exploration – the point is to offer space for reading practice, and allow scope for reflection:

1 *See* is used as a term to reference your first impression, as a straightforward (as possible) observation; it is not just a way of referring to visual communication.

2 *Hear* is not just an ableist term referring to a particular way of taking in information – it is also used here in a metaphorical way, "hearing," as in "what do you receive beyond the first level description."

3 *Shadow resource* refers to what annoys you, what upsets, creates friction, to what is missing and pushes against your reading in its absence.

4 *Joy, vibration, self* refer to aspects of the work you can carry into the future, parts that connect with you, what attracts you.

This book tries to honor many different learning styles, and most concepts are worked through more than once, with different modalities, to allow for the flourishing of a holistic understanding and engagement. On this journey, students and teachers can engage with each other as wayfarers, as explorers, and as active participants and knowledge carriers. Adapt, discard, recycle, and repurpose as you will, allow for the openness that characterizes an accessible world.

EXERCISE

The Observation Wheel: Cultural Difference and Ways of Knowing

Classrooms can keep cultural differences and cultural conventions in mind by interrogating shared knowledge habits.

When I ask students about the particular shape of this tool, and its name, students in my US mid-western classroom, built on Native land, are usually able to identify it as a structure similar to a medicine wheel. This is a culturally specific way of making meaning and representing knowledge, and one that Michigan students, whether settler or Native, have encountered in their public spaces somewhere, given where we live.

By using this structure, I am introducing other ways of knowing, not so much in content but in design and orientation. When I lived and taught in Wales, we used other visual formats, such as knots, as ways of marking the specificity of how knowledge is shaped, and how locality, colonial histories, and ways of storytelling authorize knowledge. I have found it a useful exercise to ask students to identify organizational structures like these:

• What are the assumptions/backgrounds/cultural features of these ways of organizing knowledge?
• What are the effects of design choices for diagrams – who feels familiarity, comfort, appropriation, or exclusion?

- Should we create new diagrams for use in our classrooms?
- Can you add to this list?
  - Two-part division
  - Three-part division
  - Four quadrants divided by a cross
  - Bullet points/lists/sequential arrangements
  - Mind map
  - Spiral

• •

Bibliography

Aalten, Anna (1997) "Performing the Body, Creating Culture." In Davis, K. (ed.) *Embodied Practices: Feminist Perspectives on the Body*. London: Sage: 41–58.

Adams, Rachel (2001) *Sideshow USA: Freaks and the American Cultural Imagination*. Chicago: Chicago University Press.

Anzaldúa, Gloria (1999) *Borderlands/La Frontera: The New Mestiza*. San Francisco, CA: Aunt Lute Books.

Autistic Self Advocacy Network (2014) "Day of Mourning 2014," press release, February 24, http://autisticadvocacy.org/2014/02/day-of-mourning-2014-2/.

Back to Back Theatre (n.d.) *Ganesh versus the Third Reich*, http://backtobacktheatre.com/projects/show/ganesh-versus-the-third-reich.

Baggs, Amanda (2012) "Untitled." In Bascom, J. (ed.) *Loud Hands: Autistic People, Speaking*. Washington, DC: Autistic Self Advocacy Network: 324–34.

Bahan, Ben (2008) "Upon the Formation of a Visual Variety of the Human Race." In Bauman, H.-D. (ed.) *Open Your Eyes: Deaf Studies Talking*. Minneapolis: University of Minnesota Press: 83–99.

Baizley, Doris and Lewis, Victoria Ann (2006) "P.H.*reaks: The Hidden History of People with Disabilities." In Lewis, V.A. (ed.) *Beyond Victims and Villains: Contemporary Plays by Disabled Playwrights*. New York: Theatre Communications Group: 63–108.

Bakhtin, M. (1968) *Rabelais and his World*. Cambridge: MIT Press.

Barnartt, Sharon and Richard Scotch (2001) *Disability Protests: Contentious Politics, 1970–1999*. Washington, DC: Gallaudet University Press.

Barnes, Colin (2012) "The Social Model of Disability: Valuable or Irrelevant?" In Watson, N., Roulstone, A. and Thomas, C. (eds) *The Routledge Handbook of Disability Studies*. London: Routledge: 12–29.

Bartlett, Jennifer, Black, Sheila and Northen, Mike (eds) (2011) *Beauty is a Verb: The New Poetry of Disability*. El Paso: Cinco Puntos Press.

Bascom, Julia (n.d.) "Quiet Hands", http://juststimming.wordpress.com/2011/10/05/quiet-hands/.

Bauman, H-Dirksen and Murray, Joseph M. (2009) "Reframing: From Hearing Loss to Deaf Gain," translated from ASL by Fallon Brizendine and Emily Schenker. *Deaf Studies Digital Journal*, 1, 1–10.

Bell, Chris (2006) "Introducing White Disability Studies: A Modest Proposal." In Davis, L.J. (ed.) *The Disability Studies Reader* (2nd edn). New York: Routledge: 275–82.

Bogdan, Robert (1988) *Freak Show: Presenting Human Oddities for Amusement and Profit*. Chicago: University of Chicago Press.

Brown, Steven E. (1995) *Investigating a Culture of Disability: Final Report*. Las Cruces: Institute on Disability Culture.

Burch, Susan and Joyner, Hannah (2007) *Unspeakable: The Story of Junius Wilson*. Chapel Hill: University of North Carolina.

Burke, Theresa B. (2006) "Bioethics and the Deaf Community." In Lindgren, K., DeLuca, D. and Napoli, D.J. (eds) *Signs and Voices: Deaf Culture, Identity, Language, and Arts*. Washington, DC: Gallaudet University Press: 63–74.

Butler, Judith (1990) *Gender Trouble*. London: Routledge.

Chemers, Michael (2004) "Mutatis Mutandis: An Emergent Disability Aesthetic in 'X-2: X-Men United'." *Disability Studies Quarterly*, 24(1).

Chemers, Michael (2008) *Staging Stigma: A Critical Examination of the American Freak*. Basingstoke: Palgrave Macmillan.

Chen, Eric Y. (2005) *Mirror Mind: Penetrating Autism's Enigma*. Chen Yixiong, Eric.

Chen, Eric Y. (2006) "Autism Myths," available at http://iautistic.com/autism-myths-the-curious-incident-of-the-dog-in-the-night-time.php, accessed April 2014.

Cheu, Johnson (2005) "Oats and May," *Red River Review*, August 26, www. redriverreview.com.

Clare, Eli (1999) *Exile and Pride: Disability, Queerness, and Liberation*. Boston, MA: South End Press.

Collins, Patricia Hill (1990) *Black Feminist Thought*. Cambridge, MA: Unwin Hyman.

Cooley, Jessica and Fox, Ann M. (2009) *Re/Formations. Disability, Women and Sculpture*. Available at www2.davidson.edu/academics/acad_depts/galleries/reformations/index.html.

Cooper Albright, Ann (1997) *Choreographing Difference: The Body and Identity in Contemporary Dance*. Hanover, NH: Wesleyan University Press.

Cowl, C. (1997) Small Fish, *Animated*, Autumn: 16–17.

Creativity Explored. Gallery website, www.creativityexplored.org/artists/peter-cordova.

Crutchfield, Susan and Epstein, Marcy Joy (2000) *Points of Contact: Disability, Art, and Culture*. Ann Arbor, MI: University of Michigan Press.

D'Antonio, Michael (2005) *The State Boys Rebellion*. New York: Simon & Schuster.

Davidson, Michael (2008) *Concerto for the Left Hand: Disability and the Defamiliar Body*. Ann Arbor, MI: University of Michigan Press.

Davies, Rhian (2011) "Vic Finkelstein: Founder of the Social Model of Disability: A Major Loss to the Disability Sector," *Disability Wales*, December 2, www. disabilitywales.org/1168/3406.

Davis, Lennard (1995) *Enforcing Normalcy: Disability, Deafness, and the Body*. London: Verso.

Docherty, Daniel, Hughes, Richard, Phillips, Patricia (Manchester People First); Corbett, David, Regan Brendan (Bury People First); Barber, Andrew, Adams, Michael (Tameside People First); Boxall, Kathy, Kaplan, Ian, Izzidien, Shayma (Manchester University) (2005) "This is What We Think". In Goodley, D. and van Howe, G. (eds) *Another Disability Studies Reader? People with Learning Difficulties and a Disabling World*. Antwerp: Garant: 29–50.

Doe, Tanis (2003) *Studying Disability: Connecting People, Programs and Policies*. Victoria, BC: Island Blue Press.

Eckersall, Peter and Grehan, Helen (eds) (2013) *We're People Who Do Shows: Back to Back Theatre – Performance, Politics, Visibility*. London: Performance Research Books.

Elman, Julie Passanante (n.d.) "Cripping the City," course blog, http:// disabilitysexuality.blogspot.com/p/accessible-dates.html.

Erevelles, Nirmala and Minear, Andrea (2010) "Unspeakable Offenses: Untangling Race and Disability in Discourses of Intersectionality," *Journal of Literary & Cultural Disability Studies*, 4(2): 127–45.

Ferris, Jim (2004) *Hospital Poems*. Charlotte, NC: Main Street Rag.

Fiedler, Leslie (1978) *Freaks: Myths and Images of the Secret Self*. New York: Simon & Schuster.

Finger, Anne (2009) *Call Me Ahab: A Short Story Collection*. Nebraska: Bison Books.

Foster, Susan Leigh (1986) *Reading Dancing: Bodies and Subjects in Contemporary American Dance*. Berkeley, CA: University of California Press.

Foster, Susan Leigh (1995) "Harder, Faster, Longer, Higher: A Postmodern Inquiry into the Ballerina's Making." In *Border Tensions: Dance and Discourse. Proceedings of the Fifth Study of Dance Conference*. Guildford: University of Surrey: 109–114.

Galloway, Terry, Nudd, Donna and Sandahl, Carrie (2007) "Actual Lives and the Ethic of Accommodation." In Kuppers, P. (ed.) *Community Performance: A Reader*. New York: Routledge: 227–34.

Garland-Thomson, Rosemarie (ed.) (1996) *Freakery: Cultural Spectacles of the Extraordinary Body*. New York: New York University Press.

Garland-Thomson, Rosemarie (1997) *Extraordinary Bodies: Figuring Physical Disability in American Culture and Literature*. New York: Columbia University Press.

Garland-Thomson, Rosemarie (2000) "Seeing the Disabled: Visual Rhetorics of Disability in Popular Photography." In Longmore, P.K. and Umansky, L. (eds) *The New Disability History: American Perspectives*. New York: New York University Press: 335–74.

Garland-Thomson, Rosemarie (2002) "The Politics of Staring: Visual Rhetorics of Disability in Popular Photography." In Snyder, S.L., Brueggemann, B.J. and Garland-Thomson, R. (eds) *Disability Studies: Enabling the Humanities*. New York: Modern Language Association: 56–75.

Garland-Thomson, Rosemarie (2006) "Ways of Staring," *Journal of Visual Culture*, 5(2): 173–92.

Gill, Carol (1995) "A Psychological View of Disability Culture," *Disability Studies Quarterly*, 15(4): 16–19.

Goffman, Erving (1961) *Asylums: Essays on the Social Situation of Mental Patients and Other Inmates*. New York: Anchor Books.

Goffman, Erving (1963) *Stigma: Notes on the Management of a Spoiled Identity*. London: Penguin.

Goggin, Gerard and Newell, Christopher (2005) *Disability in Australia: Exposing a Social Apartheid*. Sydney: University of New South Wales.

Gómez-Peña, Guillermo (2000) *Dangerous Border Crossers: The Artist Talks Back*. New York: Routledge.

Gómez-Peña, Guillermo (2005) *Ethno-Techno: Writings on Performance, Activism, and Pedagogy*. London: Routledge.

Grandin, Temple (2006) *Thinking in Pictures: And Other Reports from My Life with Autism*. London: Bloomsbury.

Griffis, Damian (2012) "Disability in Indigenous Communities: Addressing the Disadvantage," *Ramp Up*, April 20, www.abc.net.au/rampup/articles/2012/04/20/3481394.htm.

Haddon, Mark (2003) *The Curious Incident of the Dog in the Night-time*. London: Jonathan Cape.

Hadley, Bree J. (2014) *Disability, Public Space Performance and Spectatorship: Unconscious Performers*. Basingstoke: Palgrave Macmillan.

Hall, Stuart (1990) "Cultural Identity and Diaspora." In Rutherford, J. (ed.) *Identity: Community, Culture, Difference*. London: Lawrence & Wishart: 222–37.

Haraway, Donna (1985) "A Cyborg Manifesto: Science, Technology, and Socialist-Feminism in the Late Twentieth Century," *Socialist Review*, 80: 65–108.

Haraway, Donna (1989) *Primate Visions: Gender, Race, and Nature in the World of Modern Science*. New York: Routledge.

Hehir, Thomas (2002) "Eliminating Ableism in Education," *Harvard Educational Review*, 72(1): 1–32.

Hickey-Moody, Anna (2009) "Little War Machines: Posthuman Pedagogy and its Media," *Journal of Literary & Cultural Disability Studies*, 3(3): 273–80.

Imrie, Rob (1996) *Disability and the City: International Perspectives*. London: Paul Chapman.

Johnston, Kirsty (2012) *Stage Turns: Canadian Disability Theatre*. Montreal: McGill University Press.

Kafer, Alison (2013) *Feminist Queer Crip*. Bloomington, IN: Indiana University Press.

Keidan, Lois and Mitchell, C.J. (eds) (2012) *Access All Areas: Live Art and Disability*. London: Live Art Development Agency.

Kempe, A. (2012) *Drama, Disability and Education*. London: Routledge.

Kerschbaum, Stephanie and Price, Margaret (2014) "Perils and Prospects of Disclosing Disability Identity in Higher Education," blog post, March, http://sites.udel.edu/csd/2014/03/03/perils-and-prospects-of-disclosing-disability-identity-in-higher-education/.

Kleege, Georgina (1999) *Sight Unseen*. New Haven, CT: Yale University Press.

Knoll, Kristina R. (2009) "Feminist Disability Studies Pedagogy," *Feminist Teacher*, 19(2): 122–33.

Kochhar-Lindgren, Kanta (2006) *Hearing Difference: The Third Ear in Experimental, Deaf and Multicultural Theater*. Washington, DC: Gallaudet University Press.

Kuppers, Petra (2003) *Disability and Contemporary Performance: Bodies on Edge*. New York: Routledge.

Kuppers, Petra (2011a) *Disability Culture and Community Performance: Find a Strange and Twisted Shape*. Basingstoke: Palgrave Macmillan.

Kuppers, Petra (ed.) (2011b) *Somatic Engagement*. Oakland, CA: Chainlinks.

Kuppers, Petra (2014) "Outsider Histories, Insider Artists, Cross-Cultural Ensembles: Visiting with Disability Presences in Contemporary Art Environments," *TDR: The Drama Review*, 58(2): 33–50.

Kuppers, Petra and Marcus, Neil (2008) *Cripple Poetics: A Love Story*. Ypsilanti: Homofactus Press.

Kuusisto, Stephen (2006) *Eavesdropping: A Memoir of Blindness and Listening*. New York: Norton.

Lee, Henry K. (2013) "Oakland man kills disabled daughter, self," *San Francisco Chronicle*, August 19, www.sfgate.com/crime/article/Oakland-man-kills-disabled-daughter-self-4743718.php.

Lehrer, Riva (n.d.) "Totems and Familiars," www.rivalehrerart.com/#!totems-and-familiars/c1pyv.

Lewiecki-Wilson, Cynthia, Brueggemann, Brenda and Dolmage, Jay (2008) *Disability and the Teaching of Writing*. New York: Bedford/St. Martin's.

Lewis, Victoria Ann (ed.) (2006) *Beyond Victims and Villains: Contemporary Plays by Disabled Playwrights*. New York: Theatre Communications Group.

Linton, Simi (1998) *Claiming Disability: Knowledge and Identity*. New York: New York University Press.

Lipkin, Joan and Fox, Ann (2002) "Res(Crip)ting Feminist Theater Through Disability Theater: Selections from the Disability Project," *NWSA Journal*, 14(3): 77–98.

Longmore, Paul K. (1995) "The Second Phase: From Disability Rights to Disability Culture," *The Disability Rag and ReSource* 16: 3–11.

Longmore, Paul K. and Umansky, Lauri (eds) (2001) *The New Disability History: American Perspectives*. New York: New York University Press.

Lukin, Josh (2012) "Pity is Shadowed by Contempt: An Interview with Anne Finger," *Wordgathering*, 26.

McDonald, Anne (n.d.) "Crip Time," available at www.annemcdonaldcentre.org.au/crip-time, accessed April 2014.

McRuer, Robert (2006) *Crip Theory: Cultural Signs of Queerness and Disability*. New York: New York University Press.

Manning, Erin (2013) *Always More Than One: Individuation's Dance*. Durham, NC: Duke University Press.

Manning, Lynn (2009) "The Magic Wand," *International Journal of Inclusive Education*, 13(7): 785.

Marcus, Neil (2011) *Special Effects: Advances in Neurology*. Portland, OR: Publication Studio.

Merleau-Ponty, Maurice (1962) *Phenomenology of Perception*, trans. C. Smith. London: Routledge & Kegan Paul.

Mitchell, David T. and Snyder, Sharon L. (2000) *Narrative Prosthesis: Disability and the Dependencies of Discourse*. Ann Arbor, MI: University of Michigan Press.

Moore, Leroy F. Jr. (2012) "Krip-Hop Nation is Moore than Music," *Wordgathering*, 22, www.wordgathering.com/issue22/essays/moore2.html.

Morales, Aurora Levins, Driskill, Qwo-Li and Piepzna-Samarasinha, Leah Lakshmi (2012) "Sweet Dark Places: Letters to Gloria Anzaldúa on Disability, Creativity, and the Coatlicue State." In Saldívar-Hull, S., Alarcón, N. and Urquijo-Ruiz, R. (eds) *El Mundo Zurdo 2: Selected Works from the Society of the Study of Gloria Anzaldúa*. San Francisco, CA: Aunt Lute Books: 77–97.

Muñoz, José (1999) *Disidentifications: Queers of Color and the Performance of Politics*. Minneapolis, MI: University of Minnesota Press.

Murray, Stuart (2008) *Representing Autism: Culture, Narrative, Fascination*. Liverpool: Liverpool University Press.

Museummuseum (2010) "Gillermo Gomez-Pena and La Pocha Nostra," interview by Lexa Walsh, blog, available at http://psumuseummuseum.blogspot.com/2010/03/gillermo-gomez-pena-and-la-pocha-nostra.html.

Nielsen, Kim (2012) *A Disability History of the United States*. Boston, MA: Beacon Press.

Nussbaum, Susan (2013) *Good Kings Bad Kings*. Chapel Hill, NC: Algonquin Books of Chapel Hill.

Oliver, Michael (1990) *The Politics of Disablement*, Basingstoke: Macmillan – now Palgrave Macmillan.

O'Reilly, Kaite (2007) *Face On: Disability Arts in Ireland and Beyond*. Dublin: Arts and Disability Ireland.

Parks, Suzan Lori (1998) *Venus*. Dramatists Play Service.

Pomerance, Bernard (1979) *The Elephant Man*. New York: Grove Press.

Poore, Carol (2007) *Disability in Twentieth-Century German Culture*. Ann Arbor, MI: University of Michigan Press.

Price, Margaret (2009) "'Her Pronouns Wax and Wane': Psychosocial Disability, Autobiography, and Counter-Diagnosis," *Journal of Literary & Cultural Disability Studies*, 3(1): 11–33.

Price, Margaret (2011) *Mad at School: Rhetorics of Mental Disability and Academic Life*. Ann Arbor, MI: University of Michigan Press.

Pullin, Graham (2009) *Design Meets Disability*. Cambridge, MA: MIT Press.

Quayson, Otto (2007) *Aesthetic Nervousness: Disability and the Crisis of Representation*. New York: Columbia University Press.

Samuels, Ellen (2003) "My Body, My Closet: Invisible Disability and the Limits of the Coming-Out Discourse," *GLQ: A Journal of Lesbian and Gay Studies*, 9(1/2): 233–55.

Sandahl, Carrie (2003) "Queering the Crip or Cripping the Queer? Intersections of Queer and Crip Identities in Solo Autobiographical Performance," *GLQ: A Journal of Lesbian and Gay Studies*, 9(1/2): 25–56.

Sandahl, Carrie (2008) "Why Disability Identity Matters: From Dramaturgy to Casting in John Belluso's Pyretown," *Text and Performance Quarterly*, 28(1/2): 225–41.

Savarese, D.J. (2010) "Communicate with Me," *Disability Studies Quarterly*, 30(1), available at http://dsq-sds.org/article/view/1051/1237.

Schweik, Susan (2007) "Begging the Question: Disability, Mendicancy, Speech and the Law," *Narrative*, 15(1), 58–70.

Schweik, Susan (2009) *The Ugly Laws: Disability in Public*. New York: New York University Press.

Sedgwick, Eve Kosofsky (1993) *Tendencies*. Durham, NC: Duke University Press.

Senier, Siobhan (2013) "Indigenizing Wikipedia: Student Accountability to Native American Authors on the World's Largest Encyclopedia," available at webwriting.trincoll.edu/communities/senier-2013/.

Shannon, Jeff (2003) "Access Hollywood: Disability in Recent Film and Television," *New Mobility*, May 1.

Shapiro, Laura (2003) "A Bronx Tale," available at http://nymag.com/nymetro/arts/dance/reviews/n_8323/.

Siebers, Tobin (2003) "What Can Disability Studies Learn from the Culture Wars?", *Cultural Critique*, 55: 182–216.

Siebers, Tobin (2008) *Disability Theory*. Ann Arbor, MI: University of Michigan Press.

Simonoff, Cynthia (2011) "Mapping Gendered Language at the Queer Resource Center." The Mapping Brandeis Project, Brandeis University. Available at https://sites.google.com/a/brandeis.edu/mapping_gendered-language_queer-resource-center/table-of-contents/disidentifications.

Sinclair, Jim (1993) "Don't Mourn for Us", *Our Voice*, 1(3), available at www.autreat.com/dont_mourn.html.

Sinclair, Jim (2012) "Don't Mourn for Us." In Bascom, J. (ed.) *Loud Hands: Autistic People, Speaking*. Washington, DC: Autistic Self Advocacy Network: 15–21.

Snider, Jerry (1993) "The Art of a Shaman," *Magical Blend*, 38: 39–42.

Stinson, Liz (2013) "The Radical Challenge of Building a Dorm for the Deaf," available at www.wired.com/design/2013/08/what-architects-can-learn-from-a-dorm-designed-specifically-for-deaf-students/.

Svetvilas, Chanika (2014) The Space In Between, unpublished MFA thesis, Goddard College of Art.

Swain, John and French, Sally (2000) "Towards an Affirmation Model", *Disability and Society*, 15(4): 569–82.

Swan, Rachel (2011) "Transit, Dislocation, and AXIS: AXIS and Dandelion Dancetheater may be coming to a BART station near you," available at www.eastbayexpress.com/oakland/transit-dislocation-and-axis/Content?oid=2938408.

UPIAS (1976) *Fundamental Principles of Disability*. London: Union of the Physically Impaired Against Segregation.

Verrent, Jo (2012) "Can an Epileptic Seizure Be Art?", available at www.
huffingtonpost.co.uk/jo-verrent/performance-art-epileptic-seizure-
_b_1291923.html.

Vizenor, Gerald (2008) *Survivance: Narratives of Native Presence*. Omaha, NE:
Nebraska University Press.

Wade, Cheryl Marie (1994) "Disability Culture Rap." In Shaw, B. (ed.) The *Ragged
Edge: The Disability Experience from the Pages of the First Fifteen Years of The
Disability Rag*, Louisville, KY: Avocado Press: 15–18.

Walker, Nick (2012) "Throw Away the Master's Tools: Liberating Ourselves from
the Pathology Paradigm." In Bascom, J. (ed.) *Loud Hands: Autistic People,
Speaking*. Washington, DC: Autistic Self Advocacy Network: 225–40.

Walker, Pamela Kay (2005) *Moving Over the Edge: Artists with Disabilities Take the
Leap*. Davis, CA: Michael Horton Media.

Williams, Patricia J. (1997) "Spirit Murdering the Messenger: The Discourse of
Fingerpointing as the Law's Response to Racism." In Wing, A.K. (ed.) *Critical
Race Feminism: A Class Reader*. New York: New York University Press: 229–42.

Williams, Raymond (1961) *The Long Revolution*. London: Chatto & Windus.

Williams, Raymond (1976) *Keywords: A Vocabulary of Culture and Society*. London:
Fontana.

Williamson, Aaron (2011) "In the Ghetto?: A Polemic in Place of an Editorial,"
www.parallellinesjournal.com/article-in-the-ghetto.html.

Wolff, Janet (1997) "Reinstating Corporeality: Feminism and Body Politics." In
Desmond, J. (ed.) *Meaning in Motion*. Durham, NC: Duke University Press:
95–6.

Wu, Cynthia (2012) *Chang and Eng Reconnected. The Original Siamese Twins in
American Culture*. Philadelphia, PA: Temple University Press.

Yergeau, Melanie (2012) "*That's just your autism talking* (and other phrases
that shouldn't appear in an autism essay)," available at http://aspierhetor.
com/2011/12/.

Yergeau, Melanie (2013) "Clinically Significant Disturbance: On Theorists Who
Theorize Theory of Mind," *Disability Studies Quarterly*, 33: 4.

Yergeau, Melanie, Brewer, Elizabeth, Kerschbaum, Stephanie, et al. (2013)
Multimodality in Motion glossary, http://kairos.technorhetoric.net/18.1/
coverweb/yergeau-et-al/pages/glossary.html.

Index

Bold page nos refer to exercises

wheelchair users, 63, 123
   and dance, 115, 118, 119
   and performance, 135–6, 138
   see also Murderball
wheelchairs, **78**, 79–80, 130, 132, 134, 135–6,
   138, 141, 142
Wikipedia activism, 166–7
Wilcox, Sadie, 94
Williams, Patricia, 49
Williams, Raymond, 21, 49, 65

Williamson, Aaron, 17–18, 33
Wilson, Junius, **83**
Wobbly Dance Company, i, 129

X-Men, 137–8, **140**, 141

Yergeau, Melanie, 6, 88–9, 168
Yi, Chun-Shan (Sandie), 131–2

zine culture, **73**